Also available at all good book stores

9781785315466

9781785313929

9781785315602

9781785316258

9781785315633

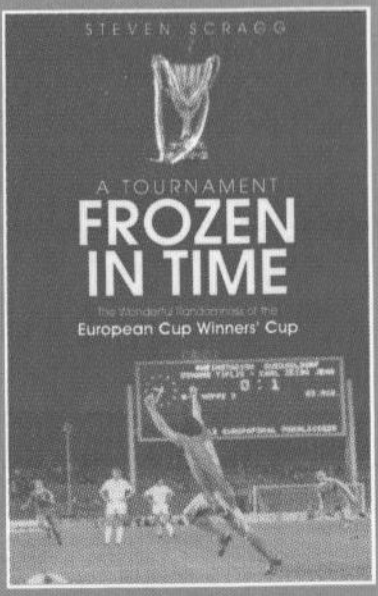

9781785315381

9781785316326

9781785316289

9781785316449

SECOND YELLOW

THE FURTHER ADVENTURES OF OUR FOOTBALL HEROES

SECOND YELLOW

THE FURTHER ADVENTURES OF OUR FOOTBALL HEROES

JOHN SMITH AND DAN TRELFER

pitch

First published by Pitch Publishing, 2020

Pitch Publishing
A2 Yeoman Gate
Yeoman Way
Worthing
Sussex
BN13 3QZ
www.pitchpublishing.co.uk
info@pitchpublishing.co.uk

A CIP catalogue record is available for this book
from the British Library.

ISBN 978 1 78531 679 1

Typesetting and origination by Pitch Publishing

Printed and bound in India by Replika Press Pvt. Ltd.

CONTENTS

INTRODUCTION

We go again.

Some of you will be here because you read *Booked!*, in which case, thank you for your continued support. Others will be newbies, in which case, welcome along. Grab a tea from the machine, pull a chair round and introduce yourself. We're all friends here.

If you're with us now it's because you love football. You may even love football as much as Graham Roberts, a man who missed his brother's wedding for Dorchester v Bridport. Apparently, 'Stephen took it badly and unfortunately our relationship was never the same again. Still, Dorchester beat Bridport 4-1.' This is the level of commitment we're looking for now, people. Go big, go home or go to Dorchester.

Our fascination with the autobiographies of football folk knows no bounds. We think it was John Betjeman, or possibly Malcolm Allison, that said 'I have come to the conclusion that every man's life must be of interest', and he's not wrong. We see the interest and value in every account of every football figure we've come across, from dry-as-a-bone David Elleray, to colourful character Mel Sterland who once thought he'd killed a man for 'challenging me to fight for twenty quid'. We are here, as always, to do the legwork and the man-hours, before placing the treasure before you.

For example, we're here to tell you that Ron Atkinson has a score-settling chapter in one of his books called 'People I Wouldn't Go On Holiday With', while Brian Laws signs off his entire book with an optimistic '... so far!', presumably in the hope that there will be a second volume to come, which is all the more ambitious when you consider that his final chapter is about doing DIY. Bermudan Shaun Goater wastes no time in dealing with the elephant in the room in Chapter One of *Feed The Goat*, by declaring of the Bermuda Triangle,

'So far as the islanders are concerned it just doesn't exist', which is better than leaving us all wondering for 300 pages. Meanwhile, Ted MacDougall shows a degree of self-awareness that one or two others could do with, to be honest, and uses his introduction to 'apologise to everyone for being such an arsehole'.

Sometimes, the most entertaining aspect of a player's book is the surprising language they employ. Jimmy Greaves eloquently describes making his debut for Chelsea as 'like kissing Jesus', while Derek Dougan goes around the place quoting George Bernard Shaw. Some overstretch slightly and come off a bit 'my first big school essay', like Neil Warnock describing his hopes at Leeds melting away like a snowman in his garden, or Jeff Winter writing: 'The big orange sun sank slowly below the horizon.' Lee Howey, meanwhile, was clearly that kid who bought a thesaurus in the summer holidays and tries to drop big words wherever possible. He liberally scatters the likes of 'emetic passages', 'eidetic memory' and 'excrescence of strawberry blond hair' about his prose – and that's just the Es. This is why we're here to pick a path through them all for you.

In doing so we've picked up a lot of wisdom and mottos along the way. Take your own pick from the likes of …

> 'There's no shame in the game staying in your football lane'. (Adebayo Akinfenwa)
>
> 'Humiliations are like power plants … you do draw energy from them'. (Jens Lehmann)
>
> On playing in front of the defence: 'If the sea's deep, a fish can breathe. If you put him just under the surface, he'll get by, but it's not quite the same thing'. (Andrea Pirlo)
>
> 'Better to wake up with a girl on your arm than a hangover in your head'. (Terry Curran)
>
> 'My golden rule is "be sensible".' (Alan Shearer)

The real gift for us in being able to expand our research has been to achieve a greater understanding of many things. For example, in our first book we dealt with Jim Smith putting on a puppet show team talk on the QPR coach to a Wembley cup final. Only during the research for this second book did we get to the root of the Bald Eagle's puppet obsession, which, thanks to information gleaned from Ron Atkinson's book, appears to date back to a celebratory dinner thrown for Smith when he got Oxford promoted to Division One. The entertainment that night was provided by Roger De Courcey and Nookie Bear, and Ron tells us that after a few drinks, 'Jim became engrossed in the behaviour of Nookie Bear', who, for those too young to remember him in his pomp, was not a real bear. 'Jim was oblivious to all of us. As far as he was concerned it was Nookie and him alone in that room, and Nookie was telling jokes. And Nookie, it seemed, had taken on a human scale. Every time Nookie told a joke, Jim just roared with laughter and punched it right in the face, almost lifting poor old Roger off his feet.' The punching we'll leave to one side for somebody else to analyse but once you know Jim had a fascination with ventriloquist acts, the monkey puppet team talk doesn't seem so daft does it? What do you mean it still does?

Along the way we've picked up other insights that have added to our enjoyment of the game, and pop culture, such as the fact that Rod Stewart was asked to star in *Escape to Victory*, or that future Man City chief executive Garry Cook (of 'AC Milan bottled it' fame) sang backing vocals on Rod's 'Rhythm of My Heart'. Because of course he did.

We learned that just before Liverpool lost the title in the last minute at Anfield in 1989, Jan Molby and the subs were on their way to get into their kit for the celebrations when the Michael Thomas goal went in. And we already thought it was funny enough.

And speaking of full kit, we've always enjoyed John Terry missing what would have been the winning penalty in the 2008 Champions League Final for Chelsea v Manchester United. Particularly because he fell on his arse while doing it. However, we've since learned from Frank Lampard's 2006 autobiography that having slipped while scoring a penalty at Euro 2004, Terry would often make fun of it in training: 'At Chelsea, John will occasionally re-enact that kick, complete with the sliding foot', little knowing that he was tempting fate and a fall was in his future. And now we can enjoy it all the more. Oh, hindsight, you wonderful thing.

What? We never said we weren't petty-minded and spiteful.

So our research has run the full gamut of these books, taking in a lot of players from many clubs and several eras. The extremes among them are perhaps best summed up by two introductions we came across. Firstly, the needlessly grandiloquent Alan Hudson:

> I was born in June 1951 under the influence of the star sign Gemini. It is represented as the Twins, Castor and Pollux. Egyptian astrologers depicted them as a pair of ghosts, while Arabian astrologers symbolized them as peacocks. Characteristics include being quick and restless. Mutable, not to be depended on.

And then the no-nonsense, nail-on-the-head approach from Roy McDonough:

> In a career that surpassed 650 games, 150 goals, 400 women and thousands of beers, I played for three England World Cup winners, tried to clog Dutch master Johan Cruyff and pulled a Miss UK finalist with half a pint of lager and £1 petrol money.

And whichever approach you prefer (and we all know really: you're not made of stone), we hope we've catered for you in the pages that follow. Enjoy.

TRAIN IN VAIN

'One-nil down against no one'

'Straight off the training ground' is a frequently heard cry from over-excited commentators, usually in response to some kind of set-piece wizardry. Think Javier Zanetti's bit of devilry for Argentina against England or a classic short corner for Teddy Sheringham to belt home. But we've looked into it for you, and it turns out it's not all tactics boards and unfettered genius down there among the balls, bibs and cones. In fact, at times it seems like some of them are making it up as they go along.

Before we get too involved in the session, it's vitally important that we stretch and warm up – all footballers must surely agree on that. Apart from Andrea Pirlo, who has views: 'I hate it with every fibre of my being. It actually disgusts me. It's nothing but masturbation for conditioning coaches.' Disgusted, you say. Well, this changes things. Pirlo was both pretty good at football and stunning to look at so maybe we should listen to him. As you were then. Just make sure your laces are tied and let's get cracking.

The stadium might be where the eyes of the world are on players, and where they get the glory and the fame, but fame costs, and the training ground, to paraphrase a great thinker, is where they start paying in sweat. It's therefore important to build a welcoming sense of camaraderie between players, to create an environment where they can relax and give their best.

Norman Whiteside tells us that he and Arnold Mühren had a nice running gag that at least one of them enjoyed, wherein the Irishman would greet the Dutchman 'with an extremely formal hello. "Good morning Arnoldus Johannus Hyacinthus Muhren," I would say. "How are you this fine day and how is your father Arnoldus Pietrus Hyacinthus Muhren?"' A bit of fun to get the day started, and no harm done, but the Man United training ground wasn't always so convivial. Dwight Yorke informs us that when he arrived from Villa with a huge price tag hanging (not literally) off of him, Roy Keane was every bit as brusque as you might expect him to be, wasting no time in fizzing a hard ball into Yorkie's feet to test him. 'I didn't control it properly and he said: "Welcome to United – Cantona used to kill them." That was his little dig at me.' It seems this was Keane's regular welcome; he did the same to Rio Ferdinand, who struggled with a similar nervy first touch. On that occasion, Ole Gunnar Solskjaer was on hand with a snide comment of 'How much?!', like a giggling Richard Hammond to Keane's bullying Clarkson, or that little puppet that sits next to Jabba the Hutt. That story comes from Michael Carrick, who says that by the time he arrived, it was Paul Scholes who 'lashed the ball at me' on day one, minute one. Nice of them. Most people just get shown where the toilets, kettle and photocopier are on their first day.

Even if Keano and the rest did this with every single new United signing[1] it still wouldn't make them as unwelcoming as Mick Channon at Portsmouth, who seems to have made making people feel bad an art form. Vince Hilaire reports that when Channon was the senior man at Pompey, he placed a lot of emphasis on Saturday's starting XI, at the expense of everyone else, claiming: 'I hate reserves' and labelling them 'parasites'. Hilaire says that Channon told him: 'Every morning, when I come in, I'm going to open that door to their dressing room and say, "Morning, Reserves" because they'll hate that. ... and he used to do it without fail.' Even if this was funny once, and we can safely say it wasn't, surely it didn't sustain? '"They hate me but I don't give a fuck." He used to emphasise the word "reserves" and he used to make it last about ten seconds: "Morning, Reseeeeeeeeeeeeeeeeeeeeeeeeeeerves!"' It's nice to be nice isn't it?

If you've managed to avoid Mick Channon thinking he's better than you, still more dangers lurk on the training field – not everyone can shield under Neil Warnock's umbrella, you know. He only afforded that luxury to his Sheffield United 'sons' Phil Jagielka and Michael Brown. The rest of you are on your own.

Look out for Alex Ferguson's 'sniper', Paul Scholes, who would ping 40-yard balls at the head of anyone who sloped off for a crafty wee in a bush on the sidelines; Dirk Kuyt, who according to Peter Crouch

1 Good luck with that, William Prunier.

'would leave a series of large tubs of hair gel in various places around the training ground so that he could dip in whenever he wanted'; and Jermaine Pennant, who kept a stash of toast 'tucked down his socks'. According to Emile Heskey, who played with him at Birmingham, 'if he didn't have the ball, he'd be bending down to take the toast out and eat it. I would be shaking my head. That wasn't professional and it was just strange.' It is a bit strange, and with breakfast and ankle tags down there, it makes Jermaine Pennant's socks out to be some kind of 'Mary Poppins's bag' set-up.

Of course, Pennant is not alone in being a bad trainer. Some players just think it's not for them. Stan Collymore claims that: 'My curse is that I've always been blessed with a great touch. I don't need to practise my ball skills. I was born with them.' Which is an interesting way of looking at things – and getting yourself out of some hard work. It occurs to us that Stan may not be the only footballer ever to suffer such a curse, and that some of his fellow sufferers might have even felt that a solid work ethic alongside such talents might be the way to success. Although Stan makes a compelling case for doing sod all, it was an approach that found short shrift with Forest teammate Brian Laws: 'I told him: "Fuck off, just get out there and DO it."' Which Laws says worked, for about a fortnight.

Having scoured the accounts of so many football folk, we find ourselves in a position to present the coaching methods of some of the finest minds the game has known. Here then is a glimpse behind the curtain of *Oz the Great and Powerful*. Here are some of the methods we've picked up. Please feel free to make notes in the margin.

JIMMY SEED – NO BALLS

Danny Blanchflower played under Mr Seed on his way up at Barnsley and seems to have succeeded as a player in spite of him. Seed's methods involved rather more snooker and rather less football skills than Danny was after. When Blanchflower requested a ball to work with he was told no, because if he wanted one, everyone would want one. Seed's philosophy was: 'If you don't see the ball during the week you'll be more keen to get it on Saturdays.' That is certainly one school of thought. Not a good school of thought, but a school of thought.

When Danny moved on and signed for Villa he says he did so on the condition they would let him train with a ball as much as he liked after official training.

HARRY REDKNAPP – OPEN HOUSE

'One of the things I changed when I became West Ham manager was to allow fans in to the training ground. When I first came they had to stand outside the gate and couldn't see anything, but now we invite them all in. And why not?' Very charitable of man of the people Harry 'Jam Roly-Poly' Redknapp. Why not indeed? Well, there was that time Alvin Martin and Matthew Rush had a big fight and Harry was almost immediately fending off phone calls from newspapers because: 'One of the fans who'd come to watch us training had raced off the moment the punch up had finished and tipped off the paper to earn a few bob.' So it's possible that opening training to the public wasn't such a good idea, and if Harry didn't learn his lesson then, then he learnt it when John Hartson almost kicked the head off Eyal Berkovic a few years later and the same thing happened again. Who could have seen that coming? That time the grateful public even filmed it.

PETER TAYLOR – MANNEQUINS

Adebayo Akinfenwa played under Peter 'briefly England manager' Taylor at Gillingham and says that the gaffer had an over-reliance on mannequins. Bayo says they were the only opposition Taylor allowed and points out the flaw with that, namely: 'you always look great against mannequins because they obviously don't move'. According to the big target man, it meant they started every game too slow as 'when we faced actual moving players, it took us a while to adjust'. Far be it from us to disagree with someone as big as Akinfenwa, but this sounds a bit like an excuse doesn't it? Surely the many years of playing against actual people was still in the locker somewhere?

CHRIS NICHOLL – YOU CAN ONLY BEAT WHAT'S NOT IN FRONT OF YOU

At Southampton in the 1980s they could only dream of mannequins. According to David Armstrong, manager Chris Nicholl had a certain 'lack of coherence in training', illustrated by a time he had them playing 'shadow football' against nobody at all, presumably to work on shape. Armstrong says: 'Colin Clarke kicked off, passed the ball to Hobson, Hobson to Case, Case to Francis Benali, and Benali back to goalkeeper Tim Flowers.' Unfortunately, Flowers was sorting the back of his net out and 'so the ball trickled over the line into the goal. One-nil down against no one. It took us a further 30 minutes to "equalise".'

Now we're sure Armstrong must be exaggerating for comic effect, but we like to imagine the relief when they levelled was palpable.

BOBBY GOULD - TOXIC

Bobby's methods are as labyrinthine and impenetrable as you might expect. At times he used a traffic-light sticker chart on the wall for players to see, with different-coloured stickers according to performance, like a cross between Opta Stats and a toddler's potty chart. At other times, Gould insisted on training in public parks on away trips, which carried predictable hazards back in the day. Before a game at Everton, his Wimbledon side were practising set pieces when, 'Eric Young headed the ball smack on then recoiled when he realised he had dog shit splattered all over his bandana. Unfortunately for Lurch, the ball hit the bar and rebounded into his face.' When it rains it pours.

Obviously, Bobby's approach to toxins was: what doesn't kill you makes you stronger, because Eric Young needing to give his bandana a thorough rinse didn't stop him playing fast and loose with poisons. As Coventry boss he took his boys, including his actual boy Jonathan, down to Aldershot barracks for pre-season training with the army. Bobby cheerfully tells us: 'Our Jonathan almost died when the players had to wear masks to negotiate a narrow tunnel that was filled with poisonous gas. He started choking, the gas got into his lungs and he needed resuscitating. I would have had a near death experience as well if Marge had got to hear what happened.'

That's real poisonous gas. It seems a bit of an upgrade on zip lines and cargo nets doesn't it? If your son's being resuscitated and your first thought is, 'The wife'll kill me for this', then we reckon you're doing parenting wrong; and if your goalkeeper is being resuscitated because you sent him through a tunnel of poisonous gas, then we reckon you're doing coaching wrong.

NEIL WARNOCK - FERRY 'CROSS THE MERSEY

Warnock prides himself on his meticulous preparation for games, and being on a ferry is no reason to set that aside. When he took his Sheffield United side to Liverpool for a League Cup semi-final he took the gang to the top deck of the Mersey Ferry, 'and went through a couple of our defensive routines up there'. Warnock improvised and used lifebuoys for a goal and set up a wall. 'Poor Wayne Allison, our centre forward, was sitting on one of the steps on a stairway and had gone very pale. He was bloody seasick on a ferry across the river.' Maybe he was, or maybe he just didn't want to look daft, joining in with the rest of you.

HOWARD KENDALL – GROG

Howard Kendall had methods, and those methods often involved booze. Peter Reid recalls a rough time at Manchester City with the side struggling and the Platt Lane training ground too frozen to get on and fix it. Reid assumed they would move inside somewhere for five-a-sides but Howard, being from the school of 'If life gives you lemons, make vodka and lemonade', decided to throw open the players' lounge and get right on it – at half past ten in the morning. 'After two hours of playing table tennis and drinking Budweiser he sent us home,' says Reidy, with a rallying cry to be at their best in training the next day. The ping-pong seems to be providing the thinnest veneer of being some kind of physical exercise. It is, after all, the sport you can play most easily with a beer in the other hand.

KENNY DALGLISH – BISCUITS

The sustenance that bound Liverpool together, at training at least, was altogether more wholesome. Alan Hansen tells us that a feeling of togetherness was engendered as 'the players had tea, biscuits and a social chat before their training sessions on Friday mornings'. That's right, Kenny Dalglish invented the PTA Coffee Morning. Over a milky brew and a selection of Lincoln, Abbey Crunch and other lost classics they 'could forget about football and just enjoy each other's company'. This sounds altogether more lovely than all that dog shit stuff Wimbledon were up to.

MALCOLM ALLISON – GO!

It's fair to say that Big Mal wasn't in his pomp by the time Vince Hilaire came through at Crystal Palace, so the winger never saw the best of him. He goes further and says: 'Malcolm was making no sense to anyone.' Hilaire recalls one particular quirk of Allison's that he wanted players to be alert at all times and that in any given situation around the club he could shout 'Go!' and he would expect players up on their toes. This stretched way beyond the training ground and could have happened when a player was sat reading a newspaper, enjoying a game of snooker or getting a rubdown. On one occasion Mal shouted 'Go!' as his team were enjoying breakfast at a hotel before an away game, resulting in 'cutlery falling all over the place and plates coming off the table because we'd all got up straight away when he shouted'. Now we suppose it depends how you measure success, but we can't work out if this is a win for Malcolm or not.

BILLY MCNEILL – EARLY AWAY

Billy McNeill didn't become the first British captain to win the European Cup by sodding off home halfway through, so why he expected to coach Aston Villa that way is anyone's guess. Yet Mark Walters well remembers being 'in the middle of a tough training session and we'd look over and see his car heading out the main gate and off into the distance. That didn't exactly endear him to the players who were covered in mud, sweat and tears and the manager is halfway home in his fancy big car.' You can see why it didn't go down well. Walters describes McNeill's short tenure as 'shambolic'. Villa finished rock bottom and the team McNeill had left to join them in September of that season, Man City, were also relegated just one place above them. So Billy can reasonably be said to have relegated two teams in one season. Walters goes on to say that 'when I eventually moved up to Scotland, he did thank me for not divulging certain things about his time at Villa'. Important to note that McNeill was at Celtic, Walters at Rangers, but that Mark decided that the Old Firm divide wasn't enough to make him a grass.

RONNIE ALLEN – MRS RONNIE

Ronnie Allen isn't the only manager to get his wife along to the training ground but none were quite so involved as Mrs Allen. Richard Edghill recalls that during Alan Ball's time at Man City, Mrs Ball was there on his first day in charge 'waving his World Cup medal to anyone who cared. Nobody did much.' But while Mrs Ball might have been around to establish little Alan's credentials, Mrs Allen was Ronnie's enforcer.

Ally Robertson tells the story of an early training session under Allen:

> She walks to the main pitch, unfolds the chair and sits down. The lads are all wondering what on earth is going on as we start working on some heading drills. All of a

> sudden this woman stands up and shouts across. 'Ronnie!' 'Yes, love.' 'That group over there aren't doing it properly like you told them to do it. And that one over there is messing about.' It was his missus! Ronnie shouts over to a group, 'My wife says you're not doing it properly, so come on.'

This may have been a case of short-term gain, long-term pain for Allen, though. As Robertson explains, 'That was Ronnie dead with the lads after that, finished on Day One. We couldn't believe it.' It seems that nothing undermines a manager's authority like having his missus in a fold-up chair snitching on players.

Any aspiring coaches among you can apply some of the above principles to your own approach to the game as you wish – you're very welcome. But there are some elements of training that are universal and override such quirks:

Everyone's got to run.

Everyone's got to hit the gym.

Sooner or later, despite what Jimmy Seed reckoned, everyone's got to kick a ball about.

Running is understandably not popular with everyone. Derek Dougan worried about a growing obsession with fitness over football in his day, warning that: 'If this attitude goes unchecked, the game could stultify, leaving the championship to be a contest between Stereotype United and Prototype Athletic.' Love the phrasing here. We get the point he's trying to make but he seems to have accidentally made that prospect sound quite good. Who wouldn't want to watch that? But we digress. On your marks, get set, go.

Andy Cole is full of praise for coach Brian Kidd's approach to fitness work, and says he would always call it 'money in the bank', but not everyone appreciates the fine arts of making people run around until they're sick. Chilled-out entertainer Frank Worthington at Birmingham says that under Ron Saunders, 'Training would have been more attuned to a foot slog across Antarctica with Sir Ranulph Fiennes, than honing the moves and skills which would send spectators home satisfied on a Saturday afternoon.' Though presumably everybody came back with their fingers and toes intact at Birmingham at least.

Surely Worthington of all people should be aware of the restorative benefits of getting a dab on. Many players report the trend of using a good shift to sweat out the alcohol after a heavy night on the sauce. John Sitton even says that a cure for a teammate deemed to be spending too much time on cocaine, bookies and booze was simply, 'They ran the bollocks off him.' So there you go. You don't get that at The Priory do you?

Some players would do what they could to get out of the long-distance stuff. Kevin Beattie says that Allan Hunter once sailed past him on a milk float on a run at Ipswich, puffing on a cigarette as he did so.[2] Steve Bruce has never struck us as a natural athlete but at least he didn't consider himself above the hard work. Having moved to Norwich from Gillingham, Bruce found himself a little out of his depth with the fitness regime at first. On one cross-country stretch, Bruce found himself second-last with only striker John Deehan behind him, when he saw Deehan fall into a stream they were crossing. 'As I reached the reserve team coach, Dave Stringer, I just managed to gasp out that he ought to go and see that John Deehan was all right. More than a little alarmed at the prospect of our top goal-scorer slowly drowning, he raced back to find him. Having rescued him and slung him over his shoulder, Dave Stringer still managed to overtake me before we got back.' Blimey, Stringer's a tough nut. You might think that a coach would be more impressed with a player that stopped to fish a teammate out of the river they'd fallen in, but maybe that's just us. At least Stringer was only lugging Deehan around in special circumstances; Gordon Hill says that sort of thing was a regular part of his injury rehab at Derby, saying, 'I was running up and down the stands with David Webb on my shoulders.' We're not sure what the selection process was for Webby to be Hill's passenger, but this can't have been pleasant for either of them. Not even Mr Miyagi had Daniel doing this sort of thing.

What with the dangers of falling in streams, being hit by passing milk floats, or as Alan Curbishley describes, getting into a snowball fight with a load of young Millwall fans with his Charlton lads, maybe we're better off inside – in the gym perhaps. Players who impressed indoors during wet playtimes include Andrei Kanchelskis, who Ben Thornley recalls 'used to do kick-ups with a medicine ball. And I'm not talking about five – he was getting towards 30' (which sounds like something Popeye might do), and Jamie Lawrence at Leicester who

2 Did he carry these with him in his kit, or bum one off of the milkman?

'would come in and bench press on the multi-gym and put the pin to the bottom and bang out 10 or 20 repetitions' according to Emile Heskey. Impressive. At Newcastle, however, boss Graeme Souness would have given Lawrence a run for his money. Kieron Dyer recalls being in awe of the gaffer with 'his top off in the gym' working out 'doing the chest press and it was like "boom". I was thinking, "my God, this guy".' Is it us, or did it just get a bit warmer in here?

A less fond gym memory, again from Emile Heskey's enjoyable memoirs *Even Heskey Scored*, is the time Igor Biščan nearly killed himself at Liverpool: 'There would normally be someone in there with you, but Igor was on his own and decided to do maximum weights on his chest.' You've guessed it: Igor came a cropper and nearly choked himself under the bar, with nobody able to hear his strangled screams. Fortunately, Biščan was prevented from dying from his own hubris by a passer-by, lived to tell the tale and almost single-handedly won the Champions League for the Reds. That's how we remember it, anyway.

Of course, as discussed, you can be as fit as you like and do all tactics sessions on a ferry you want, but eventually it will come down to the football itself. And it seems that the training matches, be they small-sided or full scale, are where the players can really get together and confront their tensions, like a family on a caravan holiday.

Throughout the world and whatever the standard, it seems to be a universal truth that training matches can get a bit tasty. David Armstrong says of the Friday matches at Southampton, 'there were fights, players slammed into walls, noses pressed into boards, furious outbursts', which all sounds a bit *Rollerball*. Meanwhile at West Ham, Jimmy Bullard says that Paolo Di Canio and John Moncur had to be put on the same team, 'or World War Three would have kicked off'. Now we don't think he means literally, but we can certainly imagine it got lively, and very entertaining. Moncur was by all accounts the supreme wind-up merchant, and Di Canio always seemed on the brink of a vein-popping tantrum at any given moment.

We don't imagine Harry Redknapp was tempted to step between them – we know we wouldn't – but there are those that would. Jason McAteer fondly recalls his boss at Bolton, Bruce Rioch, acting as his minder when Mark Patterson went through him: 'Bruce brings himself on as a sub and, within seconds, he's done Mark, six studs into his chest. He's done one of his own players in cold blood for having a go at me. And it works. Mark never comes near me again.' Chilling stuff, and not just because of that odd, present tense thing Jason does throughout his book.

Rioch must have been confident he was top dog around the Bolton training ground because the history of managers joining in with matches is a chequered one to say the least. When Tommy Docherty joined in at QPR, Stan Bowles was on hand to 'take the piss out of him', despite insisting that he liked him. 'I used to say: "Come on fatty, get it off me!" He would come diving in because he was quite fiery, and I would just slip by him. I certainly sold him a few dummies on the training ground, and used to taunt him. He was like a little dog following me around the ground.'; but at least The Doc escaped physically unharmed. He should consider himself lucky.

In our first book we mentioned Ruud Gullit being whacked by Stuart Pearce in training at Newcastle and we've since read Rob Lee's account confirming his own involvement in leaving the odd pass short to facilitate Gullit being sent 'into orbit'. Lou Macari was seemingly not popular at West Ham, and while several players were sufficiently annoyed with him to have a pop, they had just the fella to take the situation in hand. 'Julian Dicks would kick the f*** out of Lou whenever he joined in training games,' says Mark Ward. 'It was embarrassing to watch a fellow pro humiliate the manager.' Embarrassing perhaps, but not that uncommon. At West Brom Ally Robertson says they would kick Ronnie Allen in training while he pretended to be Pelé, George Best or Rainer Bonhof – it didn't matter, they all got kicked. We can only hope his wife wasn't watching from her fold-up chair. The tradition continued at West Brom long after Ronnie Allen had gone, as Ron Atkinson tried to mix games up by making them 'The Cream versus The Scum: the English players against the rest'. It sounds like training matches were volatile enough without turning them into a culture war and inevitably there were casualties. Big Ron got kicked a lot. But maybe he didn't mind because there were 'plenty of giggles', and that's the main thing.

It's not just the manager that joins in from time to time. All comers are welcome – sort of. On occasion, a bold director or chairman has been sufficiently brave to have a go. Some of us are old enough to remember when Michael Knighton came out ball-juggling at Old Trafford, confident that he was buying Manchester United imminently. Well it was all well and good for him doing it there, in front of witnesses. He may not have been so brazen out on the wild west of the training ground. Sir Elton John poured his heart and soul into Watford and says many lovely things about the club in his autobiography *Me*[3] – but that didn't stop him 'flying through the air at high speed, backwards, as a prelude to landing flat on my arse', whenever he joined in. If only we could think of an Elton John hit that involved him remaining on his feet here, to juxtapose with his predicament. Nope, beats us.

Doug Ellis is another have-a-go chairman who found himself airborne and 'being carried off in considerable pain' when he played with his Villa lads. But despite his bumps and bruises, he considers it a victory because he later caught the culprit, Brian Godfrey, boasting about clobbering him in the showers. Doug was soaping up in the next cubicle you see. It doesn't bear thinking about, does it?

The men upstairs can't even get any respect when they've had a glorious playing career of their own. Sir Bobby Charlton won the biggest prizes in the game, but long after he retired it seems that all he wanted was a kickabout with the lads. Sadly, according to Brian McClair, the lads were not having it. On one occasion, he says, 'Eric nutmegged him and he wasn't too happy about it', and another time away in Vienna, he didn't even get close enough for Cantona to shout whatever 'Nuts!' is in French. That time they simply sneaked off without him. 'When we got back to the hotel after training, Bobby Charlton came over and asked us what had happened. There was a guilty silence as we remembered that he was supposed to have been coming training with us. The manager had told him to be ready at 5.00 pm and we left at 4.15. He'd been sitting in reception in his training gear waiting and we missed him.' Something about all this tells us that the United players didn't really want Bobby playing with them. Which is a shame, because if a director of the club is taking his own training kit all the way to Vienna for a knockabout, I think we can regard him as keen. Bless him. It's not nice to think of him sitting there in his shiny boots and immaculate kit while the bigger boys have ditched him, is it? No wonder he looks grumpy all the time.

Sometimes you don't even need to be attached to the club to be allowed to take part and rub shoulders with the pros; if you had any interest at all, it seems it was worth carrying your boots with you on the off chance. Cricketers like Graham Gooch and Steve Harmison were

3 That's right, we left no stone unturned. We read Rod Stewart's for this too for Christ's sake.

seemingly always welcome at West Ham and Newcastle respectively, which must have been nice for them, because football's better than cricket – while Daley Thompson was another sportsman who seems to have had carte blanche to rock up just about anywhere and show off a bit in the 80s. Peter Reid confesses to effing and jeffing at a 'useless twat' he didn't recognise, during a training match called Vic, before being asked to ease off as he was just a local vicar giving it a go, and Paul Canoville seems to have just got his mate George along for the ride at Chelsea. Despite being no more than someone 'I was hanging out and going raving with', and being no good at football, manager John Hollins let George hang around his first-team squad, giving his all in the games, 'with his arse popping out of his too-small tracksuit bottoms'. Can you imagine this now? Not the arse; we mean the random stranger joining in at a professional football club with aspirations of being a top side. You're still thinking about the arse aren't you.

One of the most notorious joining-in stories involves Graeme Souness absolutely rattling Dwight Yorke and Yorke taking justifiable offence. For his part, Souness says he regrets it and admits he was wrong, which is quite the rarity in this genre, but at least explains his reasoning at the time. In the gaffer's words, he had signed Andy Cole and Dwight Yorke for Blackburn from Manchester United and 'felt they had come from United thinking, "We did this and that there", and allowed themselves to get in their armchairs a bit', which is such a lovely turn of phrase, we can almost forgive him for raking his studs down Yorke's shin and threatening to break his leg. Yorke spends a lot of time on this in his own book and was clearly stunned by the actions of Souness, with the flare-up bringing training to an end, continuing with a shouting match in the canteen and ultimately resulting in Yorke leaving Rovers. Fiery stuff.

This shemozzle leads us nicely into the real reason some of you are here: the scraps, the bundles, the square gos. We all know that tempers can fray and things can boil over every so often in training, even at Liverpool once the biscuits have run out. So at this point we're going to take a look at some of those flashpoints. In doing so, we're looking for those that fall somewhere between the 'I'm something you'll never be, son' posturing of Kevin Keegan with Steve Williams at Southampton[4] and the criminal proceedings of Joey Barton with

---

4 This from Keegan's biggest cheerleader, Mick 'Reseeeeeeeeeeeeeeerves!' Channon.

Ousmane Dabo at Man City. But fret not, that still leaves us with plenty to be getting on with.

SECONDS OUT:

REMI MOSES V JESPER OLSEN

As told by both Bryan Robson and Ron Atkinson, this unlikely pair went at it in a Man United session after a wild tackle from Olsen, with one-sided results. Captain Marvel says Remi 'absolutely battered Jesper' and remembers 'there was blood all over the place'. Manager Ron also mentions a hefty amount of claret and describes how Moses left the Dane 'in a sorry heap on the deck'. Oof. A pretty clear winner in this one then.

RESULT: MOSES BY KO

STAN BOWLES V FRANK MCLINTOCK

This pair had a scrap at a QPR training session with Bowles gleefully admitting 'I almost bit Frank's ear off, and he still ribs me about that to this day, but we are still the best of mates.' We're glad it was all done and forgotten in time, but we can't have this sort of thing. It's not Tyson and Holyfield.

RESULT: McLINTOCK BY DISQUALIFICATION

ANDY TODD V DEAN KIELY

This one is less a fight and more a random act of violence. After a minor disagreement over set pieces in a drill, Charlton boss Alan 'Curbs' Curbishley takes up the tale: 'as Deano went inside he walked passed [sic] Toddy in the hallway and Andy hit him. There was no row or anything like that, no shouting match.' The notoriously aggro Todd might lose points for being a bit sneaky here, but a punch and a bloody nose speaks for itself. It got Todd run out of Charlton and the booing crowd may not like it, but it's …

RESULT: TODD BY TKO

ZLATAN IBRAHIMOVIĆ V JONATHAN ZEBINA

Not Zlatan's only training ground fight by any means, but one in which he comes off as the good guy for a change. Zebina had recently joined Juventus and seems to have been employing the prison tactic of finding the biggest bloke to have a fight with to establish dominance.

He started it with a dirty tackle, then went head to head with Zlatan and stuck the nut on him. Ibra says: 'I didn't have time to think. It was sheer reflex. I hit out at him, and it happened right away. He hadn't even finished headbutting me. I must have hit him hard. He dropped down on to the grass, and I have no idea what I expected to happen.' What did happen is that manager Fabio Capello stayed well out of the way and Fabio Cannavaro gave him a wink to express solidarity. It seems that Zebina wasn't as popular, or as upright as he'd hoped to be in that moment.

RESULT: IBRAHIMOVIĆ BY KO (OF COURSE)

TREVOR FRANCIS V ARCHIE STYLES

Who knew that Trevor Francis was a fighter? Well it turns out he wasn't. What he was, according to Roy McDonough, was a 'big moaner', and when his moaning got him in trouble with the superbly monikered Archie Styles at Birmingham, he came off second best. McDonough, always a keen admirer of a bit of violence on a football field, tells us that 'Archie never said a word, he just punched Trevor straight in the nose and as he went down rubbed six studs across his pretty-boy face. Both of his eyes were blackened and he was left with tramlines down his nose.' Oof, this sounds nasty, though to be fair, if we ever found ourselves in a scrap with Trevor Francis, we'd have probably gone for the nose first too.

RESULT: STYLES WINS ON POINTS (FOR ARTISTRY)

ANDY MORRISON V PAULO WANCHOPE

This one might surprise you. The two fell out during rehab at Man City, with Morrison quite reasonably putting it down to 'two injured players, totally frustrated and at breaking point'. Morrison says, 'He mumbled something I didn't like so I belted him and threw him against the wall. Out of the corner of my eye I saw Steve Howey passing, but he just glanced at us and went on his way, probably thinking it was long overdue that we sorted this out.' Steve Howey not a fan of the 'See It, Say It, Sorted' policy there, and it was left to others to separate them. However, 'As things were gradually calming down, Choppy, who was now on his own, just ran, leapt a good few feet in the air and whacked me on the side of the head. Now I've taken some severe beatings in my time, but this was the first time I'd ever seen stars, just like in Tom and Jerry!'

Suckers that we are for a cartoon reference, this might be our favourite of these scraps.

RESULT: DRAW

PAUL WALSH V LAWRIE MADDEN

To continue the cartoon references, there's more than a hint of Scrappy Doo about Paul Walsh. A little guy who gets involved in fights with much bigger dogs, er men, and just about gets away with it.

The Madden Kerfuffle[5] took place in his early days at Charlton. Walsh was winding Madden up by calling him 'Skidders', because presumably they were still at primary school. After one warning that he would 'give you a fucking whack', Walsh did it again. 'With that he came straight for me, told me to fuck off and punched me square on the nose, breaking it in the process. I wasn't having that. I jumped on top of him, trying to whack him back and suddenly my nose just started gushing blood everywhere and we separated.' Lucky to get away with just a busted hooter we're saying.

RESULT: MADDEN BY TKO

BOBBY GOULD V DENNIS WISE & FRIENDS

Readers of our first volume will remember Bobby Gould being thrown around like a rag doll by John Hartson when he was Wales manager. This was part of Gould's infamous policy of 'having a circle' to sort out any disputes in training, in which the two contenders would be surrounded by teammates and staff, and go at it until honour was satisfied.

It's interesting that Gould was still maintaining this policy deep into the 1990s, because in truth it has seen him get bashed up quite a lot. On one occasion as Wimbledon boss, he was beaten by Dennis Wise on his own, so it's no surprise that on another occasion he was beaten even worse by Dennis Wise +1.

The threesome came about after Gould clipped Wimbledon player Vaughan Ryan round the ear for moaning after a match. At the following training session there was pressure from the squad for the two to have a circle. Gould says that at the last minute the youngster with the film star name said he wasn't up for it but then 'Wisey grabbed him, pushed him in and said "Yes, you are" before

—

5 *The Madden Kerfuffle* is our favourite Robert Ludlum book by the way.

he leapt in as well and the two of them gave me a right good hiding.' Furthermore, Gould says that as he was tending his wounds in the aftermath 'Fash and John Gayle leaned over and said: "We want a piece of you next time as well."' We're surprised Bobby kept hold of his lunch money most days at Wimbledon.

Even when he moved on to West Brom, and tweaked the format to keep things fresh by introducing boxing gloves to proceedings, it didn't stop him getting duffed up by Colin West, to cheers from the rest of the squad. Can somebody please stage some sort of intervention and tell past Bobby to stop fighting his players please? It's for his own good.

RESULT: EVERYBODY BUT BOBBY GOULD WINS

GRAEME SOUNESS V ALAN KENNEDY

And so, like the circle of life, all fighting roads lead back to Graeme Souness. This time at least, it's Souness the player who, according to Bruce Grobbelaar, took offence at Alan Kennedy despite being on the same side on a pre-season training camp in Spain. Kennedy sold Souey short with a pass then didn't do enough to recover the ball. In what can only be described as a flurry of moustaches, 'Handbags were out instantly and before anyone could stop him Graeme had punched him. It turned out that he had waited four years to do that in return for something that had happened in the past.' You might be thinking about Harry Enfield's Scousers at this point, but we're left wondering what had caused the initial rift. We reckon Kennedy once snatched the last biscuit.

RESULT: SOUNESS BY RICH TEA KO

So let's recap before we get out there amongst it.

You've warmed up – or not. You've had a run, a gym session, a tactics chat on a boat, a quick five-a-side with the chairman, a biscuit and a fight. By now you're ready to get down to some serious training. Apart from all those other distractions that might get in the way. These days we're sure that the state-of-the-art facilities are kept secure, clean and staffed entirely by serious professionals, but it wasn't ever thus.

Down at Chelsea these days it's oligarchs as far as the eye can see, but once upon a time they were just a little bit threadbare, and the training facilities were a world away from what they currently enjoy. Graeme Le Saux remembers training on pitches at Pleasington in his day that had a road between them that led to the local cemetery and crematorium. 'At regular intervals, a funeral cortège would wind its way slowly down that road with its cast of sombre mourners.' Quite rightly the Blues would stop and bow a head until everyone had passed by, which must have knocked them off their stride a bit. Maybe they used those moments to practise dead-ball situations. Dead ball. You know, because of the funerals. Please yourselves.

Chelsea's other training ground at Harlington around the same time had no such worries. There was no haunted-looking Dennis Wise telling everyone 'I see dead people' down there. However, there was a man in a bobble hat terrorising them constantly with his remote-controlled planes. Stan Ternent was coaching there at the time and says that the planes were constantly buzzing his players until one day 'without warning, his plane exploded in mid-air'. This was no accident, however; it turned out Vinnie Jones had blasted it out of the sky with his double-barrelled shotgun. It's an event that Ternent delights in telling but Vinnie doesn't deem a big enough deal to mention in his own book. Bringing a gun to training was obviously no big deal to him. And maybe he's right; it's not like he's the only person to fire a gun at a Chelsea training session, is he Ashley Cole?

Alongside Chelsea, Man City are the other nouveau riche arrivistes at the party these days. Again, it's fair to say that their current training facilities look like something out of *The Jetsons*, but there was a time in Paul Lake's day when they trained at Platt Lane with an audience of 'winos' hurling abuse at them. Lake shudders as he recalls jogging past them as they leered and jeered and had to chance their arm every time they went to get an overhit ball back from behind the goal: 'I remember one particularly creepy-looking guy who tried to put us off our stride as we completed each circuit by smiling menacingly and slowly rubbing his crotch up and down the netting', so that's lovely. If this happened these days we'd probably assume it was some 3D chess mind games from Marcelo Bielsa or something.

You can try to ignore these external factors as much as you like, but sometimes the distraction is something or someone inside the camp. These 'characters' are on the payroll but it doesn't seem like they always have the job in hand if we're honest.

Sheffield Wednesday had an ex-Marine on the coaching staff called Tony Toms, or Tomsy to his victims. Mel Sterland, no stranger to an oddball move himself as we'll discover throughout this book, tells us that at the start of training Tomsy would ask you what time it was, 'Then when you glanced at your watch, he'd grab your wrist, bend it back and pick you up off the floor. You'd be screaming like a baby.' We're never told what the aim of this was, other than to find out the time, but it seems like Tomsy was a law unto himself at the club. Sterland recalls, wistfully, going in one Sunday for treatment and finding 'Tomsy in the big communal bath with a couple of birds. I couldn't believe it. Obviously he didn't think anybody would be in that day. "Fucking get out," he shouted at me.' Mel made his excuses and left. So on top of being a violent bully, Tomsy was a sex person. It makes us wonder if those baths were always kept full though, or if Tomsy made small talk with the lucky women while he ran it for ages.

King of the training ground characters, however, must surely be Les Chapman at Man City. Les had a lengthy playing career, mostly around the North West of England, and a stint as manager at Preston, but by the time he got to City, it seems he was only trusted to be the kit man. In fairness, he was fortunate to get that job considering he arrived for his job interview 'in an ill-fitting polka dot suit from Oxfam, which was offset by flat cap, short, gravy-stained tie, and plastic trainers', before disrupting training by shouting about a lost dog, and being removed by security. When he did get his interview, Joe Royle asked him one question only, 'Were you that mad fella on the side of the pitch?', and Chappy was in. The odd get-up was part of Chappy's character comedy repertoire, which included:

> Billy Swift – based 'on his uncle Stephen, a patient with mental health issues he used to visit as a child'.
>
> William MacSwift – 'a wild-eyed, tartan-trewed Scot with wig and tam-o'-shanter hat'.
>
> And, 'a Lancastrian version of Adolf Hitler'.

You couldn't do two, maybe all three, of these today because of the PC, woke, liberal culture we live under and maybe the City training ground is all the poorer for it. Yes, they have a trophy room that's fit to burst but they no longer have a man that will dress as a punk rocker on away trips and leap unexpectedly out of bushes in full costume.

Oh Chappy. Can we start training properly now?

ISN'T IT ROMANTIC?

'Someone like Janice'

Bogota, Colombia, 1970.

The England squad, reigning world champions of the football world, are preparing to defend their Jules Rimet Trophy in the searing heat of Mexico. Sir Alf Ramsey is confident. Pundits believe that England arguably have a better team than they did in 1966. They've come to Colombia to play a match to help them acclimatise to the tough Mexican conditions. Their base is the Hotel Tequendama, which happens to feature a boutique jewellery shop in the lobby. Some players take the opportunity to peruse the beautiful items on sale. And then something momentous happens. Something that will change lives forever …

Emlyn Hughes bought an engagement ring for Barbara, the woman who would become his wife.

That one has slipped under the radar for 50 years hasn't it? With all the furore surrounding Bobby Moore's arrest for a crime he did not commit, it wasn't until the advent of Emlyn Hughes's autobiography that we discovered that something good came from that shop too: a wedding. And, later, two children: Emlyn and Emma Lynn. That jewellery shop has had a lot of bad press over the years, but this wonderful news proves there are always two sides to every story. Yes, the shop was at the heart of a plot to frame England's impeccable captain, but it was also the starting point of a happy marriage. Yin and yang, right?

And that's what this chapter is all about: matters of the heart. For many ex-pros, it's a difficult subject to address. Jamie Carragher sums it up best in his enjoyable autobiography when he explains he's comfortable talking about players or teams he likes, but discussing the woman he loves is another story altogether. Although, very sweetly, he does say: 'I couldn't have wished for a more perfect wife than Nicola.'

Patrick Vieira holds similar beliefs (about his own wife, not Mrs Carra) and states early on in his book that he won't be discussing private matters: 'I don't want to play the celebrity game – I have seen where that gets people,' he mutters darkly, possibly while mopping Vicks off his shirt. But he does throw us a small bone: 'all I will say is that I met Cheryl at a Destiny's Child concert a few years back and she has been with me ever since', which is a nice 'where-we-first-met' tale, even if the 'been with me ever since' part sounds a bit like how posh people talk about the cleaner they've had for 25 years. But then, when our guard is down, he tosses this line out: 'What I love about her is that she's an independent woman.' We hope this was intentional. A lesser man would have said: 'What I love about her is that she's bootylicious.'

Thankfully other footballers do open up a little more, generously giving us a peek behind the net curtains of their giant mansions, but even then they often find they can only do this by leaning heavily on the walking stick of classic football speak. Jack Charlton, for instance, says wife Pat 'adapted superbly' to their nomadic life, almost as if he was talking about a winger he'd asked to fill in at full-back for a few games.

Harry Redknapp is another who can't stop the classic language of football seeping into his discourse, describing, as he does, his beloved wife Sandra as his 'best signing'. Which is nice, except it does sound as if he spotted her out on a date with a non-league manager, recognised her potential, returned to see her in action a few more times in cinemas and at restaurants, and finally swooped in with an offer the lower-ranking boss couldn't afford to turn down, particularly as it had add-ons for things like marriage and kids, and a 10 per cent sell-on clause should Sandra decide to marry someone else. By Harry's own account, it's been a happy marriage too, which shows the benefit of proper scouting, rather than just watching a scratchy VHS of the best bits, like he did with Marco Boogers.[6]

Taking a slightly different sporting tack is Bobby Gould. For him, only horse racing analogies will do when it comes to the delicate matter of describing how a period of inactivity due to injury resulted

6 Your authors would like to make it crystal clear that we are not implying there is a scratchy VHS somewhere of Mrs Redknapp's best bits. This is just an analogy that we got carried away with.

in the conception of his son:[7] 'it's fair to say I failed to dismount in time due to the few pounds overweight I was carrying. The result: one bonny baby well ahead of schedule.' The problem with Bob's coyness here is that it makes his poor wife sound a bit like a horse, which seems very unfair on the poor lady.

Yes, moments of true romance are hard to find in the footballer autobiography. That's not a criticism. You have to know your audience and it's doubtful many people read about the lives of Keano, Souey or The Gouldfather hoping to find out how they proposed, whether they prefer to buy flowers or perfume on Valentine's Day, or where they went on their honeymoon. Having said that, former Southend striker Roy McDonough does give the romantic details of his honeymoon, saying the nudist beach they visited 'was packed with needle-dicked Germans who couldn't stop farting on their beach towels'. He does not reveal how he knew they were farting. Or how much time he spent matching penises to languages, but this sort of thing is the more common tone among our defiantly curable romantics.

For example, Terry Curran confesses to spending the reception of his wedding watching England v Scotland; everyone's ninth-favourite referee Jeff Winter admits to dragging wife Elaine to an England game during their honeymoon in London; and Dave 'Harry' Bassett, possibly confused by having two names, can't even remember proposing: 'Women seem to have total recall over this sort of thing … Apparently we were driving somewhere one evening when I said, "Perhaps we should get engaged."' Bloody women and their annoying ability to remember key moments in their lives. This is all a bit rich from Dave, mind, whose book showcases a Rothmans-like recall of his managerial career: 'An unusually symmetric pattern of draw, win, draw, win and so on, had seen us take 16 points from our previous eight games' is a fairly typical sentence in his forensically detailed book. If you can remember that run, Dave, you can hardly have a go at your wife for remembering the time you asked her to spend the rest of her life with you.

At least some of the more old-school players have fewer worries in offering up small romantic stories. Alan Mullery wistfully describes how he rowed to the centre of the Serpentine in Hyde Park to ask

—

7 Future Scotland keeper and gas-poisoning victim, Jonathan, no less. Who must be delighted with this detail of his parents' sex life making it into a book. Now two books.

future wife June the big question, while John Toshack and Dennis Tueart can each remember the film they saw at the pictures on their first dates with their wives – *That Darn Cat* and *The Nutty Professor* respectively, cinema fans.

Few players come off more likeable than Twitter activist and all-round people's champion Neville Southall in his *The Binman Chronicles*, although his wedding photo is a little unusual. It features wife Emma in a traditional white dress next to Nev in T-shirt, shorts and trainers. In fact, the sweet and practical idea was that they'd both wear whatever they wanted: 'She wouldn't let me wear flip-flops though … so I had a matching pair of trainers instead. It was a truly fantastic day.' It's a wonderful expression of love to compromise in this way, but the absolute best part of this story is that Nev's trainers matched his T-shirt. You can accuse him of a lot of things, probably, but when it comes to a wedding Neville Southall will absolutely make sure his outfit really ties together.

Bruce Grobbelaar is another keeper unafraid to show his loving side. He once caned it from Liverpool to the south of France in about 19 hours because his then girlfriend and future wife Debbie had gone on a girls' trip and he really missed her. At least, that's what it seems like on the surface. Scratch that surface, however, and you're left with more questions than answers. For a start, Debbie's friend can't have been impressed, with even Bruce admitting: 'We enjoyed a great holiday, though I am not so sure that Debbie's friend thought a lot of it.' More importantly, there's the intriguing detail that Bruce had had to retrieve his car from his insurance broker and friend, Gordon Dearden, who subsequently was frantically trying to contact Bruce in France because of a gold bar (yes, a gold bar) he'd left under the passenger seat: 'He had been asked to get it valued and feared that if it was not returned soon he might have difficulty in walking.' So what on the face of things seemed a romantic dash in the name of love quickly unravels into a needy goalie gatecrashing a holiday by absconding with some gold bullion belonging to a person apparently well capable of exacting vicious revenge. None of this seemed to affect Debbie, however, and they were later married, before honeymooning in 'Wankie National Park'. Nothing funny about that name. No, sir.

Occasionally, there are splendid moments of pure love and affection to warm even the most cynical cockles, such as Jimmy

Greaves reuniting with his ex-wife after his struggles with alcohol: 'Our divorce was a piece of legal paper that we have both ignored.' Beautiful. But the most romantic gesture we discovered didn't come from a player at all; it came from Tring's most famous export, Graham Poll. His story concerns a Valentine's Day many years ago. To surprise his girlfriend, he located her car in a car park and wrote 'I love you' on it – in toothpaste (presumably having rejected the other two main contenders for the job, tomato puree and Primula). The Pollster then left the manky squeezed toothpaste tube next to a rose on her bed back at her home.

We could just take this at face value, but instead we have some important questions we'd ask Graham if we ever enrolled in his Red Wine Club:[8]

1. Why toothpaste? Were you not concerned this might send some sort of message about your lover's oral hygiene?
2. Did you offer to clean it off later? Because dried toothpaste is a bugger to shift.
3. Why did you leave the toothpaste tube on her bed? Either she knew it was you, in which case no need; or, she was freaking out, thinking it might be a stalker. If the latter, imagine her terror at finding the tube in her own bedroom. What were you thinking?

Despite our misgivings, this ruse did work: she later became Graham's wife. And, come on, let's give Graham props for seeing his baffling plan through to the minty end, which is more than we can say for Marco Negri. In his book, he tells of how, in his Rangers days, he and wife Monica decided to get tattoos of each other's names – a permanent symbol of their love and commitment, if you like. So, off an excited Monica went to get her 'Marco' tattoo. At which point, Marco bottled it: 'I tried really hard to explain my dramatic U-turn and said, "You know Monica, Marco is such a common name that if we ever broke up, chances are you wouldn't have to get rid of it."' Spot

8 Graham had a gang of ref friends when he was still reffing, and together they named themselves the Red Wine Club – because they liked red wine. There's loads of this ref stuff in our other book, *Booked! The Gospel According to our Football Heroes*, if you want more.

on, Marco. There's Van Basten, Tardelli, Reus, Rojo, Veratti, Materazzi and … um … Mark Owen? Any tattoo artist worth their salt should be able to do something with that.

THE DATING GAME

But we're jumping ahead of ourselves here. Before the tattoos and the toothpaste, there's the dating. There's a school of thought (that we've just invented) that footballers' love lives often reflect the way they play the game. Look at Frank Worthington, as flamboyant in his love of women as he was with the ball at his feet. Same with George Best. Consider Frank McAvennie, Mick Quinn and Dwight Yorke – according to all their books they were as prolific off the pitch as on it. And then think of the great Zlatan Ibrahimović. How do we sum up his playing style? Direct. Flash. Ultra-confident. Lethal. Now ponder this: Zlatan met his partner Helena after spotting her zipping round Malmo in her Mercedes while he was zooming around Malmo in his Ferrari. Impressed, he somehow obtained her number, and his opening text was every bit as audacious as that ludicrous volley he scored a few minutes into his LA Galaxy debut: '"All right, how's it going? Think you've seen me around," and then I finished with "The guy in the red one" – the guy in the red Ferrari, that is – and got a reply. "The girl in the black one," she wrote.' When you're able to identify yourself, in a large city, purely by the colour of your car, that is some pretty high-level flirting.

George Graham's management career was characterised by teams that, while not unattractive, were certainly based on solid defensive discipline. This, though, was a marked contrast to his playing career, where he was not known as a worker (his nickname was 'Stroller'), but as a crowd-pleasing playmaker. Off the pitch, he had the moves too. Vince Hilaire, who played with Graham in his latter days at Palace, compared him in his book to Sean Connery in his Bond days, but if he truly was that magnetic, where does that leave Leicester legend Keith Weller? We only ask because Alan Hudson got to know Stroller and Weller at Chelsea and reckoned, in a complicated footballer-to-celebrity analogy equation, 'Weller made George Graham look like Larry Grayson in the crumpet stakes.'

Anyway, how does Hilaire choose to back up his 'the name is Graham, George Graham' (which could just sound like one long name, now we think about it) assertion? Well, by explaining how Gorgeous

George liked to honk his horn at attractive women while driving. You'll remember Bond famously employing this trick while driving his white Aston Martin Transit in *You Only Honk Twice*. Vince writes: 'He'd do it twice and then he'd mouth to her and ask why she was beeping her horn at him and they'd start flirting.' So the woman was in another car? We assumed she was minding her own business on the pavement. How did this flirting take place from car to car while negotiating the thick south London traffic? We're lost.

More evidence of George's genius comes from a story alleged by Perry Groves (we'll be coming on to his sexploits, yes, we said sexploits, later) that took place in Cyprus when they were out there for an exhibition game. During dinner one evening, Graham was eating with Kevin Keegan when the restaurant owner introduced them to a particularly attractive woman. Groves says that Keegan was, as you'd expect, the epitome of politeness, standing up and shaking hands and so forth, while George barely glanced at the vision he'd been presented with. And then 'all of a sudden, he looked her straight in the eyes and said, "Are we fucking later?" She giggled and then, after a moment, said, "All right."' Perry could only sit back and admire: 'I realised I had just seen a master operator in action.' To be fair to Vince Hilaire, this does read like the unwritten dialogue of pretty much every Bond movie.

Graham went on to manage another Arsenal maverick, Charlie Nicholas, who himself was linked with numerous glamorous women in his 1980s bachelor days, from Suzanne Dando to the Cadbury's *Flake* girl. Knowing all that, his description of what he was looking for in a woman, written at the height of his 'Champagne Charlie' notoriety, is perhaps a little surprising: 'Ideally I would like to marry a girl like my sister Janice. She isn't the most beautiful girl in the world, but she's very attractive and has a lovely personality ... Yes, someone like Janice would be perfect.' Poor Janice, damned with faint praise, yet at the same time desirable enough for one of the great heart-throbs of the era – it's just unfortunate they were related.

Charlie Nick may have had to live with the unfortunate curse of going out with models and gymnasts, but for quieter lads, like keepers, things were not quite so easy. For instance, back in the days before Tinder simplified the dating process for horny young folk, David Seaman was forced to take a more primitive route: CB Radio. That's right, in the early 80s, Spunky was a Radio Ham and across the airwaves a young Seamo was known as 'Green Giant' – you know, like the sweetcorn.

Dave explains hitting it off with one lady to the point where they decided to take things to the next level: 'I arranged an eyeball (sadly, you never forget the jargon) but I had a car by then and I knew where this girl was supposed to be waiting. I drove up and saw she was a big – and I mean very big – girl so just kept on driving.' Oh Dave. As Charlie would tell you, looks are not the most important thing – it's what's inside that counts.

In their younger years, other players had more conventional ways of convincing girls to go out with them. The old classic is to pretend to be someone you're not to seem more impressive. As a teenager on Liverpool's books, Swansea legend Lee Trundle's hook with the ladies was to claim he was a footballer. All well and good, but then he made it weird by giving them not his own name, but that of Liverpool reserve Lee Jones. This needless lie almost backfired one night when he was taken home by a slightly older woman, who insisted on waking up her Liverpool-mad son to show him who she'd enticed into their front room: '"All right, lad, how are you?" I said, trying to look confident. He turned back to his mum. "He doesn't look like Lee Jones." "Nah mate," I said. "I've just had me haircut last week." Somehow I got away with it.' It's the thought process that baffles us on this one. Trunds was much more well versed on the Mersey dating scene of the 90s than us, but was there really enough boost in Jones's name to make that lie worthwhile?

Eventually, Trundle became a bit of a star in his own right and so he was able to confidently use his real name in his nightclub negotiations – but celebrity, even localised in a lower-league context, can work both ways. He describes one occasion where he had a 'quickie round the back of a nightclub in Wrexham' and at the next home game a local copper cheerily told him he'd seen the whole thing on CCTV: '"in that case, bung me a copy of the tape next time," I said, with both of us in stitches as I ran off. It was the stuff any young lad dreams of, and you didn't have to try very hard with the whole VIP scene.' Yes, it's a common fantasy for youngsters: a quick bunk-up behind Shimmers while in a dark surveillance room somewhere a member of the constabulary whacks off to the grainy black and white footage so he can tell you all about it just before you warm up for a home game with Leyton Orient. *Roy of the Rovers* stuff.

THE MISSUS

Plenty of footballers make sure to find a space somewhere in their book to thank their other half. But some go the other way completely, lamenting that their wife or girlfriend could never quite understand or tolerate the footballer's lifestyle. And by 'lifestyle' we mean stepping out a lot with the lads, playing regular golf and going away most weekends. Some women, perhaps understandably, just don't get it.

Ray Parlour was married with three young kids by his mid-20s: 'We just didn't get on after a while,' he writes of then wife Karen. 'I would go out, she would be moaning.' Keith Gillespie's partner Vikki was similarly upset when they moved to Ireland and he filled the hours before evening training with golf: 'She complained about being stuck at home as a childminder … There was similar grief when I went for a few drinks with the lads.' And Jimmy Floyd Hasselbaink goes full-on unreconstructed male when mentioning one relationship that went south: 'You know how that goes, women aren't always the easiest to deal with.' Amirite, lads?

A little surprisingly, it turns out that Sir Alf Ramsey might well have approved of this desire to escape the wife. Not for drinking purposes, of course, but Alf wanted his players fully focused on football and not worrying about silly things like love or children. Sir Bobby Charlton remembers talking to his boss at the end of an England tour, and mentioning that although he'd enjoyed it, he was looking forward to seeing his wife and daughter. 'I was shocked by his response,' says Sir Bob who was, let's not forget, one of the best players on earth at this time. 'A very hard expression came to his face and he said, "If I'd thought that was your attitude I wouldn't have brought you on the trip."'

Seriously, Alf? You would sacrifice Bobby bloody Charlton because after some weeks away from home he might actually miss his wife and child? He wasn't complaining. He wasn't agitating to go home. He was just, in quieter moments perhaps, occasionally thinking about his closest family. That is hardcore.

Sir Geoff Hurst reports two similar stories in his book, too. On the first occasion, the wives of Hurst and Martin Peters booked into the same hotel as the players during a tour of Malta and Ramsey told Peters that if it ever happened again, he would not select either of them in the future.

On the second occasion he talked directly to Hurst's wife, Judith: 'And poking her in the chest with a finger said, "I hear you're going to watch us in Mexico in the summer. I want you to know that we're not going there for your enjoyment, and we're not going for my enjoyment. We're going there to bring back the pot and I don't want any interference from you or anyone else."'

Pretty incredible stuff from Alf, particularly the poking in the chest, which would be uncalled for no matter who he was speaking to, let alone the wife of the man who four years earlier had scored the hat-trick in the actual World Cup Final that had allowed Alf to win the 'pot' (we did love that) in the first place.

Mo Johnston may have been right up Sir Alf's street, because according to John Barnes, he was one player often keen to avoid going home if he could possibly help it. When he signed for Watford from Partick, the club temporarily put Mo and his girlfriend up in a flat above the club shop at Vicarage Road. Genuinely. In some respects, this arrangement surely held great advantages for Mo. For Saturday home games, for example, he could both sleep late *and* be back in time to watch the end of *Grandstand*. Plus, a ready supply of Watford-themed mugs, tie clips and pennants were available just feet from his front door. Imagine how happy someone like Tony 'all the gear' Pulis would be with such a set-up.

And yet, there was a downside. Mo liked a night out and when the coach would return from away games, there would be Ms Mo, wouldn't you know, at the window, looking for her beau (we thank you). But, Barnesey says, to avoid having to explain that he planned to go straight out on the town, Mo would sometimes hide on the coach, then sneak off when she wasn't looking. Later, expertly covering his tracks, Mo would tell his love that he'd had business to attend to in another part of the country and had asked the coach to drop him off en route. Such were the freedoms enjoyed by men afraid of their girlfriends in the days before the mobile phone.

It all seems a bit rum, doesn't it? We don't like to judge, but at least Parlour and Gillespie stood and took the flak (before ignoring it and going off for a pint) – this seems cowardly in comparison. Then again, the most important detail of this anecdote is not Mo hiding his strawberry blond barnet under Wilf Rostron's coat, it's the bit about Watford housing players above their club shop. At this time, Elton John was the chairman. Couldn't he have sorted a swankier pad for their new signing? It sounds like a sitcom – *Mo Place Like Home*, perhaps.

In fact, much of Mo's life contained scenes you'd usually only expect to find in a sitcom. For instance, Frank McAvennie tells a story about the time he and his Page 3 model girlfriend Jenny Blyth stayed with Mo in France. They were getting ready to go to a Simple Minds concert, when Frank caught Mo spying on Jenny as she was getting changed. 'The urge went through me to punch his lights out. "Jesus, Frank," Mo said, realising I was there, "she's got a fucking great pair of tits." And he walked away, casual as you like ... That was Mo.' This could be from Mo's spin-off sitcom, *Mo Worries*, where Mo is forced to face up to his addiction to voyeurism and all his mates are really concerned about his future.

Yet when it comes to lying to the missus in order to have a few sherbets, no story can possibly match the vast, labyrinthine anecdote related by Ian 'Snowy/Snods' Snodin in his straight-talking memoirs *Snod This for a Laugh*.

Buckle up. It all starts when Snods is injured while at Everton. One weekend in 1991, the Blues are away at Southampton and boss Howard Kendall asks Snods to take his injured leg to Port Vale v Hull to scout Dean Windass. Snods sees his chance of extending this assignment to a short weekend break, so calls up his mate, the also injured Kevin Sheedy, in the hope he'll join him. Sheeds is up for it. Course he is; this is Sheeds we're talking about. But, he doesn't think his wife Debbie would be so keen, so he concocts a story for her, claiming that Kendall has asked him to travel to Southampton with the squad so he can have a late fitness test.

So far, so good. Bit weird, but not hugely unusual. Sheeds and Snods head out on the Friday and have a lovely evening in Liverpool. Or, in Snods's words, 'It was an absolutely magnificent night and both of us were paralytic.' Paralytic to the extent that the next day Snodin slept through at least some of what turned out to be a fairly dull game at Vale Park. It was only as they drove back to Merseyside after the game that they spotted the flaw in Sheedy's plan: he'd need to have at least some basic knowledge of what happened in the Southampton game in case Debbie quizzed him on it when he arrived home.

Had it been a simple 1-0 away win (John Ebrell after 28 minutes, for example), that would have been fine. We all could have busked that, couldn't we? But, surprisingly, the game was a bit of a thriller, ending 4-3 to Everton (Mike Newell scored at both ends, a young Alan Shearer scored for Southampton and Everton brought on Ray Atteveld for Tony Cottee. Yeah, Ray Atteveld. Absolutely guarantee you haven't thought about Ray Atteveld for at least 25 years, have you?[9]).

The lads were reduced to furiously taking notes on the game from a radio match report and trying to memorise all the scorers.

Anyway, even then Sheedy somehow lost the notes he made about the game and had to frantically ring Snodin so they could go over the scorers again. Somehow, he got away with it. The perfect crime. Which is an apposite phrase, because although that *should* be where this story ends, there is one more detail: 'To add to the drama, on the Sunday we heard there had been a fatal stabbing in Liverpool in the early hours of the morning.' In fact, the boys had actually chatted with the victim on their Friday night out. Step back for a moment to appreciate the way Snodin introduced this nugget of information: 'To add to the drama'. In truth, the story hasn't been that dramatic at all – it was basically 'men secretly go on lash and get away with it'. To say *an actual murder* 'adds to the drama' of this tale is to dismiss it as a mere footnote to the enjoyable banter of the rest of the weekend. In reality, it's the one thing that makes the entire anecdote remarkable, because Snodin goes on to admit that the police appealed for people to come forward if they'd had contact with the victim in the previous few days: 'This was a problem for Kev as he was supposed to be in Southampton, so we kept quiet and didn't contact the cops.' Indeed. Don't worry about the murder investigation boys – Sheedy might get told off by his missus.

And from there, Snodin ends the story. We don't know if the killer was caught. All we know is that Sheeds pulled off a classic lads' night out without having to ask permission or getting caught in a lie *or* getting dragged into a messy-sounding homicide case. Phew! Job done.

What Snods does do, though, is drop one final bombshell concerning what Sheedy liked to do if he'd been called home early from a Saturday night out: 'Debbie is deaf in one ear so if she fell asleep with her good ear on the pillow, he'd go downstairs, climb through the window and head out for a few more drinks. If she woke up before he returned he would be in for a big bollocking. Kev and Debbie are divorced now.'

---

9 Well, unless you're a West Ham fan who remembers *that* back pass in an FA Cup fifth-round replay against Sunderland in 1992. Then you probably wake up screaming about him most nights. It's on YouTube.

Brilliant. The detail of him creeping all the way downstairs only to climb through a window is particularly mystifying, but maybe Sheedy had a really creaky front door. And if this entire episode paints a slightly frightening picture of long-suffering Debbie, don't worry: Snods says she's a lovely lady and they're friends to this day. You know, despite the divorce.

We can only guess what would have happened to Sheeds had Debbie caught him in the lie, but it can't have been worse than the fate of Mark Dennis, a legendarily hard left-back who, Frank Worthington claims in his book, nevertheless had good reason to fear his then wife Jane: 'They were a super couple, but they used to wind each other up terribly. One night Mark had been out with the lads and was just creeping in the door having arrived home at about 5am when Jane suddenly appeared and stuck a knife in his collar-bone.' Luckily her aim was a bit off – Dennis apparently reckoned she was going for his heart.

Speaking of attempted spousal murder (or hubbycide, as we like to call it, to make it seem cuddlier) of footballers by wives called Jane, former West Ham and Everton winger Mark Ward tells of the time his Jane (presumably a different one) ran him down in a car park near Ascot: 'Without warning, she pressed the accelerator and before I could react I was thrown up and over the car and landed on my backside.' Pandemonium ensued as Wardy wound up with his head against a back wheel, to the shock of their friend Kathy: 'She thought I was dead.' He wasn't, so Jane sped off, apparently grazing the pub wall in her haste. Cue the *EastEnders* doof doofs.

PLAYING AWAY

Footballers are not renowned for their loyalty. Fans demand it, of course. Loyalty is important to us fans. We despise players for being disloyal if they 'move for the money', as if every one of us wouldn't change jobs if offered a bit more cash at a better company. So, in terms of work, they're probably no more disloyal than any of us. In terms of home life, that may be a different matter. If you're a footballer and are attached to a Premier League club, you are prime fodder for a tabloid kiss-and-tell story and over the years the multitude of these stories has left the impression that footballers are overwhelmingly cads, bounders, love rats and serial adulterers, which seems unfair. I mean, none of us knows for sure how true this stereotype is, do we Keith Gillespie?

'It is true that footballers who stay faithful are a rare breed. Personally, I can't say that I've encountered many.'

Oh. Well, that's only one player's opinion. Here's David Batty's memories of that era just before he joined Gillespie at Newcastle from Blackburn: 'Players were saying: "It's class here Batts. We're out every night! You'll be divorced in six months."' Right. We should note that Batts stayed living in Yorkshire after signing and was definitively not divorced in six months, or ever, in fact. He's very much the family man who eschews lads' trips to Ayia Napa for staycations with the wife and kids, commenting 'we decided that English companies like Haven Holiday Homes could give us all we needed'. It mystifies us that Haven haven't locked the Leeds legend into a long-term advertising contract based on this glowing endorsement.

But let's return to the point. This tendency towards unfaithfulness must at least come in part because young footballers do attract the attentions of women easily – they barely need to work at their seduction technique at all. In fact, according to Mick Quinn, at Coventry the 'birds' would brazenly approach him and say, 'Take me home, I want to shag you', apparently reciting rejected dialogue from an early draft of an *Austin Powers* movie. Judging by his book, Quinn was as prolific between the sheets as he was in the six-yard box (which, even if we say so ourselves, would make a great cover quote for his book) – on another occasion, he reports that he was seeing four barmaids at once: 'In truth, I was leading a celebrity lifestyle.' Because absolutely nothing says 'celebrity' more than concurrently dating multiple barmaids.

Despite Gillespie's assertion about the unfaithfulness of players, though, the best stories we read about adultery involved managers. Back in the 1970s, there was the huge scandal that the then Manchester United manager, Tommy Docherty, was having an affair with a woman named Mary Brown – who happened to be the wife of United physio, Laurie Brown. It was easily the biggest football story involving a physio in the history of football until the hullabaloo with Mourinho and Eva Carneiro a few years back.[10]

Anyway, the press line at the time was that Docherty had 'run off' with Mary. Tommy, however, is keen to end this misconception once and for all in his book, where he reveals the startling truth that they didn't 'run off', because Tommy, Mary *and* Laurie all shared

10 Though Gary Lewin falling over and getting stretchered off at the World Cup that time comes in at a highly enjoyable third place.

Mary's mother's house together for more than a year. According to the Doc: 'He [Laurie] was occupying a part of the house upstairs. Mary would go upstairs to put her kids to bed at night and then come back downstairs to spend the night with me.' It's yet another sitcom – *Three Up, Doc Down*. It almost sounds civilised. Did Laurie and Tommy travel into work together too, on some kind of primitive car-pooling scheme? Or would that have been too awkward?

Sven-Göran Eriksson is, of course, a known lothario these days. But when the story emerged about his relationship with Ulrika Jonsson in 2002, it all felt so unreal. This ageing, softly spoken man with a funny-shaped head and a resemblance to Mr Burns was not only involved with the glamorous Nancy Dell'Olio, but had also managed to attract the much-lusted-after Ulrika (ka, ka). It was like finding out from Edwina Currie that John Major had a sexual magnetism all of us had failed to notice for years (a story, which, weirdly, emerged in the same year. It was an incredible few months for white, wealthy, grey-haired, bespectacled, middle-aged men).

But while Sven's dalliances with Ulrika and, later, Faria Alam at the FA, were pored over in minute detail because he was England manager at the time, there was less light shone on exactly how he had got together with Nancy in Italy. Their relationship had started while she was married to a wealthy Roma-supporting lawyer called Giancarlo. Eventually, as Sven and Nancy's affair became serious, they decided to come clean. Giancarlo, astoundingly, was totally cool about it: 'Whatever happened, he hoped that we could stay friends. I had made Roma play the best football he had ever seen,' wrote Sven. That must have been some proper Barca 2011 meets Brazil 1970 football. West Ham fans used to sing to Christian Dailly: 'You are the love of my life, I'd let you shag my wife.' Giancarlo could clearly relate to that sweet sentiment.

Another international manager, Craig Brown, doesn't immediately feel like the sort of person you'd expect to find in a collection of stories about philandering footballers, and indeed he did not, as far as we're aware, go off on a bonking spree every time the Scots were playing qualifying games across Europe. But we do know that he held a large torch for Marge, the wife of his late 90s Wales counterpart Bobby Gould. And wasn't afraid to let it be known, either. It all started on a course for coaches held in Malta that Gould and Brown both attended, when one day 'Broony' inadvertently saw Mrs Gould enjoying some sun without her bikini top on. Gould says that Brown was so taken with the view that from then on he would send them postcards whenever he was travelling, 'all addressed to Marge and headed: "how to murder your husband".' Later on, he called up their son Jonathan to the Scotland squad, where he would refer to him as 'Son of Mother', ensuring that Jon would constantly be aware of how much his national manager lusted after his sexy mum.

This strange story of inter-international-manager-spousal-flirtation is perhaps only topped by a tale from Peter Shilton. After a row one day with wife Sue, Shilts went out on the town in Nottingham and met up with some friends. During the course of the evening, an unknown woman introduced herself and he subsequently asked her if she'd join them all for a curry. Later, and because Shilts had discovered she lived near him, he offered her a lift home. Obviously, he'd been drinking, because this was the 1970s and drink-driving was quite the thing back then, particularly, it seems, for footballers.[11] Unfortunately, he started to think a police car might be following him, so after some overly careful driving he decided to pull off down a country lane to wait until the police had passed.

All of which sounds perfectly innocent, doesn't it? Because if you ever think the police might be following you because you are possibly driving erratically while drunk, the thing to do is to turn off and pull up down a small country lane. That kind of behaviour doesn't seem remotely suspicious, so they'll just leave you to it, won't they? That's how police work works, isn't it?

Anyway, then things get really odd. Shilton says a car drew up behind them and the woman claimed it was her husband. So, logically, her husband followed her from the pub to the Indian restaurant, and then all the way to the country lane. He must've done, surely? He can't have stumbled on them by luck. All of which would make the husband fairly terrifying and perhaps Shilton made the same calculations, because he writes: 'I had assumed she wasn't married. Not that that really mattered, seeing as my intention was purely to give her a lift home. But her husband arriving on the scene sent shock waves through my system. I really panicked at this point. I revved the engine, thrust the car into gear, let out the clutch and sped away.'

---

11 And still today! Right, Derby fans?

Sadly, Peter lost control, crashed, was knocked unconscious and when he came round the woman was gone and the police were there. And all because he had innocently given a woman he'd never met before a (drunken) lift home … stopping innocently down a quiet country road on the way … to make sure he wasn't being followed by the police … except he was being followed … by the woman's husband.

Poor old Pete. That's what you get for being a good Samaritan.

There are plenty of footballer autobiographies where football takes a back seat to the sexploits the player enjoyed in his heyday. Colchester, Arsenal and Southampton forward Perry Groves is one of the best examples: 'You could say I was a sex addict, although I think all this addiction thing is bollocks. I just liked it, simple as that.' So, as you can see, he was a big fan of a bunk-up. 'I lost my virginity when I was 16, and after that we were at it morning, noon and night.' OK, mate, more than we needed but ... 'It was non-stop for me from there on, two or three times a day. Before training, after training and one at night just to round the day off.' Righto – we get the ... 'When we returned for pre-season training I was fighting fit: I'd been running every day and swimming a lot, I was teetotal – and all that shagging helped too.' All right, Perry. We get it. The man's relentless.

Groves admits he was unfaithful to his wife Mandy 'throughout' their ten-year marriage – and also before it. We know this, because he explains that not only did he sleep with an ex-girlfriend in the lead up to his wedding, he rang his best man to tell him exactly what he was about to do beforehand. Groves says that 'there's a saying in the film world that affairs on location don't count. Well, it's the same in football. We say, "When you fly over the water, it doesn't count."' Is that the right phrase? We thought there was a more common one: 'Our own code of silence is, "What goes on on [sic] tour stays on tour."' Ah, that's it. Sort of.

Grovesy's extra-marital shenanigans are what inspired the following list – our Five Favourite Occasions Where Footballers Got Caught Having Affairs. Sorry that's not catchier. We start, as you would expect, with Perry himself.

PERRY GROVES

Poor old Perry was caught by the long-suffering Mandy the day after he'd actually ended a long-running affair. His cover for visiting the woman for a final time had been to tell his wife he was giving a presentation at a local boys' football club in Romsey. But Mandy went all Columbo on him by quizzing him on the distance to Romsey. Perry guilelessly fell into the trap by saying it was five miles, but unfortunately for him Mandy had been checking his mileage – a trick she'd picked up from another one of Perry's mistresses.

UNNAMED PLAYER

This story comes from the richly memorable memoirs of Leeds and Sheffield Wednesday full-back Mel Sterland and all it proves is that when footballers are caught, they have an excuse for literally anything. On this occasion the player in question, whose identity is protected by Sterland, had sex with a woman on tour, only realising afterwards that she was a prostitute. He thought it was just a random woman who openly approached him for a quickie or something. Long story. Anyway, the point is that she passed him an STD: 'His knob and balls were red-raw and nobody would get into the bath with him.' So, how did he explain this one away when he got home? 'I think he told his missus he'd got kicked in the bollocks playing football.' Of course he did.

KEVIN BEATTIE

Let's be fair to Beats. He was stitched up good and proper. Playing in an away match at Barcelona he was involved in a photoshoot when he was asked if he'd mind if a Spanish actress could be in the photos with him. He agreed, and was then shocked when the young lady walked in and removed a mink coat to reveal very little else underneath. Beattie squirmed about for a couple of pics, then called it off, only afterwards finding out she was a major porn star. 'I felt as though I had been stitched up and went berserk.' Poor Kev says it took quite a lot of explaining to his wife when he got home, but, fortunately, in the end he straightened it all out. Phew. No real harm done. Beattie comes out of it well – he was doing people a favour, got caught out a bit, was understandably cross, and made sure his wife knew the truth of why a sexy lady was sat on his knee in a photo wearing only a string vest. It happens to the best of us.

And then Kev loses most of his gallant points when he ends his anecdote with: 'By the way love, if you get a copy of this book – what great tits you had!' Ah.

HOPE SOLO

Come on, Hope wasn't doing the cheating. But she did suffer when an early boyfriend cheated on her with a cheerleader while she was still a student. Like a scene from a 1980s John Hughes teen flick, her swift revenge was wreaked at a carnival: '"Hey," I said, stepping in front of her. "You're a fucking slut." She smirked at me. "Tom's pretty good," she said. "You should give him a try." I punched her in the face.' Never mess with Solo.

BEN THORNLEY

Our favourite story comes from Class of 92 member Ben Thornley, who does not make any excuses for the womanising ways of his youth, freely calling himself 'an arsehole'. This story happened in Antigua, where Ben was on holiday with Huddersfield's Kevin Gray. One night, Thornley's girlfriend Catherine and Gray's wife Debbie had retired early after a night of drinking celebrating Catherine's 21st and the Grays' anniversary. Left to their own devices, Ben and Kev fairly quickly hooked up with a couple of German tennis instructors, which quickly escalated to the point where Gray was 'rattling away' with one in an outdoor gym while Thornley was naked with the other, frolicking in the sea.

They might have got away with it too, had it not been for the meddling Julie Phillips, wife of ace striker Kevin, who spied them leaving the bar and grassed them up to their other halves. Yeah, Kev Phillips was there too. And Thornley's teammate Chris Casper. Basically, this place seemed to be crawling with footballers. Anyway, Thornley complains: 'Ultimately I've got to take some responsibility for what happened but Julie's got a certain portion of the blame in all this too – as has Kevin Phillips for bringing her.' Not sure Kevin is to blame here, is he?

Somehow the womenfolk missed Gray and his Deutscher Tennislehrergesexymacht in the gym, but Thornley, who thought he was getting lucky, was not quite so lucky when the pair investigated the beach: 'that's where they caught me, otherwise engaged, lying down in the surf. Debbie came racing into the sea. I jumped out of the way and she went straight for the tennis coach and banjoed her.' Boom! Absolutely Soloed her.

This one at least has a happy, if unexpected, ending: Thornley proposed on the flight home the very next day, and Catherine accepted.

THE SENSITIVE ONES

It would be unfair of us to give the impression that all footballers spend their autobiographies boasting about conquests and admitting to affairs. Thankfully, some players are really nice about their loved ones.

Didier Drogba unabashedly describes meeting his future wife Lalla as like being hit by a 'thunderbolt'. Lawrie McMenemy says, very sweetly: 'If praising the crucial role of a wife is a strange way to end a book about football then I make no apology.' And Kevin Keegan fondly remembers meeting his wife Jean for the first time on the waltzers at the St Leger Fair.

Uwe Rösler's story of how he started seeing a Norwegian woman called Cecilie is particularly sweet. He hadn't long signed for Manchester City and his English wasn't great, so he was forced to bring Dutchman Michel Vonk, who (he knew some German) along with him to act as a kind of Cyrano de Bergerac. Seriously. And we are not going to be so crass as to make a nasty nose joke here, but … it's there, isn't it?[12] That's not our fault. We can't change classic literature any more than we can deny Vonk's most distinguishing feature. Anyway, Rösler admits he could have no way of telling what Vonk was saying, but it must've worked as Uwe and Cecilie were later married.

However, our prize for most loved-up footballer has to go to 80s Everton centre-back Derek Mountfield, as revealed by Neville Southall: 'He was deeply committed to his wife, Julie, and we used to slaughter him for it. She used to come to Bellefield and they'd get cushions out with "Derek" and "Julie" written on them and have a little picnic in his car, which was like Knightrider's [sic]. Then when he got inside the training ground itself he'd give her a call to let her know he'd got there safely.' The best part about all that is that Degsy had a car like Knight Rider's which presumably meant they could have their picnic while Kit drove them safely to the training ground.

JUST ONE MORE THING

That should have been the end of the chapter. But we can't leave it there. And we can't leave it there because of Steve Nicol and the explosive tale of his interaction with teammate Gary Ablett's wife

12 Michel Conk more like.

Debbie[13] at a big dinner following their defeat to Crystal Palace in the 1990 FA Cup semi-final. Yeah. They had a big dinner all lined up for their inevitable win! Anyway, it's a story that is in a category all of its own, but it can't go untold, so it's here.

Here they all are then, the Liverpool lads and their significant others drowning their sorrows after being downed by Pards Pardew's extra-time winner. With the meal done, Nicol lights up a fag while 'staring at Debbie Ablett and her huge lion's mane of hair. Like a child, I was fascinated by it.' Almost in slow motion, you can already see what's coming, can't you? 'Then for some inexplicable reason, I decided to see what would happen when I put my lighter next to her rather large mop.' Listen Steve, there's no 'inexplicable reason' about it. This is how science works: hypothesis and experiment. Alexander Fleming hypothesised something about mould and Petri dishes and boom, penicillin. Stevie Nicol hypothesised something about a naked flame and a hairdo propped up by a can of hairspray and, well, also, boom: 'I started bashing her on the head with my hands to try and put the fire out. "What the hell are you doing?" enquired Gary, understandably, with more than a hint of anger in his voice.' 'A hint of anger', yes.

Nicol claims he doused the flames 'before they caused too much damage', but what does 'too much' in this case mean? That she wasn't left completely bald? And finally, you have to love a man who looks on the bright side: 'At least that broke the ice after the disappointing result earlier in the day.' Break the ice, melt the ice, whatever – either way, creating a scene that looks a bit like the moment the Ark of the Covenant is opened at the end of *Raiders of the Lost Ark* is guaranteed to get people nattering.

—

13 Do not think it has escaped our attention that a solid 85 per cent of footballers in the 80s and 90s (and 100 per cent of magicians in the same era) seem to have been married to women called Debbie.

JUST CALL ME ROBBO

'Walnut Whip'

If you read our first book, *Booked: The Gospel According to our Football Heroes*, then, firstly, bless you. Secondly, you may remember that we spent a good deal of time breaking down the complex set of unwritten rules concerning the issuing of nicknames in the world of football. In the process, we discovered some absolute pearlers that bear repeating: Kevin Keegan was once 'Andy McDaft', Tony Galvin was 'The Russian' and Vinny Samways was, gorgeously, 'Vinegar Sandwich'. We thought we were done, but our further reading turned up so many more fantastic nicknames that we felt it was our duty to chronicle them here in our little sequel.

Before we reveal with not much fanfare our Top 12 New Favourite Footballer Nicknames, though, we do have some honourable mentions.

Steve Nicol (Chips, Henderson, Chico), Mick Quinn (Sumo, Bob Carolgees, Noah, Fletch) and Sir Trevor Brooking (Tricky, Lord Ted, Hadleigh, Boog, Cyril) were our winners for players with large collections of nicknames previously. But it turns out there are others who enjoy what we like to call multi-monikerism.

Steve Hodge reveals that Forest keeper Mark Crossley, for example, had a healthy three nicknames:

> 'The Future' because he once referred to himself as such.
>
> The rather cruel 'Ugly Man', which was given to him by Brian Clough for obvious, if unfair, reasons.
>
> And 'Norm' because 'someone thought he resembled Norman Whiteside'.

We are particular fans of footballers being nicknamed after other footballers, because it's a solid sign of your status in the game, isn't it? You would never be named after a footballer less well known than you, after all. No one was calling Whiteside 'Crossy' any more than Gareth Bale is being called 'Kenny' after Irish semi-professional and former Spurs youngster Kenny McEvoy (Google it).

Next we have Ally McCoist, who has at least four nicknames that we know of. There's 'Coisty', obviously, but Graeme Souness says that when he was boss of Rangers the lads began calling him '"Dudley" after I said he was "a dud" in one sharp dressing room exchange'. Ally's a man who likes to award himself nicknames, and Souness adds that because he kept leaving him on the bench, McCoist also referred to himself as 'The Judge'. Nicely self-deprecating from Dudley, there. Slightly less so, but still tongue in cheek, was nickname number four, revealed by Lee McCulloch: 'In training he liked us to call him the "Gas Man" because when he came on as a sub he'd turn the heat up a few peeps!' So Coisty managed to eke two separate nicknames out of one scenario. The man's a nicknaming machine.

And finally there's former Wales, Coventry, Wimbledon, Cheltenham (we could go on) boss Bobby Gould, who handily lists his many nicknames at the end of his book: 'The Gouldfather, Mrs Malaprop ... The Ex-Superstar, Gouldy, Gaffer, Moroccan Mule, Bunter, Father Ted, BG.' That's a grand total of nine, which must get confusing. We're fine with all of these, although he shouldn't be counting 'Gaffer' as a nickname; that's like a judge claiming 'Your Honour' as a nickname. Also, earlier in the book he says he was known as the 'Moroccan *Mole*' by his Wimbledon teammates when he had a pre-season there under Dave Bassett (before getting a better offer from Aldershot) partly because of a holiday tan and partly because the squad thought he was a spy for the gaffer. The Gouldfather doesn't mention it, possibly because of an unforgivable knowledge gap in Hanna-Barbera cartoons, but surely this had nothing to do with his tan – the lads were referring to Secret Squirrel's sidekick, Morocco Mole here, weren't they? Regardless, either this new Moroccan *Mule* nickname is a typo, or it's yet another nickname he was given because he was once involved in the drug trade. Or because he likes vodka cocktails. Probably just a typo.

One big discovery that we made previously was that Terry Curran's real name was Teddy and he was only called Terry because of a mistake in a local newspaper, which he decided not to correct and, well, things just snowballed from there. But Teddy/Terry isn't the only one who's been hoodwinking us all by using a name that's not his. There's Llewellyn Curbishley, for instance. You know, old Llewellyn 'Curbs' Curbishley. Managed Charlton for ages. Then West Ham. Then spent the next decade or so being linked with every single vacant managerial job in the top two divisions. Fortunately, Curbs clears up the confusion in his autobiography, penned under his pseudonym 'Alan': 'Llewellyn is actually my first name, but for some reason I've always been called Alan.' Thanks, Llewy.

Former Stoke forward Terry Conroy at least has the decency to explain why he was forever being called Terry despite the fact his name was Gerard – it went back to his childhood: 'I would hold my hand out and say "that" when I wanted something, but then I got really ambitious and added my name, along the lines of "Gerard wants that". The problem was the name Gerard was a little trickier for a youngster to say than anyone expected and it quickly morphed into Terry.' Did no one consider he was actually saying 'Gerry'?

We are huge fans of the complicated nickname – the ones with a long back story that require some patient explaining. As an example, Perry Groves tells us that the Arsenal lads liked to call David Seaman 'H': 'Most people think it was from "Harry Monk", which rhymes with spunk, as his name was Seaman', which, to be fair, would have been complex enough for us, but 'in fact it was from "Harry the Head" because of the size of his head. Footballers get funny nicknames, I know.' Which doesn't really explain that much – do all people with big heads get called Harry the Head? We'd have gone for Max, as in Max Headroom (look it up, younger viewers), but that's just us.

Bruce Grobbelaar's nickname for Liverpool's resident 1980s Aussie forward Craig Johnston was 'Doc Roo'. Obviously, the 'Roo' bit is self-explanatory,[14] but the 'Doc' part is a little more baffling, so let's allow Bruce to explain himself: '[It's] because he read tennis player Martina Navratilova's book and was impressed with all of her dietician talk of fibres, cholesterol and carbohydrates. He drinks water with every meal which invariably seems to be roast chicken.' Ah, now it makes sense.

And then there's Dave Thomas, QPR's brilliant winger of the 1970s, who famously refused to play with shin pads even though he had the likes of Norman Hunter and Chopper Harris attempting to stop his wing wizardry using their particular brands of stout defence.

14 Famously, Craig Johnston has a small marsupial pouch.

There must be a nickname in there, surely, even if it's just 'Shins'? But no, instead his nickname was 'Ticer', which his QPR teammate Stan Bowles tries to explain: 'This was after his grandfather, a cricketer who, apparently, used to 'tice' the ball – which means he used to 'entice' it. None the wiser? Neither am I!' Well, thanks for clearing that up Stan. We could have been guessing the origin of that for years and never got there.[15]

Now we've dealt with the Ticers, the Hs and the Alans of this world, though, let's reveal our Top 12 New Favourite Footballer Nicknames:

Player: Adebayo Akinfenwa
Nickname: Zugali
Comments: This comes from his time playing in Lithuania and Bayo explains that because he used to say 'What's up?' a lot, they called him Zugali, which is Lithuanian for rabbit, because Bugs Bunny's catchphrase was 'What's up, doc?'. Akinfenwa says he ended up embracing it completely: 'whenever I scored my celebration would be a bunny hop', which shows admirable commitment to the gimmick.

Player: Andy Goram
Nickname: Goalie
Comments: This is as route one as it gets. Everyone just calls him Goalie. We're sure it's affectionate, but it does have the ring of the rest of the team not really caring about who's in goal and just calling anyone who stands between the posts 'Goalie'. Dave Seaman was apparently known as Goalie by some, too. What happens when the famous Goalkeepers' Union has their AGM? Do they just all refer to each other as Goalie? Also, we'd like there to be more of this and fervently wish that Trent Alexander-Arnold's nickname is Full-Backy and Harry Kane's is Strikery.

Player: Gary Stevens
Nickname: Slippery or Beer Burglar
Comments: Two lovely nicknames there for the ex-England, Rangers and Everton right-back, who would've needed them, too, as there was

—

15 Incidentally, we would highly recommend Dave Thomas's autobiography, *Guiding Me Home and Away*, in which he writes about coming to terms with losing his sight in his 50s. All proceeds from the book are going to the Guide Dogs charity, because that is the kind of brilliant man Ticer is.

another right-back vying for that England squad at the time also called Gary Stevens. 'Slippery', Goalie tells us, was 'because he was always disappearing on nights out'. 'Beer Burglar', which we like because it sounds like he dresses up in a mask with a stripy outfit like Ronald McDonald's nemesis, The Hamburglar, is pretty self-explanatory: at functions he'd move between tables, joining in the chats, then suddenly grab and drink someone else's pint. Kenny Sansom also notes that Stevens and his partner up the wing at, well, everywhere, Trevor Steven, were known as 'The Hustlers': 'they were never off the pool table'. We feel a bit sorry for them there, being lumped together once again, even in the world of nicknames.

Player: Clive Goodyear
Nickname: Winko
Comments: We adore an ingenious nickname and this comes from Wimbledon's Crazy Gang of the 1980s. Bobby Gould, who managed them to FA Cup glory of course, explains that it came from 'Wingco', thanks to a tache that gave him the look of a classic World War Two RAF officer. Full marks.

Manager: Tony Waddington
Nickname: Mr Gin
Comments: Waddo was manager of Crewe and Bruce Grobbelaar tells us in his tome, *More Than Somewhat*, that he found out the reason for the nickname one evening at the Crewe Arms Hotel, when he noticed the boss had his own bottle of gin: 'It had a cardboard cut-out of his face on the neck, a little red and white scarf underneath and two cotton reels on the bottom painted to look like red and white football socks.' Tremendous commitment to the booze, that. These days, mind you, Waddo would be seen as a hipster, likely sipping his gin with the addition of an elderflower-infused Fever-Tree tonic.

Player: Malcolm Macdonald
Nickname: Supermac
Comments: Everyone knows this nickname for the former Newcastle, Fulham, Arsenal and England striker, but it came as a surprise to us, reading his autobiography from the early 1980s, to learn that he never liked it: 'I absolutely loathe it,' he writes, adding: 'When I did a book previously, the publishers wanted to call it Supermac, but I said, "No

... if you do that you can burn the manuscript."' Extremely laudable. It's the obvious thing for him to call his book, it was his tag throughout his time in the 70s where he was banging in goals all over the country, but because he didn't like it, he had no interest in trading on it. Good for him. We wish more people were that principled in life, and we include ourselves in that. We'd call our book literally anything if it would result in a bit more coin. So, well done Malcolm. Incidentally, he wrote one more set of memoirs in 2003. It was entitled 'Supermac'. Nothing is sacred these days. Nothing.

Player: Andy Morrison
Nickname: Jake
Comments: Morrison's nickname wasn't generally Jake, but Jock, for the usual reason. But while at Plymouth some new signings began calling him 'Jake' and – showing courage well beyond what we could ever dream of – continued to do so even after he had corrected them. Eventually, Morrison spoke to Gary Poole about it, who explained that they were calling him Jake after the boxer Jake LaMotta and said he should watch Martin Scorsese's biopic *Raging Bull*. Morrison says: 'That night, I rented the video from my local store and finally understood what they were on about. I accepted Jake or Jock from that point on as I assumed it was a back-handed compliment.' Well, that could have gone one of two ways. For the completists among you, former Orient manager John 'Bring Your Dinner' Sitton was also sometimes known as Jake for the same reason, although he says: 'I have never instigated or started trouble in my life.'

Player: Neil Redfearn
Nickname: Casper
Comments: Redfearn explains he received this nickname when at Palace because of the character in the brilliant Ken Loach movie *Kes* (based on Barry Hines's wonderful book, the schoolroom favourite, *A Kestrel for a Knave*, we should add). Not only is it a good nickname, it also would have been so easy for the Palace lads to simply nickname him 'Kes' – 'Casper' just takes it up another notch.

Player: Arjan de Zeeuw
Nickname: Chester
Comments: As in Chester Zoo. Straight out of the top drawer.

Player: Bryan Robson
Nickname: Robbo
Comments: Nothing special about this, you'd think. Everyone knows the England captain was known as Robbo (when he wasn't being called Captain Marvel). But the key point is that he was known as Robbo to everyone. And we mean everyone. Even his own dad (Brian Robson, we swear to God: same name, different spelling) called him Robbo. The opening line in his book, *Robbo: My Autobiography* (even his book calls him Robbo), is: 'My dad called me Robbo.' Kenny Sansom also notes that the England boys sometimes called him 'Pop', 'Because his shoulder kept popping out of its socket.' Now, we're not going to dispute that Bryan Robson spent a decent portion of the 80s having his shoulders (and hips) popped back into place (as well as his leg bones knitted back together and so forth), but surely, surely, he was known as Pop because he shared his entire name with West Ham, Sunderland and Newcastle legend Bryan 'Pop' Robson? Ken?

Player: Kenny Sansom
Nickname: Miguel
Comments: Speaking of Ken, we are big fans of this nickname bestowed upon him by his boss at Palace Terry 'Tel/Venners' Venables 'because every time I left training I'd say "I'm off to see 'me gal' now."'

Player: Gary Gillespie
Nickname: Smithy
Comments: It's Steve Nicol who brings us this one (as well as noting that Bruce Grobbelaar's nickname was at some stage 'Parlez Bleu', although infuriatingly he doesn't know why) and it's one of our all-time favourites. It's ample evidence that, and particularly in the 1980s Liverpool dressing room it seems, even the tiniest, most meaningless of errors can result in a nickname that will ensure you will never be allowed to forget your misdemeanour. Not only is this the slightest-ever reason for a nickname to be awarded, but it's also probably the only one to be given in relation to a 1980s Aussie golfer not called Greg: 'He once said Ian Baker Smith instead of Ian Baker-Finch when talking about the golfer.' And that's it. One slip of the tongue and you're known as 'Smithy' for the rest of your life.

THE MAGIC SPONGE

'Shave inside my mouth'

> Richard Ord received a cut to the head, which he shrugged off to defend a corner. John Fashanu strolled over and rubbed his hand on Ordy's wound, then licked his palm before declaring: 'I love white man's blood.'
>
> Lee Howey, *Massively Violent and Decidedly Average*

What better way to introduce our little chapter about injuries than to read about the time John Fashanu went sort of *Enter the Dragon* on a bloody Richard Ord. This could never have happened these days, mind, because Ordy would have been taken off for ointment, bandaging and a fresh shirt before Fash could possibly nip in to sample his vintage claret. Plus, if the coronavirus has taught us nothing else, it's that if you *are* planning to smush someone's head wound so you can dramatically lick their blood, you must take the time to wash your hands thoroughly in warm water for 20 seconds first. Times have truly changed.

All footballers are at the mercy of injuries, but few are able to articulate the sensation of a bad injury quite as vividly, or with such illuminating details, as former Arsenal and Germany keeper Jens Lehmann. We join the action as he is mid-air after attempting to come for a cross:

> Shortly before the landing, I hit my colleague Andreas Müller's calf; the entire motion sequence was all over the place and, aiming for an emergency landing, I needed to rely on my right leg – which, in turn, was not prepared for this and revolved around itself. Upon contact with the

> ground, I immediately had a light, buttery feeling in my knee. And then there was a crack. A crack which sounded as if a crustacean was being dissected. Although the pain kept within a limit, I knew at once that something was badly wrong. Cruciate ligament, intra-articular ligament, meniscus: all torn, such was the diagnosis later on – and the joint capsule had blown up too.

A level of analysis so deep that we almost need a translation – or at least someone to put it in ... wait for it ... Lehmann's terms.

With good care, Lehmann recovered from that knee explosion to later become Germany's number one goalkeeper and pioneer of the note-in-sock stratagem when facing a penalty shoot-out.[16] Players, then, do rely heavily on physiotherapists and doctors to help them with their rehabilitation – particularly these days, as the best players are flown all over the world to see the best specialists and are given the best facilities so that they may return to action as quickly as possible. That wasn't always the case, however: 1970s Stoke legend Terry Conroy says their physio, Frank Mountford, 'had no medical qualifications at all, and also very little sympathy ... He had a sponge and could offer you a pretty rough massage. That was it.'

That comment is a familiar one when it comes to players from past generations. In his playing days, John Sitton recalls physio Bill Songhurst refusing even to massage his hamstring on a matchday, as he claimed: 'I've got a simple rule when it comes to massaging players ... good players don't need it, bad players ain't worth it', which seems like a handy excuse to basically avoid doing any work. Worse, Derek Dougan says that at Portsmouth he once played in pain for ten weeks because doctors failed to diagnose that he had a broken ankle. 'I was really angry,' he says, with admirable understatement.

The only thing worse than no treatment, though, is bad treatment. Mainly, we're about to deal with dodgy treatment from supposed professionals, but let's not forget the time David Batty badly cut his finger on some bushes (he was tossing away a broken umbrella on a windy day, if you must know) and tried to fix it using 'a lollipop stick bound with Sellotape like a makeshift splint', possibly while

16 A technique taken to a new level by Norwich goalie Tim Krul in early 2020, when he avoided the hazards of the paper becoming soggy and unreadable due to excessive leg sweat by writing his notes on a water bottle, presumably using a Sharpie.

muttering something about fuss and nonsense. Even after stitches had been belatedly applied, however, his finger became infected anyway and the tendon 'rotted through', leaving him, as you'd expect, in agony.

That was self-inflicted pain, but if you read Norman Whiteside's book *Determined* (which we highly recommend) you'll find the sad story of how he believes his career was ruined by a physio working for Glentoran called Bobby McGregor. Whiteside describes his ordeal when he went for help on a common-or-garden groin strain as a teenager while at Man United: 'First off, he put his hands on the front of my hips and wrenched so hard I could barely draw breath. Then he moved them to my groin, digging his thumbs in on both sides, probing and manipulating so deep I felt my pelvis move.' He continues: 'From that day onwards, I lost all my pace and when I next had a medical at United they noted that I had lost the ability to rotate my hips … Bobby McGregor moved my pelvis so drastically that my hips have never worked properly again. He knackered the player I should have been.' And when you remember that Norm was tearing it up as a 17-year-old at the 1982 World Cup in Spain, that was some player he was shaping up to be.

As a schoolboy, Terry Venables also suffered at the hands of someone who thought he could work a miracle cure: Chelsea scout Jimmy Thompson. Tel remembers that Jimmy 'turned up at my house with an ointment he assured me was safe, but not something we should talk about. At that, he spread the unction over my damaged foot. I have no idea where it came from or what it was, but within a minute my foot had turned black as pitch.' Sounds absolutely fine – and indeed, off they went outside, where Jimmy ordered Tel to strike a football: '"My foot is killing me," I protested. "Hit the ball as hard as you can." I did, straight at him with all my force from the bad foot. I cracked him hard and he went down. At the same time, I collapsed in agony from the pain in my foot.' We're fairly sure this is the plot later lifted by the writers of one of our favourite comic strips ever, *Hot-Shot Hamish and Mighty Mouse*.

Venners's misfortune brings us on to the lengths some footballers will go to when seeking a cure. At Ipswich, George Burley would send his favourite player Matt Holland to bathe his limbs in the apparently restorative salt water at Brightlingsea beach, but poor Manchester City's Paul Lake went further than most as he sought an end to his particularly cruel injury nightmare. In the excellent *I'm Not Really Here*, he describes trying Chinese acupuncture, visiting a faith healer (fee: £50) and even applying some holy water given to him by a City fan: 'Despite not being particularly religious, I was really touched by this man's kind sentiments. I took the magic potion back home and, each morning for a whole week, gently dabbed it on my operation scars.'

Sadly, none of it worked for Lake. And yet there are footballers who swear by the power of faith healing. The most famous of all, of course, is former England manager Glenn Hoddle and his unwavering belief in the power of Eileen Drewery. We found out about the origins of his devotion to Eileen in his first stab at an autobiography, *Spurred to Success*. Back in the day, he dated Eileen's daughter, Michelle, and was once round their house telling them about a troublesome hamstring injury. It was then that Eileen said she could try some 'absent healing'. Glenn sort of laughed it off, but then the miracle happened: 'I woke up on Friday morning and got out of bed ... I couldn't feel any more pain in the hamstring. I remember sitting up in bed, digging my finger in as far and hard as it would go, searching for the pain. It had gone. I was absolutely staggered! ... I rushed to the phone and rang Michelle. "What's happened?" I shouted. Michelle said, "Mum did some 'absent healing' on you while you were in the kitchen last night."'

Now, for years Glenn has had stick about his use of Eileen Drewery with the England squad around the 1998 World Cup. But one thing you have to say is this: if Glenn's hamstring injury had not been fully healed overnight, surely he would never have spent so much time subsequently encouraging players to use her abilities. So all we're saying is ... something weird happened that night in Chigwell (it was probably Chigwell), and it compares favourably with Whiteside's experience with an actual professional.

But let's get on to what we know you've all been waiting for: the most gruesome injuries we read about over the course of our autobiography-reading odyssey. This will feel a little like rubbernecking: you may want to look away – but we bet you can't.

STEVEN GERRARD

Steven Gerrard wastes few words in describing his most awkward injury: 'The magic of the FA Cup was bloodied on the day my penis was cut and then stitched shut on an unromantic afternoon in

Bournemouth.' Hopefully not totally stitched shut, because ... well, we don't even want to start imagining.

Anyway, this painful injury ('my dick was stinging like fuck' says Stevie G, with feeling) occurred quite by accident when he was challenging for the ball. Understandably worried, he went to the touchline where some backroom staff formed a sort of privacy huddle so he could show the gash to Brendan Rodgers: 'Brendan peered down, grimaced and shook his head.' Still, Gerro played on, they won 4-0 and after the game he had a stitch in his knob for each goal scored.

Another Liverpool hero, David Johnson, also had a nasty incident with his crown jewels, although it was during his time at Ipswich. It happened in an Anglo-Italian Cup match against Lazio, and Kevin Beattie recalls it well: 'David Johnson was kicked all over the place and in the end one of their players went so over the top that he split Jonty's bollocks and he had to be carried off for stitches.' Christ. We've discovered previously that David Johnson was known as 'The Doc' at Liverpool because he carried a medical bag with him at all times. We bet he did. For just such an occasion.

DAVID SEAMAN

This one doesn't make great reading for the squeamish. Seamo was at QPR at this time and during training Sir Les Ferdinand accidentally kicked Sir Spunky's thumb as they went for the same ball. Dave knew immediately it was broken, but the other players weren't so sure: 'They did not believe me because I had not even taken the glove off to look. When I did, a piece of bone caught on the material and I shouted out in pain. The players looked and then immediately looked away. I looked, felt faint, and had to sit down while they phoned for an ambulance.' Worse still, this was on his ham radio hand, so the Green Giant was off the air for a good few weeks after that.

MALCOLM MACDONALD

Malc was making his home debut for Newcastle against Liverpool back in 1971 when he unfortunately took a very nasty kick in the face from Reds keeper Ray Clemence. He lost three teeth and needed five stitches in a ripped lip. Without wishing to play down a horrible experience, this is the sort of thing that quite a lot of footballers will have experienced to some degree.

So, of course, that's not the end of the story. There's something else to add. And no matter how many times we read this, it still makes us want to curl into a tiny, tiny ball and shut out the noise. Strap yourselves in: 'Because of that injury, I now have to shave inside my mouth. Where the lip has been stitched together, a bit of outside skin is now inside, and if I don't shave in there I feel the whiskers prickling my gum!' Don't try to imagine the actual act of Malcolm Macdonald lifting his upper lip so he can take a blade to the inside of his mouth because … ah, we're too late. Sorry.

TERRY BUTCHER

No, we're not talking about his famous crimson face mask that so gloriously adorns the cover of this book. We're talking about a horrendous nose injury he suffered after Luton striker Brian Stein caught him in the face when attempting a bicycle kick. Butcher, being Butcher, of course, completed the match and it wasn't until the next night when the horror started: 'I woke up and could feel the pressure mounting behind my nose. I just made it to the bathroom before the plugs burst and blood streamed out rather like a dam bursting. It didn't stop. Rita phoned for a taxi and insisted that I go to hospital. I sat in the back with a plastic washing up bowl in my lap to collect the blood. It's not a long journey but the bowl was nearly full by the time we arrived at casualty.' You read that right – he nearly filled a *washing up bowl* with his own blood.[17]

It turned out that Tel had damaged an artery and for the next few days he suffered bouts of prolonged bleeding. Nothing seemed to stop it and he was in hospital for weeks: 'I lost almost 16 pints of blood and two stone in weight.' Yet, while Butch was understandably concerned by this, the thing that seemed to really upset him was that when doctors decided to inject some dye into his veins via his groin, he needed to have that tender area shaved bald. He claims that the medic 'pulled out a cut throat razor which he started sharpening on a leather strap'. This sounds like he was in hospital at some point in the 1930s. Can this really have been true? A hospital employee gleefully having a bit of fun with a seriously ill patient by menacingly sharpening his ancient tools in front of him? Terry says, 'I didn't mind what else they did, but to shave me around there was a loss of male dignity.' Come

17 Even if this was one of those smaller washing up bowls you end up using in caravans, that's still a lot of blood.

on mate, it's just a bit of manscaping – you were years ahead of the fashion curve. According to Dean Windass, Stan Collymore used to do that sort of thing in the showers after training without so much as a by your leave.

Butcher eventually began to improve after some risky surgery to tie off the artery, but he actually puts his full recovery down to a handkerchief sent by a faith healer along with a letter: 'We have prayed for you and blessed this handkerchief. Put it to your nose at eight o'clock in the evening: we will be praying for you at that time and the bleeding will stop. At other times wear the handkerchief in the top pocket of your pyjamas.' Butcher claims he was sceptical but followed their instructions and his nose never bled again. But the biggest mystery here is, surely, how did these people know he had a top pocket in his pyjamas? And if they didn't know, but guessed wrongly, would the hankie have still worked its magic? And finally, did these healers send him another hankie after that famous match against Sweden in 1989?

HOPE SOLO

Terry's perma-bleeding nose was pretty bad. But we did read worse. And it comes courtesy of the decorated USA women's keeper Hope Solo. She was playing for the national Under 21s at the time in a match with Mexico's senior side and the injury occurred as she tried to keep out a free kick. Reader discretion is advised: 'As I dove to block it, I hit the post and felt myself get caught on something. As the ball went into the net, my body lurched in a circle, still attached to the pole, and I thudded to the ground.'

At this point, you're wondering what the injury could be. Did she hit her head? Or land badly? Apparently, her teammates didn't think anything was wrong because they urged her to get up so they could restart the game. But something was wrong. Terribly wrong: 'Something was terribly wrong.' See?

> I looked down to make sure my arm was still there because I couldn't feel it – was it still dangling from the post? The arm was there and I didn't see anything wrong. There wasn't any blood. There was no tear in the jersey. When I lifted up my jersey sleeve I gasped. A hole gaped in my forearm; the muscle and tendons were hanging out. I

> could see the yellow of the fat, the white of my bone, the maroon rippled texture of the muscle. My forearm had gotten caught on a hook on the inside of the goalpost and had been ripped wide open. I panicked, fearing that the insides of my arm were going to fall out. I took my filthy goalkeeper glove and covered the hole and sprinted off the field, with my defender, Natalie Spilger, running along beside me, screaming.
>
> Sleep well, everyone.

Fortunately, and by the sounds of it, miraculously, Solo made a full recovery and, of course, went on to win tonnes of medals. Hurray!

Clearly, we can't leave the chapter here. We all need a bit of light relief to counteract all the gore, so let's take a look at some ridiculous injuries sustained away from the game. Whenever this subject comes up, everyone's first go-to story is the time Wimbledon keeper Dave Beasant dropped a bottle of salad cream and injured his foot by trying to trap it just before it hit the ground. Poor Lurch – he saved a penalty in a cup final and that's still the first thing people think of. But it turns out there are far more of these comical injuries than we realised. Although, not all are comical, just to warn you.

DAVID SEAMAN

Following in Beasant's goalkeeping footsteps is Spunky, who admits to pulling his hamstring while watching TV. Dave says, and we award points here for his honesty: 'I reached forward for a can of Coke, without realising the can had been moved further away, I over-stretched and my hamstring pinged.'

Incredibly, that wasn't the worst injury he inflicted upon himself – as a kid, he managed to break his own leg with *his own head* after 'jack-knifing off a swing'. As you'll remember from his complicated nickname of 'H', Dave does have a big head, so this sort of makes sense.

BRYAN ROBSON

Poor Captain Marvel. World Cup 1990, his last real shot at international glory, and it was ruined by a toe injury – although, of course, that injury hastened the introduction of David Platt to a team that then almost made the final. While at the time we all assumed it was an injury sustained in a legitimate manner, the truth is a little different. Paul Parker writes: 'I will let you into a secret about that toe injury of his. It was widely reported that he injured his toe in a match but in fact he had dropped a cast iron bed leg on it during a lifting contest at the team hotel.'

The thing about this is that it's not really a secret. The same story is told in several books – including Robbo's – and sometimes includes some classic Gazza antics leading to the injury. But each time we read it, the players make out like they're taking us through the looking glass.

KEVIN BEATTIE

One of the not so funny ones, but unarguably a spectacular injury. One day, Kev was spending a nice Sunday doing a spot of gardening and decided to burn the garden offcuts in an oil drum. He set it alight, but it soon went out, so he, quite literally, decided to pour petrol on the fire: 'What I didn't know was that the fire was still alight and when I emptied the can of petrol flames leapt up from the oil drum. In a moment of panic I threw the can down, but the petrol splattered all over me. I rushed indoors and grabbed a towel to rub myself down because my shirt had caught alight.'

Beat was actually quite badly burned around the neck, and to make matters worse his neighbour managed to crash into the front garden wall while trying to rush him to hospital. 'What a nightmare!' says Beat, as casually as if he was ending a classic anecdote about how his train was delayed for work, rather than, you know, relating a horrific tale of self-immolation.

TERRY CURRAN

Regrets of a Football Maverick is a rollercoaster of a memoir, dealing as it does with Curran's eventful career, his work since (including owning a motorway cafe) and, a lot of the time, the women he's been to bed with and had pink champagne baths with. But in amongst it all is a fairly harrowing tale of the time his body reacted badly to a flu jab he had taken on the advice of the medical team at Nottingham Forest. Basically, it seemed to cause some kind of radiation poisoning: 'I spent over a week in hospital as my condition got worse and worse. I shed skin, my toe and fingernails came out and I lost a fair amount of my thick curly hair.' Luckily, he recovered, but bloody hell. Terry would not be Terry (or Teddy) without that thick, curly hair.

KERRY DIXON

It's the 1986 World Cup. The boys are all in Mexico and are as usual looking for ways to pass the endless hours between games, because for footballers sitting by a pool and reading a Lee Child thriller is never enough. Anyway, Dixon played some tennis. Some harmless tennis: 'Somehow in chasing the ball trying to make a return, I managed to hit myself in the face with my own racquet.' Never, ever let it be forgotten that Kerry Dixon injured himself, at a World Cup, mind you, by hitting his own face with a tennis bat.

ALEX FERGUSON

Sir Alex Ferguson, while still at Rangers, also ran a pub. Because that's what footballers did in them days. Anyway, one Sunday morning he was making a keg change in the cellar: 'I was releasing a spear to let the air out when a rat jumped on my shoulder. I leapt back and the spear of the keg sank into my cheek.' He drove to the hospital with the spear stuck in his cheek and then makes a great deal about how embarrassed he was when he fainted when a nurse put a needle in him.

But what gets us is that he's so blasé about the rat. Few things would terrify us more than a rat leaping on to our shoulder like some kind of diseased parrot. What kind of rat makes an attack like that? And why? It strikes us that Pixar could option this story as the basis for the long-awaited sequel to *Ratatouille*, involving a Scottish rat who becomes enthralled by a Scottish footballer/pub manager and decides to learn how to set up his own microbrewery in Falkirk. *Ratatouille Twoey*, if you like.

THAT'S ENTERTAINMENT!

'Yul Brynner and the other six'

You may have been lucky enough to meet some of your football heroes over the years, and maybe you're confident enough not to get all giddy and nervous around them. However, if, like us, you get tongue-tied and sweaty around anyone you've ever paid to see cross a touchline, then you might struggle for conversation. What we all need is a leveller of some sort – something universal that everyone can talk about, regardless of whether you once scored a hat-trick at Wembley or not.

As The Blues Brothers once told us, there are still some things that make us all the same, and those things are that we all listen to music, we all watch a bit of telly and we all enjoy films – unless we are Michael Owen. So not only is this chapter designed to give you a brief insight into what your football heroes get up to in their spare time (non-sexual exploits department), it's also designed to provide a handy guide to help you out if you ever find yourself struggling for something to discuss with, say, Paul Merson, should you one day get stuck in a lift with him, or something. The answer in that case being: *There's Something About Mary*. He very much enjoyed it.

This chapter is a bit of a bonus for those among you that don't let football rule your life 24/7. This is where football crosses over with the small screen, the big screen and the record player.[18] This is for those among you who know your Tyrion Lannister from your Gary Bannister, your Awkwafina from your Akinfenwa, and your Bruno Mars from your Bruno Martins Indi.[19]

Anyone who picked up a *Shoot!* magazine in the 70s or 80s might be fooled by the player Q&A pages therein into thinking that the

18 Or cassette player, minidisc, Discman, or whatever the latest format is. It's probably phones isn't it? It's all phones these days.

19 'Your Fellini from your Fellaini' was rejected for being a bit route one.

musical tastes of a footballer stretch no further than Diana Ross or Phil Collins, but it's simply not the case. Well, sometimes it's the case. Alan Shearer uses a diary entry to tell us that 'I like listening to Phil Collins and Rod Stewart' on his new 'stack stereo' but it really does go deeper than that, we promise. Steven Gerrard insists in his book that despite reports to the contrary, his infamous nightclub bust-up was *not* caused by his insistence that the DJ played a bit of Phil, for instance. See, we always need to hear both sides of the story.

Across the many books we've read, we've come to learn that there's actually a rich tapestry of musical tastes and influences out there in the game. Please feel free to make your own Spotify playlist as we take a trip through it.

Let's kick off with Paul Lake fondly recalling the family ritual of watching *Top of the Pops*: 'Every Thursday night, my siblings and I would jostle for position in front of the box while Mum and Dad sat at the back of the lounge, tutting and shaking their heads. "Is that a bleedin' man or a woman?" Dad would ask as Boy George or Pete Burns preened before the cameras, lip-glossed to within an inch of their lives.' A very relatable experience here to get things going. Many of us of a certain age can recognise and empathise with this set-up completely. We can smell the same dinner aroma as we read it. And while we like to think our parents weren't as disapproving as the Lakes, there was certainly a bit of that going on.

Having your favourite bands questioned certainly didn't begin and end at home though. Around football clubs up and down the land, the musical tastes of players are scrutinised for weakness, seemingly along with everything else.

For example, Ledley King speaks highly of Spurs teammate Kasey Keller, but draws the line at what he listened to, saying, 'To be honest I couldn't really class what he loved as music because it was so heavy – it was the heaviest stuff I've ever heard.' Ledley clearly regards this music as so out of step with the tastes of the dressing room at the time that he doesn't even dignify it by naming the bands Keller was into.

Safer fare to play in and around the football clubs was the likes of Bryan Ferry, as enjoyed by John Robertson in Forest's heyday, and Status Quo and Thin Lizzy, enjoyed respectively by his teammates John McGovern and Martin O'Neill – all of which get a nod of approval from Terry Curran in his book. Jeremy Goss also seems on safe meat and potatoes footballer ground musically when he pops

'Dire Straits, Journey, Queen or REO Speedwagon' on his Walkman back in the Walkman days.

Dean Windass tells us in *Deano* that 'the other lads cane me for my taste in music and never let me put it on', which seems a shame. He just seems a man out of time with his tastes, saying: 'So what if I like something a bit different? Tom Jones, Brenda Lee, Elvis and Roy Orbison. Sounds sad doesn't it but I'm happy. I couldn't give a toss what the others think.' Quite right too, Dean. This is exactly the right attitude. Let the 'guilty pleasures' tag go hang. You enjoy what you want to enjoy and don't worry about the stick from anybody. Stand up and stand proud about your favourite tunes, whether it's John Wark proclaiming the anthemic 'I Am What I Am' as his all-time fave ('I think the lyrics of my favourite Shirley Bassey song tend to sum me up pretty well') or Jaap Stam loving the Champions League theme so much that it 'is now firmly ensconced in my personal top five after the events that night in Barcelona'. We're left curious about what the other four are, but the sentimental reasoning is entirely valid for this choice, even if there's almost certainly less dancing going on in the kitchen at Jaap's place than round at Johnny Wark's. You're more likely to find the Stams standing ramrod straight, shoulder to shoulder, enjoying his favourite instrumental track.

There's a lot of sentimentality in football and it's bound to inform a player's musical memories. Ronnie Whelan is one of several members of that all-conquering Liverpool side that won the European Cup in Rome in 1984 that can vividly remember the players singing a bit of Chris Rea as they waited to go out, saying that someone 'decided it'd be a bit of a brainwave to sing "I Don't Know What it Is but I Love It" while we were lining up against the Italians in the tunnel'. It obviously did the trick and why Rea doesn't get the same credit for the win as Bruce Grobbelaar's wobbly legs routine, we just don't know. Wonder what the 2019 vintage had in their heads as they lined up in the tunnel? Rea again probably. Roberto Firmino's a massive 'Road to Hell' fan, we've heard.

Perry Groves fondly remembers an Arsenal celebration dinner at which Tony Adams and his girlfriend went 'from one table to another' performing a duet of Cher's "Shoop Shoop Song". Well that sounds lovely. What a wonderful, cherished memory for Perry. 'It was all right to begin with, but as they did it every half-hour we'd all had enough by the end of the night.' Oh no. Still, at least they were going table to table. Cher and share alike, that's what we say.

Tony Adams live: it's an enticing prospect. There's nothing quite like live music is there? Imagine if it was your job to have thousands of people turn up every week, pay good money and scrutinise your every move. You'd probably welcome the chance to do the same to someone else: to melt into the crowd and enjoy yourself. If we were to produce a pie chart of the gigs attended in these books then there would be a very large slice of Rod Stewart pie[20] and a generous helping of Elton John pie[21], but buried there in that remaining sliver are the really interesting ones.

Let's run through a few: Peter Reid likens seeing his big favourite Bruce Springsteen live as 'a highlight to almost match winning the league'; Terry Dyson says Westlife were 'brilliant' at the 02; and Neil Warnock seems absolutely enchanted by the Barbra Streisand concert he attended in New York. 'The concert was unbelievable. We were four rows back. Tony Bennett was a few seats away. Oprah Winfrey was there. I was right on the edge of the stage so when Barbra looked down at the audience, I just thought she was looking at me.' It's possible that Barbra was simply wondering where Warnock's eyebrows had got to, but we're glad he enjoyed it. It's very on brand for potty-mouthed Neil that one of his highlights of the gig was when Ms Streisand told a heckler to 'shut the fuck up and get out'. As Neil sagely puts it, 'You know what, the pressure gets to everybody, Even her.'

Matt Le Tissier got along to several gigs but seems constantly concerned that people might think he's gay for going. Why that would be a problem, or why he cares what people think, are never satisfactorily explained but it's there, time and time again.

Le Tiss has rubbed shoulders with the likes of Chesney Hawkes ('very down to earth'[22]) and Robbie Williams ('top man') and says, 'I did go and see Take That in concert with two of my aunties and I must have been the only straight male there.' See. On good mate John Beresford, he says, 'I took him to see Shania Twain in concert. I know how it sounds but I had been a big fan long before she became famous.' He says they went for a drink near the arena beforehand and ordered Malibu and Coke, 'which isn't exactly a manly drink. The look on the barmaid's face was priceless as two guys walked in

—

20 'You're in My Tart', anyone?

21 'Rocket Flan'? Come back, no more, we promise.

22 Of course he is. He had one big hit in 1991. Imagine if he was still going round giving it Bertie Big Bollocks these days.

and ordered this girly drink – and when we told her we were going to see Shania Twain you could see "What a pair of gays" stamped across her forehead.' Firstly, we assume he's talking metaphorically here as it's never advisable for people in the hospitality trade to have such tattoos; secondly Matt Le Tissier would have to be batting well above his average to be in a couple with John Beresford; and thirdly what's the problem, Tiss? Drink what you want, go where you want, enjoy what you want. Don't worry what people think so much. This unseemly gay panic don't impress us much, and if we know Shania like we think we know Shania, her neither.

Stan Collymore had his own concert concerns about joining his Nottingham Forest teammates at a Madness gig in Birmingham one night. He says the lads got into the spirit of things by buying '20 pairs of Dr Martens boots to wear', but 'I didn't go. I wasn't going to make myself look a fucking knob by jumping around pogo style with dubious BNP geezers at a Madness concert.' Feels like this is quite the generalisation by Stan here, but he doesn't strike us as much of a joiner-inner at the best of times.

Stuart Pearce is a man who will enjoy what he wants with not a bother on him, possibly because, well, who's going to tell him he's wrong? He was probably at the jaunt above that Stanley Victor opted out of, but his regular gig-going is largely punk-based. He's seen his personal favourites The Stranglers 'pushing 40 times', and subsequently made good friends with the band, but that didn't stop him enjoying a bit of musical theatre when the opportunity arose. While on tour with England in New Zealand, Graham Taylor asked if any of his players wanted to go and see *Les Miserables*, which was on 'literally over the road from our hotel'. The take-up does not seem to have been huge if we're honest but Psycho says he went along with Keith Curle, Nigel Clough and Tony Coton. Pearce says that 'within five minutes Curle was up and off followed five minutes later by TC who announced to the rest of the audience that he was going for a beer'. Such a bloody bloke. The peer pressure to join them must have been enormous, as a trip to the musical theatre might not have been seen as exactly par for the course for the other no-nonsense footballers in the squad. However, 'Nigel and I stayed and really enjoyed the show; in fact, it was so good that I'll remember it for the rest of my life.' Good on the Forest contingent here. They've been brought up properly to have a bit of respect for the show in front of them. And Pearce clearly doesn't care if 'I Dreamed a Dream' doesn't exactly fit neatly alongside his Sex Pistols 7"s. Le Tiss could learn a lot from this trip to *Les Mis*, could Le Tiss.

However, our absolute favourite gig story comes from Peter Shilton. Do tell, Shilts: 'Although I loved music and still do, I have never been one for attending live concerts. This might have something to do with the fact that the one and only gig I attended as a boy was a great disappointment.' Oh well. The young Peter Shilton, you see, had got all his pocket money out of his piggy bank (not easy with goalie gloves on) and spent it on a ticket to see Freddie and the Dreamers. For those unfamiliar with Freddie and the lads – they're no good. They rode the coat-tails of much better bands in the 60s and substituted daft dancing for songs of any substance. There, we've said it. Don't @ us. However, if we were so inclined to go along to a Freddie and the Dreamers concert, the very least we would expect to see was Freddie and the Dreamers, rather than just the Dreamers, *sans* a poorly Freddie. An understandably bereft Shilts says that 'the songs were just not the same'; well they wouldn't be: Freddie was the singer, after all. 'I felt cheated. That was the first and, to date, last concert I attended.' Writing off all concerts ever at the age of 13 seems a bit of an overreaction to us, but each to their own. It's a good job that Shilton hasn't carried this kind of bitterness about feeling cheated into any other areas of his life, that's all we can say.

If you couldn't get along to an actual factual gig back in the day, there was always the Bus Stop mobile disco to be enjoyed, fronted by none other than Micky Quinn on the decks. A youthful Quinn decided to turn his love of the likes of Earth, Wind & Fire, Luther Vandross and Stevie Wonder into some cash, by spinning the wheels of steel at weddings, birthdays and bar mitzvahs in the Liverpool area. However, he admits that the main motivation behind it was inevitably 'pulling birds'. It seems to have worked, given the exploits detailed in *Who Ate All the Pies?* but it also gave Mick and his mates access to alcohol. Too much alcohol at one anniversary party, when he got rotten on 'Pernod, whisky, gin and brandy. It was double this and double that. I was really loving it, giving it the big one on the mike and winking at the girls.' But we've all had those evenings where one minute we're on top of the world and the next minute we've been sick down our front and wet ourselves in the back of a van. Well, Mick has at least. This evening described here. Mick says he learned his lesson though, and 'didn't drink Pernod again for a decade'. Interesting to note that of that evening's potent cocktail, Quinny is blaming the Pernod for the mess he got in – he must have copped a dodgy one.

Micky's turn as a DJ might have fallen some way short of his comparatively glittering career as a goalscorer, but he's not alone in the game as an enthusiastic amateur when it comes to music. More often, of course, it's a sing-song they like. Harry Redknapp tells us that Paolo Di Canio is a big Spandau Ballet fan and that when he met the Kemp brothers, 'He was up, singing all the songs, telling them how he saw their concert in Rome and got beaten up by a policeman because he tried to sneak into the second night without a ticket.' Treasured memories indeed. If this much is true, his fanboying makes us warm to Paolo a bit. If only he didn't love Mussolini as much as he loves Tony Hadley.

The born entertainer Lee Trundle was practically a semi-pro singer in his youth, even winning competitions for it. One victory scored him some Michael Jackson tickets by singing "The Way You Make Me Feel" to get into the final before I won it with a bit of Rick Astley'. Of course he did. As we say, that man knows how to entertain.

Gordon Hill warns us that his Manchester United skipper Martin Buchan was one of those other breeds of singer – the double threat: always a bit too quick to reach for their guitar at a party. Meanwhile, Hope Solo tells us that not one, but two of her former international coaches were also too handy with an acoustic. Firstly, there's Greg Ryan who 'wore sandals and played his guitar for us'. We all know the type. Ryan would even ask for requests during USA squad downtime: 'Awkward. We all just wanted to finish our meal and go Skype with our boyfriends. We didn't really want to sing "He's Got the Whole World in His Hands" with Greg.' Ouch. Poor Greg was probably just trying to cultivate a bit of team spirit but Solo says she watched on 'fascinated but horrified'. That's fascinated but horrified – not really what you're going for when gently strumming for your players, we're guessing.

Confusingly, even though Hope was absolutely not having any of this kind of buffoonery from Ryan, she happily accepted similar from her next US coach, Pia Sundhage. When Sundhage did her own David Brent bit and sent for the guitar, the squad apparently 'listened in amazement' as she rattled off some classic Bob Dylan to inspire her troops to harmony and success and apparently it worked. Poor old Greg. We like to think he was listening outside the door, sobbing gently as Sundhage held her new charges in the palm of her hand. The times really were a changing, he must have thought, as he shuffled away in his sandals.

International squads like this one must need to strike a delicate balance in terms of music. At their clubs, players probably have a certain way of doing things, somebody who is in charge of the playlist perhaps, and you might get used to hearing particular things. At international level players come together from all over, so keeping everyone happy with a soundtrack must be almost impossible.

Peter Crouch says that there was an attempt to be as democratic as possible at the 2006 World Cup as there was an iPod playlist with a song selected by each player. 'It was an eclectic mix – a burst of Jay-Z followed by Johnny Cash and "Ring of Fire", courtesy of Jamie Carragher. The most popular choice was Michael Carrick's selection of Byron Stingily's "Get Up (Everybody)", the most hated Paul Robinson and *500 Miles* by the Proclaimers.' Poor old Paul Robinson: that one's a banger, if maybe a bit anthemically Scottish to be on the England bus. Still, it's nice to know that Scotland have had some representation at a World Cup in the last 20 years.

One alternative to every individual sticking their neck out and selecting their own song is to leave it to the gaffer, and believe us when we tell you that is not a good idea when Glenn Hoddle's in charge. In his private moments he says he treated himself to 'a bit of Celine Dion', while on the coach his France 98 squad was force-fed M People's 'Search for the Hero Inside Yourself'. Hod claims it 'was becoming something of a theme tune', but surely it left players desperate to get off the bus, and possibly desperate to get out of the World Cup if that was all they listened to. We're not saying we blame it entirely – just that it must have been at the back of the minds of Paul Ince and David Batty when they missed those penalties against Argentina.

These days it might be a case of players sticking to their own choice of music on headphones, which feels like we've lost some sense of community. At the 1986 World Cup, room-mates Viv Anderson and Terry Butcher seemed to rub along well together, going halves on a music centre and sharing it despite their tastes (Viv – 'Go West, Talking Heads and George Benson' and Terry – 'AC/DC with the volume right up') being poles apart. We wonder who kept the music system at the end of the tournament, or if Butcher simply smashed it to bits with his head when the squad got back to the hotel after that Hand of God game.

While we're chatting England and music, it would be remiss of us not to discuss New Order's (sorry ENGLANDneworder's) 'World in Motion', the official England song that broke the mould of all that had gone before it.

Right off the bat, let's all agree that it's the high point of all football singles, right? Not if you're Bryan Robson, a veteran of so many World Cups and cup finals that 'I brag to the kids that I've been in the top ten five times with United and England'. He can be justifiably proud of his chart success but we cannot get on board with his assertion that: 'The worst one I was involved with was "World in Motion".' The one chink of light here is that maybe he's confused because he misremembers the video as the one 'with Tony Adams and a bunch of other lads in a car'. He's thinking of 'All The Way', the Stock, Aitken Waterman produced effort for 1988, there. Now that one *is* bad, but it did involve an enjoyable squad performance on *Wogan*, with Bobby Robson front and centre and some of the lads at the back bizarrely messing about with gym equipment.[23] And Robbo's right about the video being a bad one with green-screen racing cars in it. We'd go so far as to say it's probably the worst thing Tony Adams has ever done in a car.

Robson says: 'The best England song has to be "Three Lions"', and many would agree, even if his United teammate Brian McClair takes the polar opposite view. Choccy tells us that Robson was very gloomy about the New Order single and wouldn't believe him when the Scottish striker wisely told him it would be a hit, but loses pop picker points by saying that 'Three Lions' is terrible: 'Ian Broudie will have to live that one down for a long time.' Sorry Chocs, the fact that 'Three Lions' is still being sung at World Cups more than 20 years after it was first released suggests it's a keeper.

John Barnes fondly remembers recording 'World in Motion' and tells us that the other players in contention to do the rap were Beardsley, Waddle, Gascoigne and Des Walker. We can't help but feel the right choice was made, and nothing in the singing careers of Waddle or Gascoigne will convince us otherwise[24] – not 'Geordie Boys', 'Diamond Lights' or that one The Waddler did with Basile Boli.[25]

—

23 Again, please do have a look if you can find it. There's a bit of it on YouTube.

24 Beardsley though. Can you imagine?

25 Seriously, we can't stress how much an afternoon on YouTube would be time well spent.

One final snippet from that World Cup comes from David Platt who reveals that the squad really embraced their new-found chart success. On the way to the semi-final the song was played on the coach: 'It certainly got us in the spirit of togetherness as everyone sang at the tops of their voices in excitement and anticipation.' Not only does this raise the tantalising prospect of John Barnes doing a live rap on the bus, it also shows that the only way to truly bring harmony to a squad through music is to make your own, wait till Bryan Robson's gone home injured, then turn it right up.

* * *

On to the screen now and let's stop off briefly for a look at some of the TV habits of a few of our football folk. Ian Snodin lists his favourites as Benny Hill and *Fawlty Towers*, while Peter Schmeichel is very enthusiastic about '*Prime Suspect*, *Cracker*, *The Bill* and *Harry Enfield and Chums*. My favourite is *Coronation Street* and the day after we won the 1998/99 Premiership I even took my family to visit the set.' A lovely image. While other players may have been jollying it up around town drinking champagne in the back of a Rolls-Royce, Peter took young Kasper and the rest down to the cobbles for a look at the recently opened 'Roy's Rolls'. Good wholesome fun.

Only slightly less wholesome, inevitably, is Micky Quinn who admits to watching 'any old bollocks' on his telly. Between the 'bollocks' and the sport though, he does express his love for *Star Trek* and particularly Captain Kirk. Of course, the nobility and stoicism of the ship's captain, boldly leading the crew into all sorts of unimagined danger – you can see why he'd be an inspiration. What's that Mick? 'I thought it was dead cool that wherever he went in the universe he always found a bird who fancied him, even if she was an alien.' Of course, it's about the 'birds'. It always is with Micky. The football, the music, the TV – the man's obsessed. Elsewhere he tells that his favourite film is *The Wizard of Oz*. He says he loves the way it transports 'you to a different world for a couple of hours', but we wouldn't be surprised if he was just into witches or munchkins. Or both.

If you're surprised by the thought of Quinny sitting down each Christmas to enjoy the Lollipop Guild strutting their stuff for Dorothy, then don't be. These people are connoisseurs. It stands to reason that in a job with a lot of free time and hotel stays, a lot of films get watched. Some of them not even porn. So if you're looking for footballers' film recommendations for a night in,[26] then you're in the right place.

Bryan Robson reckons 'I could sit and watch films all day – and did. My record during the World Cup was five in a day.' For the record, he lists some of his favourites as *The Godfather*, *The Sting*, *Gladiator* and *Troy*. Jamie Vardy, who includes *American Pie* as a favourite, may have even outdone Robbo at one point, claiming that he 'racked up hundreds of movies, viewing three a night at one stage'. Very impressive, although being on a tag and under a curfew for an assault charge at the time might have helped.

Gareth Southgate says *One Flew Over The Cuckoo's Nest* is his favourite and cheekily describes it as 'an everyday tale of football folk'. Terry Dyson likes an eclectic mix of *The Magnificent Seven*, 'with Yul Brynner and the other six'[27], *Taken* and *Beaches*, while John Barnes is your go-to guy for a steer on kung fu movies, saying 'I love *Iron Monkey 1* and *Iron Monkey 2* but my favourite films are the tales of the Shaolin temple.' We'd have to bend at the knee to Digger Barnes here. If it's not Bruce Lee or *Kung Fu Panda* we're a bit lost if we're honest.

Ian Snodin says his favourite stars are Charles Bronson and Jim Carrey, 'for his facial expressions and the effort he puts in to his performances',[28] but admits to being traumatised by seeing *The Birds* aged nine, saying 'For months afterwards I was terrified if I saw a flock of crows or starlings. It took me two years to get over it.' Two years seems oddly specific. Like Micky Quinn's ten Pernod-free years. Micky Quinn, incidentally, would surely have been very disappointed that time he rented a film called *The Birds*.

For even quicker reference we've compiled a list of some of the reviews that players have casually dropped into their life stories.

---

26 Netflix and Chilwell, perhaps.

27 Charles Bronson, Horst Buchholz, Brad Dexter, James Vaughan, Jack Colback and Gordon McQueen.

28 Yeah, Carrey really does give it 110 per cent doesn't he? The gaffer would be disappointed with anything less.

PLAYER	FILM	REVIEW
Andrea Pirlo	*Children of the Corn*	'the worst film I've ever seen'
Peter Reid	*Commando*	'the less said about that the better'
Chic Charnley	*The Deer Hunter*	'a barrel of laughs wasn't it?'
Paul Merson	*Jackie Brown*	'not very good'
Paul Merson	*There's Something About Mary*	'a brilliant film'
Paul Merson	*This Year's Love*	'Quite good'
Paul Merson	*You've Got Mail*	'which I enjoyed'
Paul Merson	*The Negotiator*	'Not bad'
Paul Merson	*Message in a Bottle*	'a mistake. Not because it was a bad film but because it was a love story'

The more observant among you will have noticed a lot of Paul Merson in here. That's because many of these come from Merse's diary when he moved to Middlesbrough, and evidently he couldn't find much else to do in the area apart from going to the pictures – at least not until Gazza turned up and they started taking sleeping pills with Jimmy Five Bellies and seeing who could stay awake the longest, that is.

Merson says at one point he saw so many films that he was able to recite large chunks of *There's Something About Mary* to Ray Parlour when he saw it for a third time, and eventually earned the nickname 'Barry Norman'.

However, both Merson and indeed Norman fall short of Gordon Banks when it comes to film critique. Check out his take on the early Connery *James Bonds*, for example, which he says, 'purveyed the fantasy that government took a laissez-faire attitude to Bond's penchant for bedding any amount of delectable women. His promiscuity mirrored the increasingly liberal attitude to sex among young people who were the first generation to have the contraceptive pill. The sophistication of the James Bond character, not only with regard to gadgets, but also food and drink, became something to which the masses could aspire.'

And why not?

Of course, it's not always simply about the film you see, but the circumstances in which you see it that makes the film experience so memorable. Andy Goram recalls struggling to watch *King Kong* in a hotel room with Rangers teammate Oleg Kuznetsov, claiming that

'Oleg couldn't understand a word and was laughing at all the wrong parts. He was driving me nuts.' This had us scratching our heads about which parts of *King Kong* you're supposed to laugh at, but Goram was sufficiently unimpressed that despite Oleg being 'a lovely man' he never shared a room with him again. All a far cry from the more harmonious and incredibly handsome room shared by Ben Thornley and David Beckham when they were each making their name at Old Trafford. Thornley remembers a night away before playing Chelsea when 'we watched *Planes, Trains and Automobiles*; when we looked at each other at the end we both tried to hide the fact that we were wiping a tear away'. This is lovely, and good on the pair of them. If you're not openly weeping by the end of that film you've got a heart of stone.

In addition to the circumstances, it's clearly the company in which you see a film that can really make the memories. And things are inevitably going to be more memorable than most if you're watching it with the High Priest of Hi-Jinks Steve Harrison. David Batty says of the England trip down under in 1991 that 'the whole tour was a bit low-key, enlivened only by the comic antics of Taylor's assistant, Steve Harrison, who is one of the funniest men I've ever met'. If Batts was bored he could always have gone along to *Les Mis* with Psycho and Nigel Clough, but at least he went along to the flicks to watch *The Silence of the Lambs* with Harrison and the rest of the squad. What could have been a terrifying experience for everyone was alleviated by the actions of one man. 'The lights came on at the interval and there was Steve, absolutely stark naked, staring at the screen as if nothing was amiss.' Unfortunately, Batty doesn't tell us whether or not Harrison tucked it under as a nod to the film's killer, Buffalo Bill, but we like to think he did.

There were equally disturbing cinema scenes in London where Stan Bowles and Don Shanks were trying to keep themselves out of gambling trouble by taking in a movie. Unfortunately for the pair of them, they chose *A Clockwork Orange* and neither of them were fans, with Bowles telling us: 'Obviously, it was an absolutely mental film.' Well yes, it is problematic and challenging for sure, but a good entry point if you're intending to start going to the cinema more as there is much to discuss. No doubt Stan and Don repaired to a neighbouring coffee shop afterwards to dissect what they'd seen. Not really: 'We never went to the cinema again. Next night it was the dog track, and for the next seven years we went down the dogs almost every night.

We would go anywhere to gamble.' That's right, *A Clockwork Orange* bent Stan's head so much that he never went back to the pictures, and instead took up gambling again. We've seen Stanley Kubrick accused of faking the moon landings before, but now we have to add this to the charges.

When Rotherham were preparing for an Auto Windscreens Final at Wembley in 1996, manager John McGovern decided to relax the lads by taking them to see *Trainspotting* at the cinema the night before. All well and good and above board, until you're reminded that Archie Gemmill was McGovern's assistant and that Gemmill actually appears in the film, with footage of his wonder goal against Holland at the 1978 World Cup intercut with an energetic sex scene featuring Kelly MacDonald and Ewan McGregor. Poor old Archie was reluctant but McGovern was insistent, telling him, 'it will do the lads good. Besides, they will give you loads of stick.' Sure enough, Gemmill sat squirming as his 'appearance in the movie was accompanied by a chorus of catcalls and whistles'. With team spirits sky-high, Rotherham went out and beat Shrewsbury in the final the following day, inspired by seeing Obi-Wan Kenobi getting his rocks off while thinking about poor Archie's best goal.

Gemmill is not the only footballer we've covered to get a mention on film. *The Damned United* told the story of Brian Clough and Peter Taylor's time at Leeds and two of the players who played under them have very different takes on it.

Duncan McKenzie is an easy-going guy. If we could jump minis and hurl golf balls the length of a football pitch like him and they didn't include those things in a film in which we appeared, we'd be livid. However, apart from his mock outrage that he was 'a tad disappointed not to be played by Brad Pitt' Mackenzie describes the film as 'a reasonable and believable portrayal of events', even if he wasn't in it much. Johnny Giles, on the other hand, did not enjoy it, saying that 'eventually, the bullshit just got too much for me'. While most of his problems with the film are with factual inaccuracies and his own portrayal, he can't resist a dig at the condition of the actors playing the Leeds team, claiming they 'look like members of a pub team at the bottom of their league'. Miaow.

Giles hints that he's earned the right to be critical having watched 'every movie made between 1950 and 1960, and one or two since', which really is quite a boast. But it's not our favourite film-related footballer boast. Nor does that title go to Jaap Stam showing off about his 'TV which beams pictures on to the wall' or his multiregion DVD player. No, sir. Our favourite boast comes from Jimmy Floyd Hasselbaink, simply because it might be the lowest rent boast by any Premier League footballer of all time. This is Jimmy Floyd Hasselbaink, remember – FA Cup winner, Golden Boot winner, international football star and former Northampton Town manager, lest we forget.

Is his film-related boast that he voiced Buzz Lightyear? Or that he was the original choice to play Ethan Hunt in the *Mission: Impossible* movies? Not quite. Jimmy boasts that during his time with Boavista, 'I had access to movies that had just been released in the cinema. For example, I had already seen *Hostage* starring Bruce Willis before it was released in England.' Well shut the front door. You know that bang average mid-period Bruce Willis thriller.you may not even remember whether you've seen or not? Well Jimmy Floyd Hasselbaink saw it before you on a hooky DVD. That truly is the stuff of Hollywood dreams. Made it, Ma. Top of the world.

YOUNG, GIFTED & BLACKPOOL

'Fat King Melon'

We know what you're thinking: the tales of childhood and growing up are always the boring bits in an autobiography, right? The sentimental bits you have to wade through before you get to the gold once the subject joins the circus/army/space programme/Wham!/Leeds United. But wait, come back. Trust us. This is where the 'we've read them so you don't have to' formula really pays off.

We've got no time for all of the romanticised guff, so we've ditched that. What remains is just the sweet golden juice from the days before our heroes joined the professional football ranks. Fires, gangs, Santa trauma and Pog guilt – we've got the lot. So strap in.

It isn't that we're cold, heartless people who can't find enjoyment in Bryan Robson's third-person descriptions of himself having a kick around as a lad ('pure delight on his face, a lifelong love in his heart and the world at his feet'). We just prefer the bit when he played chicken on his bike, lost control, hit a kerb and 'flew over the handlebars and went straight into a brick wall'. It's not a hard and fast rule that we prefer to see children knocked unconscious, but we'd be lying if we said it didn't help.

Now you're interested, hopefully, but in case you need more convincing about the value of tales from the younger days of your heroes, let's employ a tabloid tactic of splashy headline shock stories to lure you in:

KEEGAN IN SANTA DEATH RIDDLE

Kevin Keegan tells many a good tale across his three autobiographies (produced every two decades without fail), but the most poignant childhood episodes come from his first book, written in his 1970s heyday. His adolescence is so rich with odd stories that the time he decided to run more than 50 miles from Manchester to Doncaster as a teenager isn't even our main feature here. That run featured Kev's mate Dave taking a tumble midway, cracking his head and knocking himself out. Kev waited with him of course, but 'continued to jog on the spot' (as you do) until help arrived, whereupon 'I helped him into the car, making sure I did not stop the jogging.'

It's quite the image, a young KK jogging on the spot next to poor, prone Dave splayed across the tarmac. What on earth must the medics have thought when they arrived? One gets the impression that he would have told them that he hadn't cheated by stopping for a breather, even before he filled them in about Dave. It seems it's all a question of priorities for single-minded Kev. But, very much like the young Keegan, we're not stopping here. Instead we'll move on to a far more traumatic incident.

The Keegans, you see, lived opposite a funeral parlour, run by his friend's father, Mr Anderson. 'One day Mr Anderson called to us, "Come and have a look – it's Father Christmas and he's died."' You may well ask. 'Mr Anderson took us over to one of the bodies, the remains of a fellow with a long, white beard, who looked very much like the Father Christmas my mum had taken me to see at one of the big stores.'

Wow.

We can only speculate about Mr Anderson's motives for deliberately upsetting kids in this manner. Usually in such a story, showing the boys a corpse would be the absolute worst element of it, but telling them that Santa was dead takes things up a notch. What was he thinking? Maybe it was a money-saving exercise; perhaps business was bad and Mr Anderson was using the ruse to get out of showering his son with expensive gifts. Whatever the undertaker's reasoning, Keegan understandably says, 'I remember David and I were very upset about losing such a good friend.' Well of course they were. We're upset enough, and it didn't even happen to us.

We can't believe that Kev could ever truly erase this deeply troubling image from his mind's eye. We'll go so far as to lay the blame for Newcastle's spectacular 1996 title collapse at the door of the macabre Mr Anderson, going around dishing out childhood trauma willy-nilly. In fact, it's possible that even in the middle of his infamous 'I would love it' Sky rant about Fergie in the run-in, he was still seeing Santa's cadaver every time he blinked. Merry Christmas.

JFK – THE TRUTH AT LAST?

They say that everyone alive at the time remembers where they were when they heard about the Kennedy assassination. Frank Worthington is no exception. It was his 15th birthday, and it played out exactly like this:

> 'Brother Bob came running out with the news: "Oi Frank, you know that Yank who's been giving Marilyn one?"
>
> "Yeah."
>
> "Well he's just been shot dead."'

It would seem that young Bob Worthington had a flair for this splashy tabloid stuff himself. Straight to the dirt.

BATTY SLEEPS WITH TEAMMATE'S PARENTS

Inevitably, this isn't as saucy as it sounds – we've been mischievous. Though technically we are correct. You see, David Batty is, or was at least, a sleepwalker. It's tempting to think of him effortlessly running a Premier League midfield in his sleep, we know, but this was in his early days.

He tells us that he once stayed at his pal Rob's house and well, there was an incident. In the morning Rob's dad told him that he had awoke in the night with the eerie feeling that there was a no-nonsense midfield battler in the room with him and his wife. As his 'eyes adjusted to the gloom he was confronted with the spectre of me, standing at the foot of their bed, staring straight ahead and tapping my teeth, another curious childhood habit of mine. It must have scared him and his wife half to death.'

Yes. It almost certainly did. But when Rob's dad calmly asked David what he was up to, he immediately turned around and went back to bed. A polite sleepwalker at least.

FRY ADMITS PLAYING WITH HIMSELF

Barry Fry tells us that his 'favourite carpet game as a kid was tiddlywinks', but he put his own wrinkle on it. A tiddly-wrinkle, if you will. 'I turned the tiddlywinks into massive football matches – red tiddlywinks versus blue tiddlywinks; black tiddlywinks versus yellow tiddlywinks.' We sort of got the idea with the red v blue, Baz. 'I would put two Subbuteo goals at either end and this massive tournament would start and go on all day.'

This does sound lovely, and to be honest not too dissimilar from our own childhood carpet time; however, if you've got Subbuteo to use the goals from it, Barry, it begs the question, why not just play Subbuteo? You big tiddlywinks weirdo.

GROB IN RACE ROW MERCY DASH

Bruce Grobbelaar is very candid about his early years in Zimbabwe including his army days shooting at people in the jungle, and even before that when his family employed 'an African houseboy called Lummick, a poor man's au pair'. No offence, Lummick. Bruce concedes that this is not a good look and has overtones of 'black slavery' but maintains that it 'was an accepted way of life' in his childhood circumstances.

Among Lummick's thankless duties was bringing a young (and in our heads at least, moustachioed) Master Bruce home from school on a bike. We say thankless because on one particular occasion the young Grobbelaar was impatient to get indoors and, despite Lummick's insistence that he wait with him while he put the bike away, didn't even wait for him to stop. Bruce says that 'my four-year-old mind told me that the easiest way to get what I wanted and stop the bike was to put my little foot through the front wheel's spokes'. That's not really how you're supposed to do it. Inevitably they fell off, badly, but instead of cursing young Master Bruce, Lummick was a hero, scooping the infant up and running '17 blocks to the casualty ward of the local hospital. His reward when we returned home to concerned parents was for me to blame him for the crash.'

What a little git. Poor old Lummick.

BATH-TIME SECRETS OF FOREST STARS

Two tales now from the other side of the bathroom door, where things got hot and steamy, and blue. But calm down, we're not talking about anything saucy, we are of course referring to the time Brian Laws turned blue in the bath. You heard.

There are echoes here of the very niche 1970s children's cartoon *Little Blue*, about a baby elephant who turned blue in the bath.[29] In

29 In a book full of niche references, we'll admit that *Little Blue* might be the most niche of all. But we didn't dream it, honest.

Little Blue's case he 'bit his mummy's fountain pen and broke it in two', while in the bath. For poor little Brian Laws, he was even less to blame. It was entirely his dad's fault, as he explains: 'the bath was getting a bit rusty and my father daubed it blue with some paint he'd brought home from the shipyard. It was my turn to have first dip in the newly painted bath. The paint started to come off because of the hot water and I became blue from head to toe. I cried my eyes out but all my dad could do was laugh because it looked funny to him.'

How did this ever fly as an idea among the adults in the household? It was doomed to fail and poor little Brian paid the consequences while his hapless dad chuckled away at his Smurf-like son. And this was years before the Blue Man Group, so they couldn't even put him into some showbiz work until the paint wore off. The next day at school must have been quite formative we imagine.

Then again, maybe Laws should think himself lucky. If he'd grown up with John McGovern, there would have been no blue on him, or mud, or dirt and probably not much skin. It seems that McGovern's grandmother was in charge of bath times when the young John would come home caked in mud from wherever he'd been playing football. Her solution to the mess? 'It involved a scrubbing brush, her deep porcelain bath and DAZ washing powder. I swear it's the reason I have lovely soft skin to this day.'

We can't work out if this is brutal and wrong or just a revolutionary skincare idea. If what McGovern says is true, then the cosmetics industry is going to be in disarray.

SHARPE'S PUB SCAM SHAME

Lee Sharpe talks touchingly of his grandad in his book *My Idea of Fun*. Unfortunately, the great man died when Lee was still a schoolboy, but it seems that they had a bond forged over having fun together, including sneaking into pubs and sitting Lee on the bar with him. 'He even bought me a little suit from the market, used to dress me in that and tell landlords I wasn't a kid, I was a dwarf, so they'd let me in.'

Did landlords really fall for this? Or just turn a blind eye? Either way it makes us regret all those times as children when we'd borrow a great long coat and stand on each other's shoulders to try and pass ourselves off as grown-ups in the pubs round our way. Too much effort. That one was always rumbled when you passed a second pint into your coat at crotch height.

SOLO'S SICK BOMB SONG

US goalkeeper Hope Solo had an unusual upbringing on the banks of the Columbia River. Apart from Solo, her hometown of Richland is most famous for its part in manufacturing the bomb dropped on Nagasaki at the end of the Second World War. Solo says: 'in my hometown, that incineration is still celebrated. The logo of my high school is the nuclear mushroom cloud.' Good grief. She says that this logo appeared on the 'basketball court, emblazoned on T-shirts and the backs of varsity jackets'.

This all seems a bit much, but at least they didn't sing about it, right? Oh yes they did. 'We don't do politically correct in Richland. When I was in high school, one of our school cheers was "Nuke 'em, nuke 'em, nuke 'em till they glow!"' Till they glow, mind. Don't just nuke 'em. Nuke 'em till they glow. If they're not glowing, you're not nuking them enough. That's what they're getting at here. Nice people.

SOCCER STARS' COMIC CAPERS

Some of our players appear to have grown up within the pages of a *Beano* or *Dandy* comic. Whether it's daredevil wheezes or slap-up meals, it's all there.

We have Ally Robertson telling us about hurtling 'down the stairs on a tray' and Mel Sterland with the childhood classic – getting your head stuck in some railings. He had to be freed by firemen in front of his whole school. After that, playing full-back in front of a baying mob must have come easy.

In the slap-up feed stakes, Kenny Sansom says he would have 'bread and dripping and two jam doughnuts' for breakfast each day. For breakfast, mind. This is an acceptable lunch, but never breakfast. He excitedly says, 'Mum put this fandabydozy grub on the table to ensure I had a contented belly and my tank was full for the day.' It feels like he's stopping just short of telling us he had a massive plate of mash with 20 sausages sticking out of the side, or one of Desperate Dan's cow pies.

You wouldn't have caught Rodney Marsh eating doughnuts as a kid. Playing keepy-uppies with them, yes, eating them, no. He tells us 'I would practise with anything, oranges, coins, even Bakewell tarts. I would throw a tart up in the air, catch it with a foot and then flick it up again and catch it in my mouth. My concentration was excellent, because I happened to like tarts.' Cor!

If some childhoods are ripped from the pages of *The Beano*, then John Sitton's seems like it comes straight out of *Viz* – Biffa Bacon to be precise. His book is littered with fights he didn't start and phrases like 'Bang. I hit him' when somebody is rude to his mum. As a thoughtful man, Sitts says it was never just about the scrap, but rather it 'gave me an early insight into false bravado and people being out of their comfort zone when they're not in a gang'. This particular story involves the brothers of one of his victims seeking him out for revenge, at which point his Aunt Nell stepped in. Rather than defuse the situation completely she said, '"he'll take you on one at a time. If the other one jumps in I'll jump in." She then turned to me and said "If you don't stand your ground and take your own part I'll give you a good hiding when you get home."' Rules are, it would seem in the Sitton family, rules. Any transgressions of those rules were met with the fury of Aunt Nell and Sitton's mum, as his dad found out. Sitton's dad had an affair and in John's words 'she'd caught him with some blonde slosh pot called Patricia. The fallout was unbelievable.' During the row between these formidable women and the man with the wandering eye, Sitton says, 'I turned to see my Aunt chin my Dad and my Mum pull him down by his hair and tip a saucepan full of boiling gravy all over him.'

So there you go. Do not mess with these women. That old slosh pot Patricia's lucky they never got hold of her.

For some, violence like this is just the norm. Alan Mullery speaks very matter-of-factly about his dad's penchant for a dust-up at the pub. He even tells of a time he was posted outside the saloon bar with a cricket bat himself, to swipe at a chap his dad was going in to sort out, should he come bursting through the doors. The young Mullery, about nine or ten at this time, did his duty when he eventually saw the right man running out: 'I belted him with my bat, then Dad caught him and gave him a hiding.' It's nice to have hobbies that fathers and sons can enjoy together, isn't it?

* * *

We're sad to say that some of the childhoods we examined showed our heroes to have feet of clay, with petty theft rife among the ball-kicking youth community. Ian Snodin starts us off small admitting to pilfering sweets from his local shop as a kid, while Micky Quinn's low-level crime has an inevitable sexy edge, stealing 'pens, sweets and wank mags from W.H. Smith's'. Steven Gerrard preferred to nick his stationery from Woolworths. His parents had given him the money but he spent that on 'a Coke and burger instead at McDonald's'. It sounds like a foolproof plan but 'as I was sticking pens in my pocket and paper inside my coat, the Woolies security guard clocked us straightaway'. Gerrard was grounded for this but he's not alone. Enough footballers confess to stealing from Woolworths that it's no wonder they went bust. Kenny Sansom describes 'nicking Mars Bars' from there as if it was inevitable. Even after bread and dripping and two doughnuts for breakfast, Kenny's out robbing Mars bars. But more on Kenny's life of juvenile crime later.

Petty theft also unites two giants of the game in Zlatan Ibrahimović and Neil Warnock – two men that despite being in the same profession for many years have almost certainly never been mentioned in the same breath. The young Zlatan nicked bikes you see. Despite his claims that it 'was quite innocent', we're not sure how he comes to that conclusion. We didn't spend ages as kids having the police come round the school and stamp our bikes just so gifted Swedish strikers could steal them all and claim it as innocent fun. He admits that he 'got a buzz from that' and one time 'took a massive pair of bolt cutters and nicked a military bike'. What's a military bike? Is it just a bike belonging to someone in the army or is it a special bike? We're imagining The Batpod until someone tells us different. Warnock, meanwhile, bitterly regrets the time he stole from his mum's purse to buy fireworks, but is full of praise for the way the attending police officer dealt with the situation, giving him 'a clip round the back of my head and said if I ever did it again, I'd be in prison'. Inevitably Neil says 'I don't think it did me any harm', but we'd argue that maybe it did. Something clearly hurt him along the way, anyway.

Not everyone stuck to theft though. Others branched out into tormenting a neighbour until he set his own shed alight. What do you mean that's not a criminal offence? Well just maybe it should be. In the otherwise charming and adorably named *What's It All About, Ralphie?*, Ralph Milne cheerfully admits that he and his brother would torment his neighbour to distraction by pinging nails at his windows. One night, when it had all got a bit out of hand, Ralph says, 'I pulled the curtains back and saw Mr Grumpy's shed well alight. What we didn't know until later was that the guy was a bit of an alcoholic and he thought whoever was responsible for hitting his windows was hiding in his shed so he torched it! That was the end of the nonsense.' Poor old Mr Grumpy; first he's saddled with that name, then he has to cope with those pesky Milne lads next door driving him mad, then he sends his own shed up in flames.

Fire you say? Look no further for more of that than Steve 'Chips' 'Chico' Nicol. Stevie, you may recall, has form for setting the hair of Gary Ablett's wife ablaze, but the twisted fire starter was sparking up long before that. As a youth, he once went back to his mate Gordon's house after the pub and 'went to sleep on the couch in the living room after I finished my cigarette – or at least I thought I had finished it'. You're ahead of us again aren't you? The still-lit cigarette set fire to a sofa and soon the house was in flames. Stevie managed to get himself out through a window and Gordon got out too but 'unfortunately Gordon's dog – a boxer – had not been so lucky and suffocated because of the smoke'. All because of a careless cigarette. We wouldn't mind but we were constantly being warned about this sort of thing back in the day. Flammable sofas and smoking without due care and attention we mean – there weren't public information films warning of the dangers of Steve Nicol. Although it seems like there should have been. Despite killing his dog and burning him out of house and home, apparently 'Gordon couldn't have been more understanding'. That is a solid friendship right there. They must have got along like … well, you know.

The Steve Nicol story blurs the lines a bit here. It's not actually a crime, but there is a fire and there are victims. Steve Bruce, however, definitely committed a crime, but he might argue that it's completely victimless. It is, however, probably our favourite youth crime story of them all.

The young Steve Bruce spent his apprenticeship at Gillingham; just a young boy, far from home, all the while missing his girlfriend Janet (later his wife), who was still at home in the North East. Love-struck phone calls from phone box to phone box[30] were both time-consuming and expensive, until Steve developed a cunning plan of 'reversing the charges to Janet's box. It worked, so whenever I was a little short of cash I used the same trick.' All well and good, but Bruce claims that somebody else in the area was pulling the same trick and the exchange began listening in to calls from Gillingham to the North East to find

30 Phone boxes – ask your mum and dad.

the culprits. It seems that they were determined to get their man, and launched a major operation that frankly must have cost more money in personnel hours than Bruce was getting away with. 'One day I was telling Janet about being sent off during a game against Swindon and it did not take Sherlock Holmes to deduce from the newspaper reports the next day who had been making the call. When I came to my next call, the trap had been set.'

This seems like a tremendous effort in terms of investigation and surveillance, all for a few reversed charge calls. It's like something out of *Zodiac*, but this time they caught the culprit. While they were on the next call Steve heard sirens getting closer but didn't dream they were there for him: 'before I realised what was happening, four police cars and a van roared up outside my telephone box. There was a moment of horrid realisation that I was the target of the manhunt. I just had time to scream to Janet "Run, run; they've caught us!" before I was nabbed.' It all seems a bit excessive and heavy-handed doesn't it? But we do like to think that the four police cars pulled up on the four sides of the phone box, trapping a startled Bruce inside. We also like the image of Janet dropping the phone at her end and making good her escape. The County Durham Constabulary were obviously a bit slower than their Kent counterparts. Or maybe they just had some proper crime to deal with instead of persecuting these star-crossed lovers for having a chat.

Back to Kenny Sansom. You remember Kenny from Crystal Palace, Arsenal, robbing from Woolies and doughnuts for breakfast, right? Sansom reckons that 'playing "Knock Down Ginger" filled hours of potential boredom and by the age of 8 we had progressed to nicking lead from roofs'. Maybe we've led a sheltered life, but this doesn't seem like a natural progression to us; quite a leap in fact. Kenny says, 'The scrap-metal man must have heard us coming from streets away as we pushed a pram full of lead towards his yard.' Eight-year-olds, dude.

David Seaman is another who got himself involved in nicking lead from roofs and selling it to unscrupulous scrap men, but he says he got cold feet and never actually went through with it. We believe him, the big old softy. He would have never had the minerals for Sansom's biggest crime caper then: the time he and his brother and their gang 'happened upon an old factory with a smashed window'. Now this sounds like the enticing opening act to any number of school programme dramas we watched in classrooms with the blinds down on the big telly. We're intrigued.

Kenny says that the young villains glanced through the window and thought they'd stumbled on a marbles factory, the mother lode for kids of a certain era. However, 'We scrambled through the broken glass and found ourselves gawping at Aladdin's cave. From the outside, the building had appeared to be abandoned; but it wasn't. It was a bloody chandelier factory, and the marbles were bloody crystals.' The youngsters filled their pockets regardless, with the honourable intention of taking some 'jewels home to our mum', but thoughts of having won the lottery didn't last for long. As they were leaving, 'police sirens screamed down the lane and flashing blue lights came into view'. The crew scattered but collars were unfortunately felt, including the Sansom boys. Kenny's defence for his kiddy crime capers is that: 'We never went out looking for trouble. Who does?' Well, for a start we'd argue that if you go nicking lead off roofs and breaking into factories, you sort of are looking for trouble. Not to mention eating into poor old Woolworths' profits.

If marbles would have made the ideal haul for children of the 70s, then for a brief time in the 90s the equivalent would have been Pogs.[31] And that's where Jermaine Pennant comes in. Young Jermaine says that one day he and his mates were messing around when he found the Pogs. 'I saw them in a skip in a pile of magazines. I don't know if they were faulty or what, but they'd been thrown away. I took an absolute load of them and I put them all in my cupboard.' All well and good you might think, and good luck to him. This appears to be an open and shut case of classic finders keepers. However, a few days later the police raided his home and he was terrified they were after him for the Pogs. They weren't. Instead they were after his dad who was involved in some unfortunate business that we'll draw a discreet veil over here, but the sight of loads of police boots clumping up the stairs was enough to put the wind up our young hero: 'I've never been so afraid, so scared and so terrified of what my dad would say.' After his narrow escape, the enterprising Jermaine decided to move the hot goods on, and make a tidy profit as he did so. He took them to school and sold them – £2.50 for 20 packs, since you ask.

31 Pogs were decorated milk cap disc type things. We're not even sure we can remember what you had to do with them, but they were very collectable, and very popular.

Ah, school, the furnace in which our personalities are truly forged. A sink or swim, only the strongest survive, kill or be killed environment. We've literally all been there. Some thrived, like Alan Hansen with his multitude of O and A levels, while others, like Pat van den Hauwe, were dead against it. Pat dismisses the entire education system as being forced to learn 'how many degrees a circle contained, how to make something useless out of wood or how to dissect a frog, for fuck's sake!' Pat's really nailed what school is there, to be fair.

Some just remember the peculiarities of school, like Jimmy Greaves with recollections of the nit nurse, and the even more invasive 'cough and drop' nurse: 'I suppose she came to make sure our testicles were hanging properly, but to this day I ain't sure why they had to know this. I mean, even if they weren't, what were they going to do about it?' It's a fair point and one that clearly troubled him for some time. But at school you just accept some things as normal and sometimes they really, really aren't.

Norman Whiteside brings us news of the odd punishments meted out by one Mrs Caters, at his school. It seems that she had a three-tiered system of punishment:

- 'A stick like a sergeant-major's baton that she called "Sam Stinger" and which she used to whack your behind with.' Awful stuff, but probably depressingly common in schools in the late 70s. Though not always with a pet name.

- The second, 'a sort of strap with a hook on the end called "Willy Wobbler", with which you'd have your knuckles rapped'. Okay, getting weirder and nastier. Corporal punishment is bad enough but now we're into a bizarre choose your weapons scenario. But wait for it …

- Punishment number three involved being forced to sit under her desk 'and play "Mousey, Mousey", which entailed running your fingers up and down her stockinged legs from ankle to mid-thigh for several minutes while she continued with the class'. Mrs Caters, it seems, was not a well unit, and we can only hope that eventually somebody told her this was wrong. Norm is happy to laugh it off but it's a long way from being right.

If you weren't scarred by what went on in the classroom, then the playground was often more brutal. We remember that having the wrong bag or haircut could make you the subject of ridicule – shoes could be a similar issue, of course. The late Norman Hunter recounts a bit of childhood trauma in his book, brought on because all the other boys at his school had black wellies, while his were red, like the girls wore, because they were his sister's hand-me-downs. He recalls, 'Kids can be very cruel and I had to suffer a lot of stick from my mates about those red wellies.' Bless him. The thing is Norman, you've just got to own it. Red wellies or not, walk your own path and don't let them get to you. Be more like Gordon Banks, who must have had an awful lot of charisma because he managed to pull off wearing clogs to school without being beaten up four times a day. He even says that 'my father, in an attempt to extend their life, had fixed steel bars across the soles'. Banks managed to turn this into a virtue and ingratiated himself to the other kids as he would allow them to 'take me by the hand and drag me across the school playground to see who could make the greatest number of sparks fly'. Good innocent fun from back in the old days. Kids didn't shut themselves away playing non-existent PlayStations back then; they were too busy dragging future England goalies in clogs across a playground. Banks even suggests it might have helped him have a longer reach in his chosen career. You see, this childhood stuff is important – no clogs, no save from Pelé.

Norman and Gordon managed to avoid fights at school but not everyone was as fortunate. There are several accounts of what we understand the kids these days call 'Beef'. Swashbuckling England captain Bryan Robson admits to 'a few fights' at school, which is what you might expect. On one occasion he was picked on by 'two ginger nuts' and exacted revenge by getting them one at a time, on his dad's advice. Another time he dispensed justice for a friend who was having his apple taken from him by a bully. Robbo grabbed the apple to put himself in the firing line and told the 'big lad' that he wasn't getting it today. A noble scuffle ensued with young Bryan fighting with truth and justice on his side. The result? 'He battered me.' Oh Robbo, that's a much better story if you'd won, but that's what happens if you set yourself up as some kind of apple sheriff.

Charlie Miller of Rangers fame is another one who got himself in a terrible scrap on the side of the angels, defending a woman's honour, no less, against some kind of braggart or cad. 'I asked him, "Did you call Michelle Thompson a cow?" Quick as a flash, he replied, "Aye." I was hoping he might have answered differently and we could have left it at that, but I had no choice.' The detail Miller goes into involves a fearful tear-up, with headbutts, kicks and a punch that broke his hand. We can only hope that Michelle Thompson appreciated the effort.

What with all the scrapping, creepy teachers and clogs, it's easy to forget that some people actually had lessons going on at school. Here then is a quick report card of what some of our stars got up to once the bell went to start the day.

NAME	SUBJECT	REPORT
Jamie Vardy	PE	It seems young Vardy had a prodigious throw on him and held the school record for throwing a cricket ball, long after he'd left. He fondly remembers telling the teacher he would need to stand further back and delighting in sending him 'frantically running to try to get near to where it landed' when he sent it sailing over him. Probably cupped his ear at him to celebrate, too.
Les Ferdinand	PE	Sir Les says, 'Rugby wasn't my game, that was for sure, but it was really a rugby school and we all had to do it. We used to call it "roughby".' And we thought Les was a hard nut. We had to do rugby at our school too, and we suspect that if we'd called it 'roughby' we'd have never recovered from it.[32]
Graham Poll	Drama	Graham appeared in a school play called 'Fat King Melon'. Us neither.
Bryan Robson	Food & Nutrition	Didn't fancy Metalwork or Woodwork, so chose Cookery, quite rightly thinking it would be useful. 'I was the only lad in the cookery class. The trouble was that we had to take our cookery stuff to school in a basket, so I used to get a girl from down the road to take mine in for me.' Not very Captain Marvel, that.

32 Les was actually taught rugby at school by the father-in-law of one of your authors. So were Dennis Wise and Marcus Gayle. No rugby players though.

Mick Quinn	Food & Nutrition	Has his own reasons for taking the Cookery option: 'I opted to do CSE cooking – or Food and Nutrition as they grandly called it – rather than woodwork because there were fifteen birds and just two lads doing it.' Of course.
David Platt	Business Studies	Not strictly classroom but Platt set himself up with a playground sweets business. He would come back from lunch at home with Black Jacks, Fruit Salads and all sorts bought from the local shop, which he then sold at an extortionate mark-up. His profit margins were through the roof apparently. He's like Gonch from *Grange Hill*, if Gonch from *Grange Hill* went on to score a late winner against Belgium.
Mark Walters	Business Studies	Him and the bad crowd he fell in with ran a school gates protection racket. They even kept their ill-gotten gains in a safe. Well, you can't trust anyone can you? It's a proven business model at least, but he does say, 'I acted appallingly and I'm ashamed to have been a part of it'. It was, of course, good old football that put him on the straight and narrow and his life of organised crime was over by the age of nine.

Those without money taken with menace or their own young enterprise scheme had to supplement their pocket cash by more conventional means. Ron Atkinson worked for his uncle's dairy, delivering milk on a handcart, Peter Schmeichel worked in the 'dyeing department of a textile factory', Kevin Keegan worked at a brass works where he says he 'quickly discovered that women in packs can be far worse behaved and far cruder than men'. Sensitive soul is our Kev, and a bit sexist in his younger days. Hope Powell balances out the gender politics with her account of working in a men's clothing shop: 'I was almost exclusively dealing with men. It gave me the confidence to engage with people who maybe don't perceive you as someone who knows what they're talking about in a male-dominated world.' We can't think what she's getting at here, can you?

One of the oddest accounts of a childhood part-time job comes from Rob Lee, who feels that the romantic idea that he once worked the turnstiles at The Valley is overblown. He says that he only did it a few times but the idea has stuck. You can see why; it's a nice story. 'That's the problem,' says Lee, 'people like the idea. In the match programmes all you see is "former turnstile operator Rob Lee ...", which could not really be further from the truth!' Well you DID work on the turnstile, Rob. It's not *that* far from the truth is it? If they said it and you'd never seen a turnstile in your life it would be further from the truth. If they said you were a teenage helicopter pilot, it would be further from the truth.

Howard Webb wasn't always a boring referee; in his younger more dynamic days, he worked in a bank. Calm down girls. Form an orderly queue. Webb was a rebel though, and the Yorkshire Bank James Dean got the sack for swearing all over the official literature. In a bored moment, young Howard took a bank diary from a pile and wrote some choice phrases throughout it like 'WHAT A LOAD OF BOLLOCKS' and 'KNOBHEADS', but instead of binning it 'that defaced diary somehow ended up back on the customer pile'. A customer duly found it and got the vapours and Webb was sacked shortly after. That defaced diary can now be found on eBay going for £876, probably.

The young Dwight Yorke had no gainful employment growing up on the edge of poverty in Tobago, so had to improvise. In one amazing tale, Yorkie bet a sports shop owner that he could stand in a bin outside his shop and juggle a football 100 times on his head in exchange for a pair of boots he desired. The shopkeeper was game and the bet was on: '"It's a hundred, and nothing short of a hundred and you've got to pay for them if you fail," he said. There were six or seven people in the shop amused by all this and acting as witnesses.' Those witnesses saw history in the making as young Dwight completed his unusual challenge (even throwing in an extra ten for showboating) and walked off with the boots into the sunshine of a glorious beckoning career.

It goes without saying that each and every one of our football scribes was brilliant in their youth. You know that player at that club that you've never rated? Well, even he was much better as a kid than the likes of us ever were. It stands to reason, therefore, that on occasion, some of their paths crossed. Steve Hodge boasts that both Brian 'Killer' Kilcline and Mark Hateley came into his orbit as a youngster. Hodge claims that Killer at 13 was already six-foot tall and 'had a beard and he would scare everybody to death'. We can well believe it.

West Brom legend Ally Robertson tells a beautiful story of rubbing shoulders as a kid in Philpstoun with future Rangers striker Colin

Stein. 'Stein was five years older than me, and because of this you could never get the football off him, no matter how hard you tried. He was rougher and tougher than anyone because of his age.' Robertson's career arc can then be seen as a spiteful mission to claw his way up through the ranks until he finally played against Stein when the bigger boy was at Coventry. 'I remember telling my team-mates, "I'm marking Stein!" After I whacked him a few times he turned to me and said, "You're not that little kid in the village any more, are you?"' Some people say 'the best revenge is living well' but actually it's waiting years and years then kicking someone up the arse.

Of course, being a good young footballer can take you into the rarefied air where good things happen and legends lurk. Paul Lake fondly recalls his Denton Youth side being invited to New York on tour where they watched a Cosmos team including Beckenbauer, Carlos Alberto and, er, Dennis Tueart. That was all after they'd been introduced, pre-match, to Pelé. Lake says: 'As I was introduced to him I couldn't stop grinning, imagining what Mum and Dad would say when I told them that I'd shaken hands with the greatest footballer of all time.' We think he's miscalculated here as he didn't meet Ian Bishop till a few years later, but Pelé will do for now. What a trip, though! We remember one of our clubs taking us on a trip to Wembley but Pelé wasn't there. In fact nobody was there. Although we did manage to pinch a piece of turf to plant in the back garden and they showed us the big baths, so that's not nothing, is it?

Not everyone had to travel so far to meet the great and good. Jamie Carragher played against Paul 'son of Kenny' Dalglish as a lad and that gave Carragher Snr every opportunity to get into a touchline row with Dalglish Snr. Carragher's side were awarded a dubious penalty and King Kenny raised a protest, causing Jamie's dad to swing into action. '"Keep your fuckin' mouth shut, Dalglish," he said. "You should know all about dodgy penalties after the amount you get at Anfield every season." Before I knew it, Kenny and my dad were virtually coming to blows.' All very undignified and not to be encouraged, especially with a true legend of the game involved. It does sound a bit like it probably wasn't a penalty though, right?

The righteous indignation of the Carraghers was almost certainly borne out of the fact that young Jamie grew up blue. Not like Brian Laws and his bath-time mishap you understand – he grew up in an Everton household, and so was naturally very anti-Liverpool. He says that he rationalises his split loyalties by thinking: 'There are two Evertons in my life: the Everton before Liverpool, and the Everton after. The club I loved in the 1980s and the team I see now are poles apart in my mind. I refer to the Everton team of the eighties as "us" and the modern Everton as "them".' Whatever gets you through the night, Carra. He is, of course, not alone in taking a ferry across the Mersey divide. Liverpool legends Fowler, McManaman, Owen and even Rush grew up with Everton tendencies while Peter Reid freely admits he went the other way – idolising Liverpool as a lad before turning blue later.

This does take us into an interesting area though. We all enjoy a player being 'one of our own' but that remains a rarity. More often than not, a player's younger days will have been spent supporting someone other than the side he plays for. In David Platt's case, his boyhood allegiances are entirely in keeping with his peripatetic playing career. He freely admits that his earliest memories are of liking Chelsea because they won the cup, 'the following year I changed allegiance and became a Leeds fan', then it all changed 'around the age of ten when I finally settled on Manchester United'. It doesn't take Inspector Montalbano to notice that Manchester United also won the cup in 1977 when glory-hunting David was around the age of ten. The rotter.

Hope Powell's football heroes as a girl were chosen on an even more flighty basis, with Kevin Keegan and Ray Wilkins competing for space on her bedroom wall – Keegan 'because he was the player of the moment' and Wilkins 'because he had nice legs'. Go on Ray. Tremendous. The legs of Ray Wilkins bring us on to tales of sexual awakening among our teenage football prodigies. Many is the tale of a player losing their focus once the hormones kick in, which in Micky Quinn's case seems to have been from the age of about four.

Perry Groves won't have been far behind him either. Obsessed he is, even saying of his first ever Sunday league goal, 'I never felt like that again until I started shagging.' Even on his way up to a trial at Wolves on the train, when most lads would be full of nervous energy, Perry tells us that he 'eased the tension in the same way as generations of schoolboys had done before me – by reading copies of the girlie magazines *Parade* and *Knave* that I'd bought at Euston'. He says he hid them inside a copy of *The Sun* to save face. It's all about personal choices, of course, but we'd be more inclined to hide a copy of *The Sun* inside *Knave*.

Perry's grubby train porn is both figuratively and literally thousands of miles away from Malcolm Allison's prosaic retelling of an early sexual encounter while doing national service in Vienna. 'To get to her room I had to pass the place where her father slept. He was a 17-stone butcher. I crept past the foot of his bed, my army boots hanging round my neck. I never knew what reassurance could come with the sound of a snore. Nor the feeling of pride a young man carries with him from the bed of a supple young girl and on to the early-morning streets of a great city.' Beautiful stuff, with undertones of *Before Sunrise*, *An Officer and a Gentleman* and *Jack and the Beanstalk* to it.

Jackie Charlton's national service stories have a different tone again to them. He spent much of it stationed at Windsor, which he claims was 'full of gays', a sweeping statement that he backs up by elaborating that: 'It was quite a well-known thing that young soldiers would go off with businessmen and suchlike, and we used to exploit this to a degree that was criminal at times. We used to go to a certain pub where they would buy you drinks all night. They would become very friendly at closing time, but we'd just say, "well thanks very much, see you now", and walk off.' Jack Charlton there, cock-teasing it up all over Windsor, playing a dangerous and very unfair game. Still, free drinks.

Sex and drink aren't the only vices that can steer a promising football career away from the path of righteousness. Derek Dougan, for instance, was almost led astray by his own grandmother and her snuff habit. 'Now and again she would give me a little to sniff, and of course I would sneeze half a dozen times.' Snuff – just say no, kids. What chance have you got when even your own family is a bad influence?

Football, fighting and the other sort of effing enthusiast, Roy McDonough, happily describes his dad as 'the porn king of Solihull, with a shop full of grubby videos shelved under the bed and a black bag full of dirty mags hidden in the wardrobe', so it's fair to say that the sexy apple didn't fall too far from the sexy tree there. Lee McCulloch recalls his mum's somewhat robust methods of dealing with his discipline problems at school, saying of one suspension: 'When I told my mum she'd just give me a right hook to the jaw. Honestly, she had quicker hands than Muhammad Ali!'

Joey Barton's home life inevitably had an air of violence around it too, but at least his dad channelled it into fatherly advice about how to fight. Barton Snr told him a series of key moves as follows:

1. 'grab the other boy's neck as hard as you can. Grab his school tie or shirt, and never let go.'
2. 'put your head straight down' because 'They'll just hit the top of your head, which is the hardest part of your body.'
3. 'Keep punching. Pop, pop, pop. Eventually they will raise their chin with the effort. All you need is to connect once on the button, and they're gone.'
4. 'Never let go of that neck until they stop.'

Now we can disapprove of the nature of this advice. We can become amateur psychologists, put the points of our fingers together and ponder the extent to which this kind of environment led directly to Joey's problems with violence in later life … but we're all also storing this advice away aren't we? Just in case things get a bit tasty down Yates's one Friday night.

It's not all bad news though. Among the nicer parent/child relationships is that of Mark Walters and his mum. Money was tight at home and Mark seems forever grateful that his mum used her job in lost property at the West Midlands transport authority to get him the odd pair of trainers. 'Mum would come out with these stunning trainers or even football boots. I suppose I should be thanking the forgetful folk of Birmingham, and maybe even those who jumped on a bus after they'd had a little too much to drink, for my footwear!' Lovely. Good on her.

Mark Walters's dear old mum seems just the right level of supportive of her son's burgeoning playing career. Making sure he kept on the straight and narrow and getting him some decent boots where she could. We all know not everybody stops there, and naturally, in the ranks of future pros we are not short of a pushy parent story.

Emlyn Hughes's dad, for example, was always very keen on his son having a career in football. Even to the extent of trampling over any other sporting dreams he might have had. The young Emlyn was once picked to play rugby league for Barrow Boys – a proud day for any northern youngster. But as he came off after a game against St Helens, he recalls, 'my father came towards me, put his arm round my shoulder and said, "Son, you want to forget all about that game. That's the worst I have ever seen anyone play."' Oh well. At least the old man was considerably more enthusiastic about his early football days at Blackpool, writing anonymous letters as 'Seasider' to the local paper with comments like: '"When is Hughes going to get his first-team chance? What a fine prospect this lad looks!" He had other nom-de-plumes such as "True Tangerine" and "Blackpool Forever", so that it seemed the clamour for my inclusion appeared to be coming from all quarters.' Very sneaky. We like to think that his father was still doing likewise years later when Emlyn was on *A Question of Sport* – bombarding *Points of View* with letters of support and spreading lies about Bill Beaumont.

David Platt says that from a young age his dad would take him over the field and throw balls at him, insisting that he had two touches with his weak foot only to control and shoot. All well and good until he lets slip that 'if I accidentally did use my stronger right foot I received a clip around the ear. I never did get in touch with the NSPCC!' We can all laugh about it now can't we, because of all the success and all of that, but how many other poor little sods are getting the same treatment, only to be tremendous disappointments to a father trying to live vicariously through them?

Not even Sir Stanley Matthews was exempt from the pushy dad syndrome. Stan, you see, was a nippy nipper, and his dad would enter him into races and run a book on them. What's a little exploitation between family? Stan's dad told him to 'run like hell and don't stop running' when he heard the gun, and little Stan duly did as he was told, crossing the line and running way beyond it while his dad gave chase to eventually make him stop. 'His pocket was bulging with copper and silver coins and on the way home, we stopped off and he bought me a goldfish. He said, "Now Stanley, if your mother asks, just say I let you run off some steam and bought you the goldfish as a present."'

We're almost done with our sepia-tinged trawl of the early years of our heroes and we're sure you'll agree we've been thorough. But it would be remiss of us to pull the ladder up before we touch on a bit of character-forming sibling rivalry. Some of it, like Gary Neville praising brother Phil's superior talents and insisting that 'teams wanted me; they begged to have Phil', seems otherworldly and unattainable. The rest of the tales of scrapping, accidents and throwing a dart into your sister's head like Mark Ward's brother did, seem all too real. Although even we would draw a line at chasing your brother up the road with a hammer like Mel Sterland did. It seems on that occasion that only a passing police car stopped him doing some very real damage. But then with Mel you have to remember The Goldfish Incident (please see our 'Four-four-two-by-two' chapter for the full, startling details of that little tale) and accept that everything was a bit, what we used to call, nuts.

Another set of footballing brothers, Lee and Steve Howey, don't seem to have been as lofty and focused as the Neville siblings. The Howeys seem to have spent so much time knocking lumps out of each other, it's a wonder either of them made it as far in the game as they did. Lee Howey is the storyteller in his candid and magnificently titled book *Massively Violent and Decidedly Average*, and recalls pinning little brother Steve down on one occasion: 'I had my knees on his arms and was happily and repeatedly whacking him. Unless he was about to bite me on the bollocks, his escape was impossible. So he bit me on the bollocks.' A painful lesson learned for Lee there and a blow struck for little brothers everywhere by Steve. When it comes to fighting between siblings, prison rules apply – anything goes.

Steve Nicol was another who found that out the hard way. Sparring with his sister in the kitchen one day 'just dicking around', young Chico says, 'She tried to hit me so I swung my head out of the way but I only succeeded in whacking it against the wall. I collapsed like a sack of spuds. To this day, my twin sister Susan claimed she knocked me out but it's not true!' Oh we think it is, Steve. Perhaps that was all part of her cunning plan, and like we say, anything goes. David Seaman will tell you similar. In his house you even used violence to cure problems caused by violence. In what some (not us) would call an incredibly Yorkshire fight over a 2p piece, David's brother managed to swallow the coin. But Spunky had a plan: 'For some reason – watching kung-fu films I suppose – I decided a karate chop across the neck would do the trick. All it did was make him throw up – but the 2p stayed wedged.' Funny, that. It's surprising how rarely a karate chop across the neck is what's required in a medical emergency isn't it? 'Colin was panicking by now, choking and shouting out, "I'm gonna die". Mum came out to find out what all the fuss was about and found me holding Colin upside down by his ankles, trying to shake the coin out.'

Eventually they got young Colin to hospital, they got him to swallow it, and as with all feel-good stories, ultimately it ended with somebody shitting out a 2p coin. In our version of events, and if he was any kind of brother, David would have been squatting behind Colin with his goalie gloves on for the next 24 hours, ready to catch the coin as it fell. And it would have been at that moment that he realised that fighting with his brother over 2p was silly, and he would have known that he was destined for a career between the sticks. Or something.

BEFORE THE GLORY

'Clockwork rituals'

'I think it was Gilbert and Sullivan who wrote, "When constabulary duty's to be done, to be done, the policeman's lot is not a happy one." I suppose much the same could be said of the lot of football apprentices. When it comes to cleaning boots, blowing up footballs, etc, many of them wonder where all the glamour is.'

Liverpool legend Phil Neal unexpectedly proffering a Gilbert and Sullivan quote there, while apparently not being 100 per cent sure that, indeed, the quote is from Gilbert and Sullivan. Well, who's got the time to check?[33] Still, his point stands. While everyone assumes the life of a footballer is impossibly glamorous, what with the goals, the glory and the going to film premieres, it takes time to reach that stage – or, at least, it used to. We've learnt about the brutal youths, but now we've signed the forms and we're on the club books. This is a look at a time when apprentices were still apprentices rather than the cosseted, mollycoddled 'academy players' of today – and life was pretty tough.

Still, it wasn't that bad, surely? We found some beautiful, sepia-hued memories from players recalling their apprentice days – like this, from Paul Lake: 'We relished being allowed to use the VIP entrance because the waiting City fans would often thrust their autograph books into our hands, giving us the chance to scribble the ridiculously showy signatures that we'd spent years practising in our bedrooms.' Living the dream. Marco Negri of Rangers admits that apprentices would 'be the butt of innocent jokes', but also says they'd often receive gifts from the pros, 'such as new boots or t-shirts'. What he's describing there feels like a happy, healthy family life doesn't it?

—

33 Well, us. It *is* Gilbert and Sullivan, from *Pirates of Penzance*. Although, as we're sure you spotted, it's a slight misquote – it's '***a*** policeman's lot' not '***the*** policeman's lot'. You are very welcome.

Mickey Thomas, meanwhile, dreamily reminisces about how he and Joey Jones would 'have races up to the top of the floodlights to see who could be the first up the pylons', when coming through the Wrexham ranks together. Typical Mickey there, displaying the same devil-may-care attitude that once saw him doing rude things with a lady in the centre circle (under the lights, mind you) at Stamford Bridge.

Or how about Kevin Beattie, who joined Ipswich with barely a penny to his name and was therefore concerned about how he was going to purchase the 'collar and tie' that the club expected players to wear to matches? Simple: 'Mr [Bobby] Robson realised I had a problem and that is why he and [coach] Cyril each gave me a shirt and a couple of ties for good measure.' A fantastic gesture, perhaps only bettered by Coventry youth coach Pat Saward, who, Bobby Gould reports, would gather the apprentices together 'to give us dress sense lessons on a Monday afternoon and show us how to coordinate our clothes. He was always immaculate and suave.' Well, this is above and beyond, surely? Every Monday? Did this lecture series last an entire season? Or just a semester? What, exactly, was the syllabus? And was there an exam leading to a BTEC qualification? Bobby, you cannot just drop that nugget in and not expand just a little bit.

Whatever the ins and outs of Pat Saward's 'Sky Blue Eye for The New Guy' sessions, we have now provided proof of just how lovely it was to be a football apprentice back in the day.

Yerss ... that's until you realise these were pretty much the only unambiguously positive apprentice stories we read about. Most of the time apprentice life seems pretty, well, shit.

Obviously, asking people to feel sympathy for professional footballers, even in the old days when they weren't being paid the kind of coin they get today, is something of a thankless task. But let's remember that apprentice footballers were not professionals. They were young hopefuls, brought in because of their talent, but paid very little. Derek Dougan, as usual, has some strong views on the subject: 'They look after the boots of all the pros, changing the studs, cleaning them, seeing that they are dried. Under supervision they clean the bathrooms, wash the toilets, sweep the place up generally, and polish any brass doorknobs there may be. Sometimes they wash the manager's car, and the trainer's, and even the secretary's ... I have often said during my time with six clubs that in many ways this is nothing but cheap labour, with nothing to do with being an apprentice footballer.'

Yeah, back in them days, you had to make sure the door knobs were polished enough so that the gaffer could see his face and sheepskin coat collar in them. Doog's disapproval at this finds him, as we'll discover, very much in the minority, because most ex-pros now are pretty appalled at the easy lives young players have today, and believe the old system to be far more beneficial and character-building.

'Character-building' is often a euphemism for being forced to endure some kind of unnecessary pain or hardship, and that seems very much the case with apprentice life. The phrase in these environs feels like a sort of free pass for pros to treat hopeful teenagers with contempt. Take the experience of Jeremy 'Gossy' Goss, who endured being Mick Channon's boot boy at Norwich: 'Let me say, for the lovely, cuddly, friendly image he cultivates, he made my life as an apprentice hell. He'd leave his kit all over the place, or throw a pair of socks or shorts up into a tree and expect me to climb up and get them. Then he'd want them all cleaned and back again before I even had a chance to get started.' Such are the mental scars from Channon and the other Norwich seniors having their fun with him that Gossy actually tells this story twice in his book.

But if you thought Channon being a bit unreasonable was surprising, strap in, because in Rio Ferdinand's *#2Sides* (#PleaseStop) he digs the dirt on lovely, genial Tony Cottee: 'I heard someone shouting my name: "Where's that fucking Ferdinand?" I came out and saw this five-foot-nothing stocky geezer standing there. Tony Cottee.

"Where's my fucking boots?" he said.

"What boots?" I said.

"You're my boot boy. Where's my boots?" he said. I said they were hanging on his peg in the boot room where I'd been told to put them. He said: "I want my boots with my training kit, wet top and track suit in my place every morning." When I said that wasn't my job, he got angry: "You're my boot boy and you'll do what I fucking say."'

Tony Cottee! Our world is crashing around our ears.

Brian Laws served his apprenticeship at Burnley and remembers polishing the boots of his seniors, Leighton James and Steve Kindon, 'until I could see my face in them'. Clearly, to a lot of footballers, the state of their boots was of paramount importance, which you can completely understand. Yet that doesn't begin to legislate for Kindon's actions on one occasion: 'Kindon would always warn me never to get boot polish on his laces. One morning he bawled out: "Lawsy, what's this?" He had some boot polish on his fingers. He grabbed me in a headlock and rubbed it all over my face. Then he banged me into the dressing room wall.' Remember: these people do sport for a living.

It wasn't just cleaning boots and laying out the kit, though. John Sitton used to hate sweeping the terraces at Chelsea when he was just starting out, describing it as 'A filthy mind numbing horrible bastard of a job … Filth, litter, dust, puddles of urine. It was a nightmare.' And that was just Ken Bates's office. Ha, we jest. He's a litigious man, and wasn't even at Chelsea in those days. Sitton, though, is one of the very few who doesn't lament those days: 'It got phased out thank Christ.'

At least Lee McCulloch says his pros Billy Davies and Paul Lambert at Motherwell 'were good to me', but at the same time, 'they demanded I TippExed different logos onto their boots to protect their sponsorship deals. I'd have to do that every week because on match days the TippEx would come off after about ten minutes.' Maybe he needed to try some emulsion – that bastard stuff never comes off.

Weirder still, Andy Morrison, who does describe his Youth Training Scheme (YTS) days at Plymouth 'as among the best of my life', recalls how 'a senior pro got one of the new apprentices to go into the toilet and warm the seat up before he had a shit'. The only other time we'd heard of this dubious practice was when we read author Roald Dahl's first memoir, *Boy* – it was an act he regularly had to undertake for a 'boazer' (prefect) at Repton School in Derbyshire. Bit public school for us, Clive.

Another of Dahl's jobs at Repton was to clean the 'office' of a boazer each Sunday, and his work was subsequently inspected by the older student donning a pristine white glove and running his fingers over every surface in search of missed dust. If any were found, there would be a beating. Maybe there was a time when players and managers were aficionados of *Boy*, or at least the practices of boys' boarding schools, because Kieron Dyer experienced this exact scenario at Ipswich, where he was tasked with cleaning boss George Burley's large office: 'So George Burley would be running his finger along his desk like some sort of old-school headmaster, checking for dust', although we assume Kieron wasn't caned if any specks were found.

But all that, as the Four Yorkshiremen once said, was luxury compared to the life led by Alan Mullery when he started at Fulham and was assigned to help the groundsman, an old boy called Albert. Mullers says that the worst job was reseeding the pitch, a back-breaking labour that involved shovelling fish manure (we looked that up – it's a sort of slurry made up of fish carcasses – yes) all over the playing surface.

By the time they finished this chore, Mullery explains, they did not smell particularly sweet, but unfortunately the dressing rooms – and therefore the showers – would be locked, as everyone else had knocked off for the day. Faced with little option, Alan and his mates cast glances towards the nearest source of water they could find: the River Thames. Hardly pristine now, the Thames was essentially a sewer back then – the Natural History Museum actually declared it 'biologically dead' in 1957. So what did Al and his mates do? 'We had a big rope and we took it in turns to tie it round our chest and under our arms, before climbing down the bank and jumping into the water. Three or four of the other lads held on to the other end of the rope. The current would drag you downstream, then they'd pull you back up.' That's right. They removed the fish slurry from their person by risking drowning in a river so filthy that, as Alan mentions, 'People caught polio by swimming in the Thames in the fifties.' This entire operation sounds like a set-up for one of those harrowing health and safety videos we were forced to watch at school that end with one of the kids *actually dying* for chasing his ball on to a railway or shinning up a pylon or jumping into a biologically dead river with a current so fast it needs several other people to drag you back to the bank with a rope. You win, Alan. You win.

At least there's training. That's what they're there for, after all. Learning their real trade, practising their skills, receiving expert coaching from men who've had a lifetime in the game. All the Thames baths you could stand must have been worth that? Well, not so much.

Paul Lake may have enjoyed the perks of using the big doors at Maine Road, but some of his memories of training with City legend Tony Book ('Skip') sound more like some kind of army boot camp. On one occasion, he ordered all the players to wear studs, but one unnamed player defied him, saying that his rubber soles were more comfy. This sent Skip into something of a rage: '"well if it's f***kin' comfort you want, f***off home on your f***in' comfy bus, go and sit in front of the TV on your f***in' comfy couch with your f***in' comfy slippers and watch f***in' Saint and Greavsie. Now f*** off."

We have to admit, that entire plan sounds absolutely lovely. We miss *Saint and Greavsie.*

Still at City, Joey Barton received a more physical example of why not to annoy the senior professionals. He and the YTS lads were mucking about one day and Barton drew a short straw to kick a ball at Andy Morrison during training. This is the Andy Morrison, you will remember, nicknamed 'Jake' by some of his teammates at Plymouth after Jake LaMotta on account of his monstrous temper and willingness to fight anybody, anytime. The Andy Morrison whose book, *The Good, The Mad and The Ugly* (it's mainly the latter), makes *American Psycho* look like *The Gruffalo.* In fact, we're so terrified of Andy Morrison that those aren't our real names on the cover of this book.[34] Anyway, Barton kicked the ball, but wisely didn't actually hit Morrison. Still, Andy was not best pleased: '"Who kicked the ball?" he said, in the sort of tone that told us this would not end well. "I am going to hit every fucking one of yous if you don't tell me."' Courageously, Joey owned up, mainly because it was obvious most of the other YTS lads were on the verge of ratting him out anyway. And we don't blame them for a second. 'He ordered me to lie face down, and pushed my head into the floor with the palm of his hand. I was determined not to whimper and show him he was hurting me, but he just kept pushing and pushing. The pain was indescribable. I didn't cry, honestly. But my eyes watered with the pain. When he let me up he simply said, "Never fucking do that again."' Joey says he didn't hold it against him, but, and we say this with the greatest respect and from behind the sofa, this seems a tad over the top for someone kicking a football in your general direction. Where we come from that's normally called a pass.

At Nottingham Forest, Steve Hodge and his young chums were subjected to an unusual test every Friday by coach Ron Fenton to check they'd been doing their stomach exercises. First, he would line them up against the wall, as if about to face some kind of firing squad – which wasn't that far off the reality: 'Fenton would walk along the line and each week he'd pick someone and say, "Tense them!" The unfortunate apprentice would then get punched ten times in the stomach. He rained them in quickly one after another, and Ronnie was a strong man. Some lads would crumple up after two punches and we'd all be in the background laughing but if it was your turn

34 As you can see, some of us try harder than others with making up pseudonyms.

you just had to take it, and it did hurt.' Well, being punched ten times in the stomach does hurt. Just ask boxer Apollo Creed – it was the body shots that eventually took their toll in his 15-round war of a rematch with Rocky Balboa back in 1979 (although in truth the fight should have been stopped a lot earlier and that weird KO decision is still controversial to this day). Anyway – you can't put this down to banter – that's just abuse, isn't it?

The sense is, however, that there was a time when you could do pretty much anything to the apprentices and get away with it – whether it was punching them randomly in the stomach or, as at Palace, just acting in a disturbingly odd manner. To be fair, Vince Hilaire says that under Malcolm Allison the youth players were treated extremely well because Allison rightly saw them as the future of the club. Big Mal would not have allowed his young charges to catch polio in the Thames, no sir. However, his assistant Frank Lord was not completely on board with Allison's methods. One day after training Lord asked Hilaire if he would kick his mother to score a goal. Hilaire's understandable hesitation to this bizarre question proved foolhardy: 'He hit me round the back of the head and told me that I was no good to him. He said that he'd kick his mother, his gran, his wife and his kids to score a goal, and exclaimed, "That's why I'm Frank Lord!"' If that tale ended there, you'd think: 'Well, it's unusual, but there's a message in there: to be a footballer, you need to be ruthless. Fair enough.'

But it didn't end there.

Frank Lord made Vince line up eight balls on the six-yard box in front of an empty net, and then ordered a puzzled Vince to watch as he slammed them into an empty net, as if it was some kind of feat, before yelling again: 'And that's why I'm Frank Lord! I'm ruthless!' Vince notes: 'I didn't know what he was trying to teach me.' Neither do we Vince. It seemed reasonably clear at first, but whacking balls into an empty net does little to back up his point. We do hope after Hilaire scored his next goal, though, he ran around yelling 'I'M FRANK LORD!' and maybe lifted up his shirt to reveal a vest with 'I'M FRANK LORD' written on it.

You might think this sort of madness might stop once an apprentice makes it into the first team. But no. Even there you're still vulnerable. At Palace, Ian Wright says Scottish defender Jim Cannon 'behaved like the playground bully' when he broke into the first XI. Wright does concede Cannon was nice to him on matchdays, apparently because he wanted his win bonus, but then adds: 'The only other time I can remember him being nice to me was when we played up in Grimsby and they'd given every player a massive fish to take home. He'd go round to everybody asking, really nicely, "Hey, are you going to be taking your fish?" Even though I knew my mum would have loved it, I'd give it to him hoping to placate him or something. He'd take the fish, then on Monday he'd be back to his regular, miserable, bullying self.'

The main point to glean from this, as far as the subject of this chapter goes, is to note that becoming part of the first team doesn't always mean immediate integration. We're not quite sure of the timescale, but clearly some older players feel the need to dish it out for some time after the graduation before a youngster truly becomes one of the gang. But, of course, this entire anecdote leaves us with many, many supplementary questions, mainly about this fish and how Wrighty seems to be giving Cannon the fish in order to placate him, as if he's some kind of Pagan God at harvest time. So, for the record:

1. Why are Grimsby giving people fish? It's not just Wrighty who mentions this in his book – Elton John does too. They are really embracing that stereotype there. They've even put some fish and a trawler on their badge for goodness sake.
2. The coaches home must have stunk to high heaven. (Maybe that was why Grimsby did it? Sort of a gag under the guise of appearing kind?)
3. What was Jim Cannon going to do with 12 fish if everyone gave him one? Did he flog them? Freeze them? Donate them to the hungry?
4. What sort of fish were they? Wrighty's very coy on this (there's a pun that works better in speech than on the page).

THE HORROR

Amazingly, all we have spoken about so far is mere child's play compared to the worst excesses that poor apprentices were forced to endure as part of their acceptance into their clubs. It's treatment that veers from the unacceptable to the downright disturbing, but let's don our biggest wading boots and, well, wade in.

First up, let's take Christmas. It's supposed to be a joyous time of year: peace, love and goodwill to all, etc. But for apprentices, it's a nightmare – and not even a fun nightmare like *The Nightmare Before Christmas*, but a really horrible nightmare, like *Jingle All The Way.*

For a start, there's some unwritten law that when it comes to mixing apprentices and Christmas, there should be nudity. Just because. For example, Chris Sutton remembers a winter when he was a youngster at Norwich where it snowed over the (altogether now) *crucial festive period.* This led to a snowball fight between the first team and the youth team. And, as with any half-decent snowball fight worthy of the name, it ended with some of the youngsters being stripped naked. 'It was a good learning experience all the same,' wrote Chris. Indeed, many of that youth team trace their knowledge of how snow feels cold against bare skin back to that very day.

Sutton also recalls having to sing carols in the dressing room to earn a Christmas tip from the players they looked after, which is fair enough – that seems like a harmless, potentially fun activity.

Except, of course, they had to be naked then too. Just like the newborn baby Jesus. And if they weren't any good, objects were thrown at them. Sutton insists it was 'a good adrenalin buzz' but, and call us unadventurous fuddy-duddies if you like, we prefer our adrenaline buzzes to come from things like running for the bus or having medium sauce at Nando's.

The naked singing at Christmas seems to be something of a tradition at most clubs, but the thing with traditions is that they often become warped, with weird things being added for a lark one year, before they somehow become normalised and no matter how odd they might be, no one can argue against them because, 'tradition'. Michael McIndoe, a midfielder probably best known for his spells at Bristol City and Yeovil, was an apprentice at Luton, where they loved to add some unique touches to their festive apprentice sing-songs: '[It] had to be done standing on a chair, naked, wearing a piece of tinsel wrapped round your knob, and a pair of wellies stuffed with flour and eggs.' At least the tinsel is Christmassy, but what's with the eggs and flour? If you're going to humiliate people, at least stick with the theme.[35]

35 May we suggest brandy butter?

McIndoe adds: 'The two singers voted the worst would have to race around the pitch completely naked in front of even more people', so in his first year, everyone watched Matt Spring and Emerson Boyce sprint round Kenilworth Road, dangly bits flopping in their mad haste as they tried to avoid further punishment. 'Springy lost and had to face the first team in the tunnel. He was drenched with ice buckets but took it all in good humour, as it was intended.' Well, thank God all that ritual humiliation was done with the intention of good humour and not with being really nasty. Otherwise, you know, it could come across as really nasty.

Are we being a bit po-faced about all this? Maybe, as people who never came close to becoming professional sports people, we just don't quite get what gels a team together. Yet we can't help feeling uncomfortable about some of this stuff – McIndoe says that 'the following year one of the apprentices pissed himself he was so nervous and embarrassed', and after a parental complaint, the tradition was ended. You'd think that if it's getting to the stage of someone losing control of their body, things may have gone beyond a bit of fun, but McIndoe has none of it, and after the inevitable nod to the ritual being 'character-building' he comes up with a, let's face it, nonsensical rationale of the whole ordeal: 'How can you perform in front of tens of thousands of people confidently, but not be able to sing starkers in front of your own teammates? After all, players have to have a thick skin to deal with the media and fans.' What he's saying there is that if you feel uncomfortable singing a song naked with your junk decorated like a Christmas tree while people chuck tomatoes at you (that was also part of it), then you can't be a professional footballer. It's ridiculous, right? We're not mad to think that are we? It's like saying … okay, it's like saying, 'How can you expect to be Prime Minister if you won't slip your willy into this severed pig's head.' Insanity.

According to Paul Parker, the Christmas singing at Fulham also involved wellies (but not flour and eggs), but was different in that they had to play air guitar with a broom. Okay, well, that's not too bad. Oh, sorry, Paul wasn't finished. They were also naked. IT'S THE LAW. And also this: 'Then we had string attached to our penises, which our audience were not slow to pull, and there were buckets of cold water ready to be thrown at us if our performances were considered to be poor.' Sorry, what? *They yanked on your penis with some string*? Like they were flushing an old-fashioned toilet?

Parker refers to this as 'the deepest humiliation', adding that teammate Dean Coney 'hid in the toilet of the Riverside Stand' in a desperate attempt to avoid the whole thing, so you'd expect PP to be well pleased that this sort of todger-tugging has been thankfully drummed out of football. You'd expect it, but that's not what he thinks. Far from it. Indeed, Paul takes the opportunity for a bit of social commentary: 'It made us mentally stronger. One of our problems, and it will catch up with us eventually, is that the young players today are not as mentally or physically as strong. There is no smacking at home and kids cannot contemplate leaving home because it is too costly until such time as they get a proper wage. Society strikes me as being softer, so, therefore, are our young footballers.' Well, it's an opinion, isn't it? People are softer because they're not beaten as children anymore, and footballers are not as strong because older footballers are not allowed to attach string to their knobs and yank on it for fun.

At Everton, things were even more bizarre, with the singing being just another part of a much longer ritual. Mark Ward was an eyewitness: 'Each apprentice was stripped naked and a pair of football socks stretched over their eyes to form a blindfold. The entertainment was provided by two apprentices who were ordered to fight blindfolded in front of the senior pros. As the fight was in progress, the pros would smear each youngster in boot polish.' And we thought cockfighting had been outlawed. It was only after the fight that the singing would commence. Like others before him, Ward remembers it as being 'very humiliating', but defends it as 'a test of character'. And maybe he's right – he falls into the same category as plenty of other footballers who believe either that this kind of thing helped shape them as men and footballers or, at worst, that 'it didn't do me any harm'. Despite that, though, you do wonder if some promising players were broken unnecessarily by what is, essentially, bullying.

At the end of Ward's account there you will have noticed those two words 'boot' and 'polish'. Footballers, it seems, are obsessed with using boot polish as a tool of torture. That and Deep Heat – clearly, they are adept at turning the standard accoutrements of a sports dressing room into instruments of painful hilarity.

Boot polish in particular was used at most clubs during the hazing of apprentices. At Leeds, David Batty says they had regular court-style trials (it had to be at Leeds, didn't it?) where apprentices were tried for crimes 'such as failing to polish a pro's boots to his satisfaction, or not putting enough sauce on a sausage sarnie'. Naturally, no one was ever found innocent. 'The guilty party,' writes Batty, 'would be stripped naked in the dressing room, tied to a treatment table, plastered from head to toe in boot polish – with maybe a more painful substance for the private parts – and probably doused in water.' After that, they'd be tied to a goalpost at the training ground, still nude.

At Manchester United, as befits a club that likes to project itself as the home of a certain type of swaggering style, they preferred to get creative with the polish. Gary Neville claims that they'd somehow scuff a version of the entire United kit on to the apprentice's bare body: 'the shorts, the shirt, even the number on your back – rubbed on to you in dubbin with a wire wool brush. I can still feel the sharp bristles ripping my skin.' After acknowledging that this sounds excruciatingly painful, we would like to praise the artistry here. Faced with a struggling young body, how exactly were the details of the kit applied? Did they just sort of do an outline of the kit? Or was the entire body coloured in, with spaces avoided for the number, badge and so forth? These days, with the number of different-coloured boots about, the polish available must allow a real artist like, we suspect, Paul Scholes, to do some stunning work.

Peter Reid had to take his turn at Bolton, too. The initiation there inevitably involved singing while being bombarded with boots and so forth, before the end game arrived: 'I was held down while they blackened my bollocks with boot polish.' Reid described the whole thing as 'very Darwinian because only the fittest would survive', although if that was the case we'd expect modern-day footballers to have evolved some sort of callous on the scrotum and shaft to help ease the torment of these attacks.

Even without boot polish, footballers could get as creative as any number 10 you care to mention when it came to doling out punishment. Back at Man United, Keith Gillespie confirms Gary Neville's tales and also says that on one occasion, 'Russell Beardsmore was left in the sauna with ten tracksuits on and had to fight to get them all off before he was let out', which at least seems more fun than most of the other stuff, although you do wonder how on earth they managed to get ten tracksuits on him in the first place. Meanwhile, Lee Sharpe (corroborated again by Nev) recalls a particularly vicious sanction: 'a player had to put his face in front of the space between the legs of the treatment table and people had to volley a ball just right, through the space and into the guy's face'. Nasty, but we suppose it has the upside that it was helping to hone the key skill of volleying. That's probably how Mark Hughes got so good at it.

But the absolute worst of the lot appears to have occurred at Sheffield Wednesday. It's unclear how the rituals and traditions travelled from club to club, or how and when it all started, but at one stage at least, Wednesday seemed to just gather and meld all the torture tactics, brought perhaps by signings from all over the country, into one horrific observance known simply as 'blacking'. For this, we go to a book entitled, and with good reason, *Boozing, Betting & Brawling*. It's Mel Sterland, who explains that 'blacking' started with getting a bit of a kicking: 'You had to put a fight up because if you didn't, you'd have it done to you again a month or two later, so you had to smack a few.' Once that was over, it was time to start playing some of the classics, which naturally began with being stripped and the usual weapons of Deep Heat and boot polish roughly applied to the most painful areas: 'Vaseline would be rubbed in your hair, up your arse and in your ears.' 'Up your arse', mind, which must've set some alarm bells ringing. If they weren't already.

Still not the end: 'I was the "bog brush man", I'd get a really hard toilet brush, shove it into their bollocks – which were covered in Vaseline and boot polish by this time – and twirl it round. They'd be screaming in agony, which was great because I'd had it done to me by Craig Howard.' So there's also a revenge element, here. Only, the revenge is not being wrought against Craig Howard, it's being wrought against some poor wretch from the youth team. In turn, of course, Howard was punishing whoever did it to him, and back and back, maybe as far as Wednesday God Derek Dooley in the 1940s and 50s – a scrotum-scrunching history of misdirected, violent vengeance cutting into the very core of the club for decades on end.

Still not the end. The apprentice would then be 'tied to the treatment bench, carried out onto the pitch and left in the centre-circle … some were left there for six or seven hours.' That's six or seven *hours*.

Still. Not. The. End. To be fair, this last bit (mercifully) was not always used, but it is here where we finally reach rock bottom. After the Vaseline and polish, the player would be chucked in a skip used for dirty kit: 'We'd then take the skip into the shower area and piss on him while he tried to cover up his head.' This is starting to sound like a horrific reboot of the *Hostel* series, only set at a nightmarish football club. Then again, how can you expect to become a footballer if you can't take a group of grown men urinating over your beaten, battered and boot-polished body?

What puzzles us about all of this, apart from how cruel and unnecessary it all is, are the specifics of it all. How do they arrive at these rituals? Are they carried from one club to another by sadistic professionals and built up as they go? If a player transferred from one club to another would he say: 'I see you put boot polish on the bollocks of your apprentices here. It was whitewash at my last club.' And then, in the spirit of compromise, somebody would suggest doing both.

Player 1: 'We make them sing.'

Player 2: 'We strip them naked.'

Player 3: 'Hey guys, why can't we all get along? Why not both?'

Finally, yet another player with a flair for Christmas decorations decides that what's required is a bit of tinsel around the cock and balls, and hey presto, you've got yourself a tradition in which many trophy-laden years to come are surely forged.

As players related their horror stories in their books, they almost always ended their tale by mentioning that with apprentices and the YTS system now gone, so have the rituals, the hazing and the initiation ceremonies. Very few players speak against what used to go on, but Kieron Dyer offers a genuinely interesting and thoughtful appraisal of that culture. He first recalls an occasion when he was a trainee at Ipswich where he continually 'ran rings round' one of the senior players in training, eventually embarrassing him to the extent that this 'big player at the club' took his revenge by deliberately soiling himself – in front of young Dyer: 'He took it [his slip] off and splattered excrement all over the floor. He pointed at me. "Clean that up, you little shit," he said.'[36]

Then, Dyer says that on an England youth tour to Malaysia he and some teammates 'decided it would be funny if we all took a shit in a plastic bag and went to hang it on [coach] Ted Powell's bedroom door. Don't ask me why we thought that would be amusing or acceptable in any way, but we did.' Dyer suggests that one of the reasons they thought this would be so funny had 'something to do with the culture

36 Dyer was 17 at the time, so you can look up the Ipswich 1994/95 squad and try and guess who this might have been. It's a fun game. We've got it down to about one of five we think. Best not speculate here, mind.

that existed at a lot of clubs in those days', and links it back to the actions of that experienced pro at Ipswich.

In contrast to most players who believe the loss of faeces-based hilarity and old-fashioned pummellings and humiliations has resulted in softer footballers, Kieron makes a much more interesting point and wonders if one of the reasons England has not won a tournament since 1966 is perhaps rooted in the culture that took hold, it seems, sometime in the 1970s (often held up by older fans as the halcyon days of the English game, yet a decade in which England failed to qualify for either the 1974 or 1978 World Cups): 'A lot of our failings are there in that image of that bag of shit. Think of everything it shows: a lack of respect, a lack of decency, a lack of professionalism, a lack of seriousness, a lack of intelligence, a lack of responsibility, and a football culture that's shot to pieces. Can you imagine Riquelme or Aimar taking part in something like that? No, you can't. It's not the way their players are brought up, but it was the way we had been brought up.' He has a point, doesn't he? He continues: 'We make fun of authority, we don't respect it. We laugh at authority, we don't learn from it. And when we want to establish supremacy or superiority or make each other laugh, we smear shit on dressing room floors or hang it on hotel room doors.' One of the finest pieces of analysis about the English game we read in any autobiography. Or anywhere else, actually.

The 2018 World Cup showcased, for the first time, an England squad that were brought up in a new system, with young players who would certainly have had to put up with mickey-taking and silly rituals on their way up, but hopefully not (for the most part) have had to put up with basic bullying. And it was the most refreshing, exciting team we have seen at a tournament for at least two decades, arguably more. That may just be coincidence, but it surely does prove that using the excuse of character-building to defend some pretty gruesome behaviour doesn't hold a lot of water. Or urine.

WATCHING THEM WATCHING US WATCHING THEM

'Uncle Arthur'

As football fans, our fascination with footballers is well established, bordering on psychotic. But what do *they* think of *us*? Do they know what it's like to be a fan? Do they even care? Do they like us, or just tolerate us as a necessary evil? Before we find out, let's hear from one non-footballer who really thinks he 'gets' us. It's the much-loved former chief executive of Leeds United, Peter Ridsdale. He gets us, because he *is* us:

> Yet we remain the same: *real* fans; those hard-core followers who belong to the non-exclusive, fully paid-up, fully dedicated band of men, women and children who make up the army of British football supporters; fans who know what it is to go hoarse from chanting, to burn the roof off your mouth on a half-time meat pie, to have collected the match programmes, and stacked them in prized collectable piles, as tokens of loyalty …

Brings a tear to the eye, doesn't it? A hot pie-fuelled breath away from 'jumpers for goalposts'. He goes on, too. And on: 'Football is not a sport – it's a bloody fantastic, nerve-racking adventure that makes the heart race with its beautiful anticipation, it's ninety minutes of adrenalin, its irrationality, its heroes and villains, its joy and heartbreak.' We've all said it, haven't we? Now irretrievably lost in his misty reverie, he reaches his climax: '… and only we can know the searing, scream-enducing pain that comes from watching our team come *this* close to the Champions League Final one year, only to be relegated twice in the next six years in the face of crippling financial problems thanks to horrendous mismanagement at all levels of our club.'

Okay, we may have made that last bit up. But the rest genuinely came from the start of Ridsdale's lengthy self-justification piece, *United We Fall*. Ridsdale is, obviously, acutely aware of what fans think of him, so he kicks off with pages of this poetic guff, desperately hoping to get a few fans onside before he attempts to explain away the horror show he was part of at Elland Road (quick summary, if, like most Leeds fans, we understand, you don't fancy reading the whole thing: yes, mistakes were made; the Seth Johnson contract is a myth; the tropical fish weren't that expensive in the grand scheme of things; and everything would have been all right if only Martin O'Neill had agreed to become manager on one of the many times he almost did but didn't[37]). It's his way of saying he's just a normal guy doing an extraordinary job. For which he has been badly misunderstood. Oh come on – maybe he's right after all. Things are going pretty damn well at Preston.[38]

Whether Ridsdale's efforts to show us how much he understands fans' pain break through our defences or not, he is obeying an important football law: don't criticise the fans. Ever. Well, unless they've done something really horrible, like trashing a quiet Spanish town or running on the pitch to clout the Villa captain. But apart from those obvious situations, fans are beyond reproach. Players and managers must respect them, must thank them, and must clap them in that peculiar footballer style of hands held horizontally above the head at the end of games.

Few players risk publicly criticising fans, and when one does, it is big news. After all, we pay our money; we can say what we like, even if we're not great at taking it back. Players appear reluctant to say much about us in their autobiographies either – perhaps understandably, as we're the only ones likely to buy their books. We fans aren't completely ignored, but it's unusual to get a nice, broad overview of what they really think of us, perhaps because, and this is pure speculation, maybe they all simply hate us and slag us off to each other daily at training.

37 You're welcome. It's what we do.

38 On a pre-season break in 2018, Preston players were pictured having a jolly time while a group of bikini-clad women carried placards spelling out Ridsdale's name. We haven't got to the bottom of that one yet.

When you think about it, why wouldn't they? Time for some, as we believe today's teens might say, 'real talk'. Football fans, overall, and we include ourselves in this, are a bunch of arseholes.

We're fickle. We're finicky. We're impatient. We think we know everything. We're judgemental. We're entitled. We are *cloyingly* sentimental. We're drunk. Perhaps more than anything, we are wildly hypocritical.

Take transfers and contracts. Let's say you have a player the fans believe has been a flop, but that player has chosen to sit out his nice, fat contract, even though he's stuck in the reserves. For fans, the solution is obvious: the player should do the right thing: leave to get regular football, and if that means taking a pay cut, then a pay cut must be taken. Fail to do this, and he is a greedy parasite, sucking the blood and money out of the club.

Now, this might be reasonable if fans were more accepting when a good player wants to leave for a bigger club and/or more money. But we are not. In this case, the player should not be allowed to move. The player should be forced to stay, to 'honour his contract'. Honouring the contract, you see, is bad if you're bad but good if you're good. Every player is walking a precarious tightrope between being a parasite or a mercenary. No wonder they all look stressed. For players, it's a minefield. That's right: a tightrope over a minefield.

Just listen to any football phone-in show. *That is what we sound like*. Terrifying, right? The footballers won't tell us, but maybe it's time we faced some harsh truths. Ready? Here it comes. Your club isn't special. There, we've said it. Your stadium is not special either. Neither is your club's supposedly sacred number 7/9/10 shirt. Also, fans of other clubs absolutely do not think that you have a proud history of 'trying to play the game the right way'. And if a player or pundit says anything about the fans being 'special' or 'different' at your club, they don't mean it. Fans are the same everywhere. Yes – even yours, Liverpool, and yours, Newcastle. Only the Crystal Palace Ultras might have a case of being really different and cool.[39]

Don't get us wrong. Of course, all these things are special to you. All of our clubs are special to us. We bloody love them. But let us reassure you that nobody outside your own club thinks your club is

39 They don't, but this notion will really annoy some people. We like the Palace Ultras. They're cute and silly.

special. In fact, if anything, they find your club a bit annoying. And that should be absolutely fine by all of us.

You won't read much of that sort of thing in autobiographies, mind, so what can we glean from the mentions we fans do get? There are certainly a few who seem to connect to fans on a different level to others. QPR icon Stan Bowles writes: 'I regard the crowd as an audience, who wanted me to go out and perform for them. I could talk to them, and get close to them, almost saying: "Look, I'm the same as you, really." That created a certain rapport between the crowd and players like me.' This noble attitude is shared by Mark Walters: 'Throughout my career I was aware that I was part of the entertainment industry. Supporters worked hard all week and wanted to relax at the weekend. They wanted to be entertained, whether that was by going to the cinema, the football or whatever, so I always had that in mind.' While Paul Scholes notes: 'It is important, though, that the fans share our joy. Everything we do is not just for ourselves, but for them as well.'

It helps, perhaps, if you can remember being a fan, and no one is more touching in that regard than the great Nobby Stiles when reminiscing about his idol Eddie Colman ('my little home-town god') and his feelings at becoming his boot boy when he joined United as a youngster: 'I wondered if he [Colman] would ever know how it was that his boots would shine so much brighter than any others, how much passion had been involved.'

Four players, then, that are very aware of our existence and how important we are to their chosen career. But beyond that, what do the rest of them think of us and what are they prepared to commit to print?

THEY LOVE OUR ADULATION

This is a vital part of the relationship. Players thrive on the fans. Not all perhaps, but many. It's actually difficult for us mortals to comprehend how it would feel to hear thousands of people melodically singing our name in adulation. It's a strange tradition when you think about it, and one that's pretty much confined to football matches (or cricket matches attended by football fans). No one chants Benedict Cumberbatch's name at the end of a play or movie, after all, and not only because it doesn't scan well into any traditional terrace tune.[40]

40 Go on, try.

But being serenaded on a weekly basis for being good at your job must be pretty intoxicating. No one puts this better than Derek Dougan in *Doog*, one of his (too) many books on the game: 'Consciously or subconsciously, footballers respond to cheers; they wallow in the adulation of the stands and terraces.' You see? They wanna be adored. 'They like to see their pictures in the papers, their names in the sports columns, and the ball at their feet. When all this is stripped away, as inevitably it must, life drops several degrees. The unknown stretches before you. For the first time, you are on your own.'

Yeah, gets a bit bleak at the end, but you get the point. And it is nice when players reminisce fondly about how much they enjoyed the adulation from fans. Brian McClair feels particular warmth towards a freezing game in Košice, when Man Utd fans ran through their entire repertoire of songs for each player, but substituted his name for the usual one each time: 'It is always good to hear your name sung, on whatever basis, and it warmed up a bitterly cold evening.'

Shaun Goater writes that one day he was warming up with Robbie Fowler at Manchester City when Fowler said, 'These people love you, don't they Shaun? I'd give anything for a bit of this.' Fowler, then in the back end of his career, was clearly feeling the pinch Doog described, and was wistfully harking back to the days when he was revered as a God by the Kop at Anfield. At least he did have the experience of eventually going back to bask in their love once more – few get that chance.

Jermaine Pennant, meanwhile, managed to maintain the adrenaline buzz of fan adoration even while he was doing a short stint inside following a drink-driving conviction: 'Girls sent me letters, knickers, pictures, the lot. It was a bit crazy. The guards must have seen a few things! They probably got a right eyeful. The thing is that, because you're bored, you write back. I was asking for a few more pictures! By the end, I had a whole big bag of stuff – clothes, underwear, all sorts of stuff.' Now, firstly, Jermaine was only in for a month, so that is some impressively rapid pen-pal work from both him and his admirers (hats off to the postal service say us). And secondly, we now love to think of him leaving prison in his civvies, squeezing through one of those tiny doors that you see in films, holding a bin bag full of kecks and mucky piccies and wondering what he's going to do with them all now that he would get regular, unfettered internet access again. Who knows, maybe there's another forgotten sports car left out there somewhere, parked at an airport with a boot full of drawers and nuddies.

Lee Sharpe was similarly sought after by female fans, but one passage of his book is a lot more innocent. Younger readers may not quite remember what a sensation Lee Sharpe was when he signed for Manchester United. He was quick, skilful, deadly and extremely likeable. People hated United with a real fury back then, but few hated Sharpey. How could you hate Sharpey? Even Roy Keane liked Sharpey. But it was women in particular who loved Lee – so much so that he decided to give something back. With his mum doing the admin, he commandeered supporters' coaches to bus girls in from all over the country for special sorts of 'Meet Sharpey' days. He remembers: 'We used to get 2000 turning up. They would be taken round Old Trafford first for a guided tour, round the museum, and for the grand finale Keith would do a disco for them at the Discotheque Royale.' Two thousand! We can only hope he laid on corner flags so they could all mimic his famous goal celebration to the strains of 'Relight My Fire'. 'We'd have a couple of bands on, a DJ, a raffle, and I'd make a little speech, tell them all to have a brilliant afternoon. They'd scream their heads off and then afterwards I'd sign autographs for all of them.'

In the hands of almost anyone else, this would run the risk of seeming a little sleazy, but with Lee Sharpe, it feels sweet. They held a raffle for heaven's sake.

There is a kind of more old-fashioned adoration, though, that can be quite useful when you're trying to write your autobiography. We learnt about this from an entry in Alan Shearer's *Diary of a Season* from 1995 (exactly as fascinating as you'd expect): 'I meet my agent Tony Stephens on the M6 and then further down the motorway we pick up David Platt. We call in at Tony's house and meet Margaret, a grandmother, who is David's number one fan and has 58 scrapbooks of his career. David is writing his autobiography and wants to borrow the scrapbooks for the next few days.' Now, there are some curious things about this anecdote (why did Alan meet Tony on the M6, then go back to Tony's house? And why was Margaret at Tony's house, possibly alone, while Tony went to meet Alan on a motorway?) but the important stat is that Margaret had filled an amazing 58 scrapbooks – Platty wasn't even 30 at this point. Not only that, but her diligence – her *love* – provided a priceless resource for a guy trying in vain to remember who fouled him in that game against Holland.[41] Forget terrace chants or knickers in the post; this is proper, valuable adoration that any footballer would appreciate. Shearer also mentions that Margaret's daughter-in-law had started a Shearer scrapbook, leaving us hoping that this family zest for cataloguing England goal-getters has continued through the generations, with Margaret's granddaughter keeping tabs on Michael Owen, perhaps, and her great-granddaughter now getting busy with the scissors for articles on Harry Kane.

THEY DO NOT LOVE OUR ADULATION

Or, at least, not all of it. Terry Curran, maverick 80s forward and ace ladies' man, certainly enjoyed the perks of being a well-known footballer – but he had some reservations: 'I could have done without some of the hassle that comes with the lifestyle. Ok, I could cope with women falling at my feet but being recognised everywhere you go has its drawbacks … I wanted to be left to myself – or the girl I was trying to pull – rather than be drawn into a conversation about my football career. Don't get me wrong, I've got time for the fans but there's a time and a place.' All right, Tel, you can't have it both ways. If you can 'cope' with the attention from women, you have to 'cope' with someone telling you what a good goal you scored that time.

Peter Schmeichel would sympathise with Curran's unwillingness to engage too much with fans. In his fairly dry autobiography he relates one story that took place on a driving range while he was on international duty during the 1998 World Cup: 'I played 80 balls and hit about 60, of which 40 were sliced, and it was driving me mad! While I was standing there slicing a school group returned from the course with their teacher, and they all stood there to watch Peter Schmeichel play! They wanted autographs and photos, but when I declined, explaining that I was training, the woman teacher told me that I was arrogant, which prompted me to call her a bitch. I'm not sure who came out on top of this exchange, but apparently there's nowhere where I can be allowed to be just Peter and work on my golfing technique.' You may not know who came out on top in that exchange, Pete, but everyone else does. And also, don't try and claim you were 'training'. You were down the driving range and you refused to take five minutes out for some fans because you were annoyed

41 You'd think she'd get an acknowledgement in Platt's book for her dedication, but we checked and she gets sod all.

about how badly you were playing. Those poor kids, Pete. They only wanted a photo.

Emlyn Hughes was another who had mixed feelings about adoration – it seems he did enjoy it, but at the same time it reminded him of the brevity of a football career, and he was determined not to let the fans get too close. In *Crazy Horse*, he's really appreciative of the welcome Liverpool fans gave him on his return to Anfield with Wolves because 'I had always kept the supporters at arm's length … I always felt the closer a player got to the crowd, the more they would hurt him when the end came.' But if you don't open your heart, Emlyn, you'll never experience true love. In fact, Hughes says he never acknowledged them when they chanted his name, 'because I thought that as soon as I was at the end of the road they would stop the chanting and that would bite hard'. Still, a little wave wouldn't have hurt? He's like the child who denies themselves the pleasure of a helium balloon because they're scared it'll float away to the stars. It's a shame that he built that shield around himself, though, because when you think of how Anfield reveres its heroes, from Shankly to Klopp, Dalglish to Konchesky, it seems he's made something of a miscalculation there; he would always be loved as a huge part of a great side, regardless of how he left the club.

OPPOSITION FANS CAN GET NASTY

Patrick Vieira has nothing but praise for English fans in his book, as he swoons: 'There's huge respect for players in England. All the foreign players who come over notice the difference.' Well, that's nice. 'You can meet a Tottenham or a Man U supporter and he might tell you that he supports another team but he won't insult you.' He knows his audience doesn't he? Well, partly. He goes on to say: 'When it came to supporters, though, the first ones to really impress me were the Liverpool fans. When they sing "You'll Never Walk Alone", it's unbelievable. The atmosphere in their stadium is magical: it's the ultimate football atmosphere', which seems a bit of a slap in the face to the famously deafening noise produced by Arsenal fans. The first part was a lovely sentiment though – it's just that Vieira's kind words are contradicted by some pretty rough tales related by other footballers, a fair bit of which make for grim reading.

Lee Howey received several threats of death and violence from Wolves fans after injuring first Geoff Thomas and then John de Wolf in separate matches. Howey insists in his book that both instances were justified payback for earlier naughtiness from his opponents, and while we've no reason to disbelieve him, his spectacular description of the Thomas tackle in particular is unlikely to smooth over any lingering bad feeling: 'I won the ball; one foot went into the middle of it, my other foot skimmed over the top of it and hit him just below the knee, leaving him spinning and ululating, like a Janis Joplin LP.'

Lee Trundle was also mailed death threats for his part in (accidentally, he says) holding up a flag that said 'Fuck Off Cardiff' after Swansea won the EFL Trophy, and while Graeme Le Saux wasn't told he might find himself sleeping with the fishes, he nonetheless received some unpleasant messages from Man Utd fans after he was badly hurt while playing for Blackburn: 'One of the United fanzines ran a cutout advert on one of their pages with a message. The message was: "Dear Graeme, we are just writing regarding your horrific injury. Just to let you know, it's the best Christmas present we could ever have. Don't get well soon." They suggested the readers cut it out and send it to me – and about thirty of them did.' Classy.

Elsewhere, both Shaun Goater and Gary Neville report on frightening incidents that occurred while they were playing for Man United. Goater, still a youngster, years before his City days, was once out for a stroll to the shops with fellow United teenagers Lee Sharpe and Giuliano Maiorano when a man pulled up in a car and, waving a crowbar about, claimed he had something for them: 'He looked at us and shouted, "I f***ing hate Man United!" and started chasing us down the street. I took one look at him and set off – there was no way he was going to catch me!' Apparently, their Adidas tracksuits had given them away. By helpful way of explanation, the would-be attacker yelled at them that he was a City fan as he pursued them with his weapon. Or maybe they somehow misunderstood the whole thing and he just wanted tickets for his daughter to one of Lee Sharpe's raffles.[42] The Nev's ordeal came courtesy of Liverpool fans: 'I've had Liverpool fans try to turn my car over on Salford Keys [sic] on the way back from a match. They tried to force open the doors, and when they couldn't get in, they started to rock me over.' Nev managed to execute a deft escape in the end, but it sounds genuinely terrifying.

42 By the way, *Sharpe's Raffles* is our favourite Bernard Cornwell book.

In Scotland, Graeme Souness witnessed first-hand when he was manager of Rangers how the Old Firm hatred is bred through the generations by some fans, with kids taught nice and early exactly who the villains are: 'I saw a kid being dragged towards me by his dad until they stood about two yards away from me. Then the dad pointed at me and said, "There you are, son, there's the bad man." So in his house, when I came on the telly, I was "the bad man". The kid was pulling away from his dad as he said this. It made me chuckle at the time, but afterwards it made me quite sad.' That kid must be completely unable to watch *Super Sunday* these days.

So that's players experiencing all kinds of abuse from opposition fans. But they can expect better from their own fans, right? Nah, not really.

YOUR TEAM'S FANS CAN ALSO GET NASTY

When Tony Cascarino went to play for Celtic, he was wary of the abuse he was likely to receive from Rangers fans, so he wasn't surprised one day when he was stopped by a supporter in the street: '"You're fucking shit, you," he hissed. "You're a useless big bastard." Glasgow is the world capital of tribal hatred and friends had warned me not to react when approached by Rangers fans, but this fellow was absolutely raving. "You're a fucking wanker, a useless bastard." "Look, mate," I pleaded, "give me a break. Can't you see I'm with my wife and son?" "You're fucking shit," he said. "And I'm a Celtic fan."' Ouch. That's got to hurt, but you have to admire the timing.

We all recognise this, don't we? One of the most awful things to experience as a player must be to receive a cheer when being substituted – not a cheer of thanks, but a cheer that finally you will not be stinking up the joint any longer. Fans can be merciless – especially to their own. And players know it.

Garry Nelson, who's groundbreakingly honest, interesting and amusing autobiography *Left Foot Forward* paved the way for dozens that came after it, had a very similar experience to Cascarino; in this case it was even more galling because it came after he agreed to a photo with a woman and her son: 'I watched the birdie and said "Cheese!" and she thanked me as did the boy. He then advanced upon a further topic of conversation. "You know Nelson," he said. "You're useless these days. Rubbish. You ought to be packing it in."' Now come on. The guy just posed for a photo with you – he didn't Schmeichel it and call your mum a horrible name. You can't talk to him like that, and if you really can't help yourself, at least use his first name.

Managers possibly get it worse than players. Poor Terry Yorath tells a heartbreaking story about the time he was watching his Sheffield Wednesday side lose at home to Millwall when he received a tap on his shoulder: 'I turned round to find this woman looking at me. "Yes?" "Terry," she said, "You're a lovely man but please do the best thing for Sheffield Wednesday and resign." Her words haunted me through the night and I decided she was right.' *Haunted him.* A 'sacked in the morning' chant is cruel, but nothing is quite as painful as the heartfelt words of a fan of your own team pleading with you to just go away.

David O'Leary really struggled with criticism from the fans while managing Leeds. In his controversial but ultimately dreary *Leeds United on Trial* diary, he gets so upset by the naysayers that he enters a weird fever dream: 'I would love to have a supply of beacons I could place on each and every one of the boo-boys in our crowd. Then, in the good times, when everyone is cheering, I'd be able to look into the crowd and identify the ones who have shown little or no tolerance or support when we have really needed it.' This sinister idea leaves us with a range of questions. For a start, what kind of beacons? Would they be battery powered? How would they be attached to the boo-boys? Would they have to wear them at all times, like an electronic ankle tag? Or would they be fitted only when they arrived at Elland Road for each game? Would there be some way of the fans redeeming themselves so they didn't have to wear beacons anymore? What if *everyone* booed? Would the whole crowd have to wear beacons? And finally, what would vengeful O'Leary do when those fans do cheer a goal? We imagine a severe look that says: 'you may enjoy this, but remember, I know your past. I know all. Thanks to my beacons.' We laugh, but Ridsdale probably would have signed off on the purchase of such beacons in a bid to make Dave's dream a reality.

This kind of symbolism is a lovely idea, though. Imagine if fans took beacons to games to indicate their dissatisfaction with particular players. A system like this at Arsenal, for example, would see Héctor Bellerín pretty much working in the dark, but for Granit Xhaka it would look something like Adele playing Glastonbury.

So there's plenty of rudeness and abuse about. But we haven't touched on one absolute no-no as far as players are concerned. The starting of a Mexican wave. This is because, as we all know, Mexican waves can have dire consequences on the pitch for your team. At least, this is the belief of Kevin Keegan. It comes from his second autobiography, written in the late 90s, and concerns a UEFA Cup tie against Athletic Bilbao. Picture the scene: it's the 1994/95 season and Kev's buccaneering Newcastle side are on the rampage. They've already put ten past Royal Antwerp over two legs and now they're 3-0 up in the first leg at St James' Park and look all set to progress. They don't, though. Bilbao grab two back and then win the return leg 1-0 to send the Magpies out. For Keegan, it wasn't his all-attack style, some rank defending or just a couple of very good goals that did for them. No. It was The Wave: 'With 20 minutes to go we were three up … when the supporters began a Mexican Wave. I think our players must have joined in mentally if not physically, because we lost concentration and gave away two silly goals to Ziganda and Suances. I'm certainly not trying to blame the fans …' Hold on Kev, it certainly *sounds* like you're trying to blame the fans. You just said the fans doing a Mexican wave made your professional footballers forget they were playing in a match …

'... but the time to start the Mexican Wave, if you must start one at all, is when you are three-up in the final with one minute to go. That's about as much criticism as I've ever made of our fans. I can understand their delight, but that was the turning point … It wouldn't have happened at Anfield because their supporters would have been more blasé. I hate the Mexican Wave at the best of times. The first time I saw it I thought it was fantastic, but once was enough. It might be good fun for the kids, but it is a major distraction to other spectators or players.'

Like the teenager that gets drunk on Malibu at 15 and can never touch the stuff again, one shot of a Mexican wave was enough for Andy McDaft.[43] Also, was there really any need for that line about Liverpool fans? Also, we've watched the highlights on YouTube, and at 3-1, none of the fans are doing any waves of any sort – surely they can't be blamed for both goals? And while we're here, another also: if you can only do a Mexican wave in the 89th minute of a cup final when you're 3-0 up, almost none of us will ever get to do one, unless we're Mexican, presumably. We hear they're at it all the time.

Anyway, we all know that Keegan says some odd things, like the time he claimed cramp is worse than a broken leg, or the occasion

43 See *Booked!* for a full explanation of this bizarre nickname.

he asked the police to let him lay waste to a group of suspects with a baseball bat, etc., so perhaps we should let this one slide. It's not like any of the Newcastle players of the time would ever dream of blaming the Mexican wave for their carelessness, would they, Rob Lee? 'We were cruising at 3-0 up, but then we lost our concentration. The crowd started a Mexican wave and unfortunately this seemed to transmit itself to the pitch and the performance clearly dipped. We gave away two silly goals in the final 19 minutes and in the end that cost us a place in the next round.' Well, that and losing the second leg (with no Mexican waves) 1-0, Rob, yes.

FANS LIKE TO CHUCK STUFF

Being a fan can make you feel a bit impotent. You're stuck in your seat, unable to do much other than shout and scream when things go wrong. There is, however, always the option of throwing something, be it programme, season ticket, piece of fruit or, like that time with Luis Figo, a pig's head.

It's far from a new phenomenon. During a tour of South America in 1969, the England squad was forced to dodge missiles thrown by Brazilian fans – and England weren't even playing. This story is so memorable that both Gordon Banks and Jimmy Greaves relate the same anecdote in their books; only they have conflicting memories of exactly what happened. They both agree that Sir Alf Ramsey's side went to watch Argentina v Brazil from the sidelines of the pitch, and that things began to get ugly when Argentina went 3-0 up, but then things start to diverge.

Banksy reckons: 'When the third Argentinian goal went in, Ray Wilson was hit on the shoulder by a tomato. Ray immediately took to his feet, turned to face the Brazilian fans and held up three fingers on one hand and none on the other to remind the Brazilian supporters of the scoreline. "That's right, Ray," said Jimmy Greaves, "you try and appease them."'

Yet Jimmy himself doesn't blame Ray Wilson. He says it was Johnny 'Budgie' Byrne who 'unwisely chose this moment to do an insane thing. He stood on the bench again to face the fans and, holding up three fingers, invited them to join him in a chant of "Three-Zero ..." It was the worst joke of Budgie's life.'

For the record, Byrne and Wilson do not look remotely similar. From there, Banks reckons the fans became angry and were shaking their fists a lot, while Greavsie ratchets up the terror by saying there was an avalanche of 'bricks, fireworks and rubbish' that led to Sir Alf giving 'the shortest tactical talk of his life: "Run for it, lads."' Banks, though, is more respectful of his old boss, and recalls him acting quite differently: 'The atmosphere was turning very, very ugly and Alf Ramsey, a model of self-control, got to his feet. "Gentlemen, there is no cause for alarm, simply sit and –" Alf never finished what he had to say. An apple rocketed through the air and hit him square on the back of the head. It was too much, even for Alf. Still exuding calm authority, Alf bent down, picked up the offending apple and carefully placed it on a bench. "Gentlemen, be so kind as to follow me," he said.' So either it was various pieces of fruit, or bits of terrace, and Ramsey was either extraordinarily calm and sensible, or not particularly calm, but still quite sensible. Great stories, nevertheless.

In both his books, Neil Warnock recalls an incident where he too beat a hasty retreat from some wild fans. In his case, it occurred when he was managing Scarborough against Wolves … *in a friendly*: 'Then their fans started smashing the ground up and when I went over to try and calm things down, with Wolves manager Graham Turner, a Coke can whizzed past my ear. I picked it up and realised it was full of sand. If it had been a foot closer it would have probably killed me.' The perils of managing a team based by the seaside.

And fans don't only hurl stuff at players – they'll take aim at other fans, too. In Michael McIndoe's at times eye-popping memoir he tells of how his dad had a flat overlooking Hearts' Tynecastle ground, and if things were going badly for the away side they would turn round and start flinging coins at the windows decorated with Hearts flags behind them. Windows did get smashed on occasion, but McIndoe would at least make a few quid from it: 'I used to run down after the match into the gardens and collect the money that had been chucked, earning me a good £5–£9 most weeks.' Not enough to pay for a new window, but not bad.

If that sounds hairy, Norman Whiteside's report of intimidation from Liverpool fans is genuinely terrifying. When they arrived at Anfield for a key match in February 1986, a brick was thrown and 'caved in' a coach window. Not unheard of, but rough all the same. Then: 'Two minutes later we got off the bus and were walking through the entrance when a Liverpool fan threw a CS gas canister at us and we had to run straight on to the pitch because our throats had started to burn and our eyes were watering. It's amazing that the game went ahead and, though Ron [Atkinson] had to re-jig his starting XI because one or two of the lads had been seriously affected by the smoke, we still emerged with a draw.' There's throwing missiles, and there's germ warfare, isn't there?

Far rarer than things being thrown from the stands are things being thrown into them by players. On one occasion the mildly hot-headed Chic Charnley (who, lest we forget, once successfully took on a fan brandishing a samurai sword while armed only with a traffic cone) was so incensed by the abuse of one fan that, as he went to take a throw, he snapped: 'Sure enough, I heard the words, "Charnley, you're fuckin' crap." Now I've admitted I could hardly hit the target that day, but I couldn't possibly miss this loudmouth. As I motioned to pick up the ball for the throw-in, I simply hammered it in his direction. Bingo! It was a direct hit. The ball thudded into his face, and I'm sure I saw a pair of false teeth take off into orbit and the bloke collapsed backwards.' After that, apparently, the fan was less vocal in his criticism.

In a way, it's remarkable something like that doesn't happen more often, but the only other incident we found came courtesy of incurable romantic Perry Groves. While at Colchester he started seeing Mandy Farrell, sister of one of his teammates, Andy (Mandy and Andy Farrell, yes, what of it?). Mandy would come and watch them play at Layer Road, and during the warm-up one day Groves kicked the ball towards her in the crowd and went to retrieve it. As he did so, he produced a pair of knickers from his shorts and shouted: '"Oi, you left something in my car last night!" and threw them at her.' Reader, she married him. Also, reader, she divorced him.

FANS LIKE A SCRAP

Most of the time, players are forced to ignore or accept any abuse that comes their way. Occasionally, though, they're left with no choice other than to front up. Andy Goram once laid out a mouthy Dundee United fan in Tenerife who challenged him to a fight after a couple of nights-worth of abuse. Goram was briefly worried that the fan's mates would take revenge, but then: 'The biggest of them just clapped me on the shoulder and smiled. "Well done. We've been wanting to do that all week."'

Andy Gray, meanwhile, came a bit of a cropper in some nightclub bogs with a group of Dundee fans when he was at Dundee United:

'They gave me a right hiding, but after they left I staggered back into the club, rounded up my pals and went after them. This time I ended up getting a pint pot smashed over my head. With blood gushing from a cut I ended my evening having stitches in the local accident and emergency.' Bloody hell. Football is different in Scotland, isn't it? Andy Goram says that at Aberdeen there's a pub where you can piss on the faces of Rangers players in the urinals. It's hardcore.

If you are going to risk having a go at a player in public, though, it's worth choosing your victim carefully. Choose someone placid, someone who doesn't like getting into scrapes, someone who doesn't enjoy making waves. In other words, not Tony Adams or Ray Parlour. Some Spurs fans tried this one day in a restaurant, constantly needling the Arsenal bezzie mates while they were trying to have a quiet meal. After they finished, Parlour decided he'd had enough and asked Adams to remove the pin from a nearby fire extinguisher: 'It was so powerful that it went over my head. I couldn't get control of it, I sprayed the whole lot everywhere. The pictures were coming off the walls, chairs tipping over, all their pizzas got drenched and everything. I promise you, I soaked them properly. We had paid the bill already, so I put the fire extinguisher back on the stand and we walked out. A couple of other diners were laughing and said, "They deserved that" as we left.'

The one ex-pro you absolutely should never mess with, though, is Malcolm Macdonald. While playing for Arsenal, Malc was about to sit down to Sunday lunch with his family when he noticed a posse of cars pull up outside: 'Out came about eighteen really tough looking lads, and they're all leaning on the fence, talking to each other and pointing to the house.'

Now, before we continue, try to imagine what you think Supermac might have done next. Call the police? Or a friend? Shout out to them from the safety of the house and see what they want? Just ignore them and see if they go away? If you chose none of the above and guessed 'go outside and confront them while armed with an actual sabre', then award yourselves a gold star. Because that was Malc's solution: 'I got Julie to go through to the study to get a big "Wilkinson" sword that I'd been given at the "Player of the Year" awards. I took it out of its sheath and started walking down the drive with it. "What the hell do you lot want?" I asked the lads, shaking like a leaf. One of them said, "We wondered whether we could have your autograph?" I have never felt so stupid in my life.'

Only in the 1970s would a player have been awarded a lethal weapon at an awards do. But what a gambit from Supermac. No checks, no warnings, just straight out there with a massive sword like Bruce Willis descending the stairs to face Zed and the Gimp in *Pulp Fiction* – although Butch took a lot longer (some would say far too long, given the circumstances) to choose his weapon. No weighing up hammers and electrical gardening tools for Macdonald. Just bring me the samurai sword, Julie – I've been waiting for this moment since the player of the year dinner.

PLAYERS CAN HOLD GRUDGES AGAINST WHOLE SETS OF FANS

Relatively few players openly criticise fans in their memoirs, but it does happen, and it can be charmingly catty. Take Mick Quinn, who had a spell on loan at Vicarage Road, but has little nice to say about their fans, moaning about 'their egg and cress sandwiches' and savagely blasting 'Vicarage Road is hardly one of football's hotbeds.' This seems harsh on Watford, who are surely not widely seen as some kind of quiet, posh sandwich-eating, middle-class club (that's Fulham's domain).

Stan Collymore's another one who knows just how to ingratiate himself with a fanbase: 'In the Midlands, it's the Wolves and West Brom fans who are the heart of the Black Country support and Birmingham fans dominate the city itself. But at Villa, one week you can get 20,000 turning up to watch and the next week you can get 48,000. They are very fickle. Most of the new supporters that had jumped on the bandwagon because I was arriving were Range Rover drivers from Worcestershire who brought the kids.' Blimey, they must love you, Stan. And what's he suddenly got against Range Rovers? Very roomy in the back we understand.

Gary Neville was used to getting abuse from fans at away games, and unsurprisingly, he didn't enjoy it when the same thing happened while playing at Wembley for England: 'There would be groups of West Ham and Chelsea supporters, lads who had come not to cheer England but to get pissed and hammer a few United players on a Wednesday night. I'd be running up and down the touchline, playing my guts out for my country, then I'd go to pick up the ball for a throw-in and hear a shout of "Fuck off Neville, you're shit!"' That would certainly be annoying, but it's Nev's visceral follow-up, dripping with venom, that is particularly juicy: 'I was delighted when that tired old ground, with its crap facilities and its pockets of bitter fans, got smashed into little pieces. I never mourned the Twin Towers, not for a minute.' It's not the Towers' fault Nev. Don't start blaming the Towers.

Perhaps the most vocal player about a particular set of fans is Frank Lampard (Junior, not the proper one). He devotes so very many pages of his book to his complicated relationship with West Ham fans, and the club in general – it's like he can't get over them. They're Frank Butcher to his Pat Wicks. He laments how much he was booed when he went back with Chelsea: 'I laugh when I see it written that "I am an ex-West Ham favourite who the fans have now turned against." Bollocks. I was never a favourite. They booed me almost every week when I was there – for years. Now they are creating a myth that the way I am treated is a direct result of my own actions.' Now we're sure most West Ham fans would concede that the young Franky Lamp got a bit of stick from some quarters, but everyone does at some point don't they? We can't help thinking he's exaggerated what he endured while there. Most will also recall enjoying him as a player. He's the son of a legend, he scored many great goals for them, and they love a local boy, as fans do at all clubs. He also sure did kiss the badge a lot for someone who wasn't having a nice time.

It's possible, of course, that the frosty atmosphere was caused by Lampard leaving for London rivals Chelsea, to which those in Frank's corner would point out that Joe Cole did the same thing, without the long-term acrimony. However, Lampard himself points out that the two England midfielders had very different reactions to their boyhood clubs, best illustrated when other results were being read out in the post-match Chelsea dressing room. 'Joe would ask about the Hammers. If they had been beaten, he would turn away in disappointment. My wounds from my West Ham days were still very much open then and I would greet the news with a wry smile. That's how deeply I felt. I wanted West Ham to lose.' That's not the sort of thing that's going to win over hearts and minds now is it?

Other reasons Lampard gives for leaving West Ham in his book are that he couldn't stay once his dad and uncle Harry Redknapp had been sacked, and that he was lied to about Rio Ferdinand being sold, and these ring much truer as legitimate reasons, so why is he so bitter? He returns to the feud again and again. And again: 'If I were to run out at Upton Park now and get cheered I would throw it back in their face. I don't want it now.' Luckily, West Ham remain the grudge-holding world champions and this scenario never arose while Lampard was still kicking a ball.[44]

With Frank rocking a gilet on the touchline these days, you would like to think that enough water may have passed under the Stamford Bridge for attitudes to have mellowed. Maybe at some point everyone can kiss and make up, and Frank can at least feel comfortable once more back at his first love. But we wouldn't bank on it. Those early years when sections of the crowd saw favouritism in his selection clearly caused deep scars, and Frank found sanctuary across town where 'Thankfully Chelsea fans are more generous with their patience.' Yeah, whenever anyone talks about Chelsea fans, the first thing they say is 'well, they are very generous with their patience'. Famous for it, they are. You will remember how lovely they were when Lampard went off to play for Man City that time.

FANS CAN BE FUNNY

If there's one thing the terraces are famed for, it's wit. Obviously, it can vary from country to country. In America, supporters will often proudly hold aloft a witty sign they've made and brought to the game, which is something you rarely see in Britain. US women's keeper Hope Solo wrote in her book that when her team made it to the World Cup Final in 2015, there were signs in the crowd that read: 'HANDS SOLO', 'THE FORCE IS WITH YOU, SOLO' and 'MARRY ME HOPE, I'M SOLO'. Of course, Hope didn't; she married a gridiron player, perhaps because the soccer fans all seemed to be *Star Wars*-obsessed nerds.

Over here, the comedy from the terraces will more often come in the form of verbal banter. As the great Micky Quinn wrote in his book when reminiscing about fans dressing up as him and doing the Harry Enfield-inspired 'calm down' chants when he had a barney on the pitch, 'I had always loved terrace banter, especially when it was humorous.' Yes, banter is especially good when it's humorous, and players can really appreciate that.

Steven Gerrard, for example, writes about how opposition fans sang joyously for years about the time he slipped over and let in Demba Ba to score for Chelsea, thereby costing Liverpool their title dream: 'I would get used to it,' he says, no doubt through tears of laughter.

---

44 It's also fair to say that Frank's book itself didn't help matters much.

Meanwhile, Peter Reid was once moved to ask his new signing at Sunderland, Lee Clark, about what his hometown club, Newcastle, were singing about him. Lee was forced to admit they were singing about his 'monkey's heed', saying in his book: 'There was always going to be the unavoidable issue of him having a monkey's head.' Of course, it is completely avoidable in day-to-day life, but on the terraces, fans feel it's imperative that Reid is regularly told what they think his head looks like.

Peter Reid's autobiography was one of the best we read, and he comes across as one of the most likeable, thoughtful and genuine characters of the game. We highly recommend picking it up because it is full of little gems, including a proper nugget of terrace brilliance. Reid grew up in a family split along Liverpool and Everton lines (in his formative years, he was very much in the red half). In one particular Merseyside derby, he fouled John Barnes and received the wrath of the Liverpool fans: 'Among the avalanche of voices, one could be heard louder than the others. "Hey you, you dirty little bastard," came the shout. I looked and saw it was my Uncle Arthur. He was a warm man, very tough, but an absolute gentleman and he loved Liverpool Football Club. He wanted me to do well … but, on derby day, all bets were off. I wouldn't have had it any other way. "Fuck off Uncle Arthur," I shouted back at him and got on with the game.' Magnificent.

We can't be sure of Uncle Arthur's response, but Paul Lake relates a story about a fan having an impressively sharp response to turn around a potentially embarrassing situation. It occurred when Lake was sitting in the stand watching Manchester City when an irate fan nearby finally lost his patience with what he was seeing and yelled, 'Get Lake off, Machin! Get bloody Lake off! The lad's crap!' Lake, and we're sure he enjoyed this, decided to set him straight: 'I tapped Old Man Steptoe on the shoulder. "I am off mate," I said. He turned around, squinted at me, glanced back at the pitch, and turned around again. "Blimey, that's the fastest you've moved all bloody season."' Bravo.

There was plenty of good-natured fun between Sheffield Wednesday fans and players after the squad pulled into a service station on the way home from beating Hartlepool in the League One play-off final of 2005. Manager Paul Sturrock recalls: 'Four or five thousand Wednesday fans – I kid you not – spotted the players and were all dancing the can-can up the escalators to the toilets which were on the upper level. It was a really great moment when players and fans were as one in support of their team. It is a football moment I will never forget.' Sounds magical, but – and call us health and safety killjoys if you like – several thousand people performing the can-can on an escalator seems a trifle dangerous. Surely a conga would have been a wiser choice? But then, maybe it *was* a conga – none of us can possibly know what the strength of Sturrock's grasp of formation dance really is.

This sort of chance interaction between players and fans at transport hubs must be reasonably rare, particularly these days when luxury team coaches come complete with, we assume, full bathroom facilities, fitted kitchens, pastry chefs, hot tubs and really fast internet, thus rendering service stations almost obsolete. But when it does happen it's not always quite as sweet as Sturrock's fond memory. Paul Walsh had his own experience while playing for Manchester City. In his early days there he struggled a little, perhaps not helped by the fact he was initially commuting from the south. He was forlornly heading home from another unsuccessful match when he stopped in Sandbach Services[45] (superb recall of detail there from Walshy, we're sure you'll agree) to grab a bite to eat: 'I was about third in the queue and feeling a bit fed up with everything when about five or six coachloads of Man United fans poured in – obviously going back to London – and they soon spotted me in the line. I had a glance around and they were all staring at me. Then it started. They all started singing, "What a difference you have made! What a difference you have made!" and pointing at me. It seemed to go on for ages while I waited for my food, then scurried back to my car and set off with the raging hump!'

Now, this all seems fairly friendly and Walsh does add that 'in hindsight, it was pretty funny', but we do have a couple of thoughts on this. Firstly, we can only applaud the fact he can't resist a subtle dig at United fans in the middle of his anecdote. And secondly, are we alone in thinking that this is a bit of an odd chant? Maybe the United fans were caught off guard and one of the lads who doesn't usually start chants piped up with 'What a difference you have made' (we imagine this is to the tune of 'you're not singing anymore' – a song we, ironically, don't hear enough of these days) but, still, it's not one you hear regularly is it? 'What a waste of money' is more usual,

45 Rated just two hamburgers out of five by the visitors to motorwayservices.info, incidentally, which makes Walshy's plight even bleaker.

but maybe they felt that a bit too harsh for the innocent travellers at Sandbach Services grabbing their Little Chef Olympic Breakfast? In the end, we're filing it under friendly banter, even if it didn't feel like it to poor Walshy at the time.

PLAYERS APPRECIATE FANS GOING ABOVE AND BEYOND

We've read a lot of negativity towards fans in this chapter, so let's end on some more positive notes. Despite all we've read, players do love us and they do understand the sacrifices we make to go and watch our teams. Two instances in particular deserve special mention.

The first tale comes from Terry Dyson who went with Spurs to Poland for a European Cup tie with Górnik Zabrze in 1961. This place was so cold and remote that only one Tottenham fan made it and, brilliantly, Dyson still remembers his name: 'They had 70,000 while we had just the one, a travelling student called David Mummery.' Now that is dedication to the Tottenham cause, even if he was possibly only in the area by chance. We've heard fans sing 'You could have come in a taxi' at away support, but this guy could have come on a unicycle.

And then we come to the ultimate away day. Keep your trips to Millwall or Leeds or Galatasaray. Try Germany in front of Hitler and Goebbels in Munich in 1938. Yeah, bit tougher than an August afternoon at Craven Cottage, that one. It was a match fraught with politics: Sir Stanley Matthews writes in his entertaining autobiography that the FA had insisted they give the Nazi salute before the game, something the players only reluctantly agreed to after being told it needed 'only a spark to set Europe alight'. Now that is pressure.

England won 6-3, with Sir Stan saying they took heart from two English lads behind the goal, armed with a Union Jack in a sea of swastikas: 'As we left the pitch I glanced over to our source of inspiration. Our two fellow countrymen had taken their Union Jack down from the perimeter fencing and were dancing a jig, manically waving it above their heads. I looked up at the VIP section of the stand and there was a row of empty seats where Goering, Goebbels and other members of the Nazi hierarchy had been sitting. We later learned that with some ten minutes remaining, and with no chance of Germany getting back into the game, they had stormed off in a strop.'

So much to enjoy here – who on earth were the two Englishmen courageously showing colours in the home end? And when the Nazi top brass flounced off in anger at their team's humiliation, did those brave lads start singing 'Is there a Reichstag fire drill?'

The roar of the crowd is so important to players, and as The Doog said at the start of this chapter, it's something players can never get back once their career is over. It's no wonder, then, that they can recall certain atmospheres with real clarity, and without doubt the best description of such we found anywhere comes from Spurs legend Danny Blanchflower's autobiography *The Double and Before*. His memory, still fresh when he wrote it, relates to an FA Cup tie during Tottenham's famous double-winning season at Sunderland's old ground, Roker Park, justifiably famed for its 'Roker Roar'.

The atmosphere that day was so intense, in fact, that Blanchflower's teammate, Terry Dyson, also remarks on it in his book, but it's Danny's description that'll stick in our minds forever. Spurs are one up, but Second Division Sunderland are all over them, desperately searching for a leveller:

> A corner … the possibility … the equaliser … you could feel the tension behind that goal. They shouted and whistled and screamed and fainted with expectancy. The noise was unbearable: I could not feel my senses or clear my thoughts or concentrate properly because of the shrieking din …
>
> The pandemonium increased … Over it came again … and in the frothing panic it was smashed into the net. The equaliser. They shot over the fence on to the field, hundreds of them, like mad Hindus waving their arms to the glory of Allah for the Equaliser.

Now that, Peter Ridsdale, is a true, heartfelt description of the wonder of being a football fan in the middle of a maelstrom of madness. Absolutely perfect.[46]

Except, well, for that confusing bit about Hindus and Allah. Different times.

46 Not least for his capitalisation of 'Equaliser', as if he's referring to Edward Woodward or Denzel Washington.

FOUR-FOUR-TWO-BY-TWO

'I like pigeon pie'

Eagles and Seagulls and Canaries. Lions and Tigers and Shrimps. The links between football and animals have always been strong. Not for nothing is the name of Pickles the Wonder Dog writ so large across the fabric of our national game. We love football, we love animals and the two are natural bedfellows. Think of the thrill when a squirrel or a cat steals on to the pitch, causing mayhem. That's why, in the current golden age of mascots, clubs will so often reach for a cuddly creature to portray the softer side of their brand. Huge foam Owls, Bears and Hornets happily bestride the touchlines of the country without a care for scale or perspective, and we all recognise it as their natural habitat. Arsenal have even managed to make the magnificent Gunnersaurus an acceptable household name, even though keener students of palaeontology will know full well that it isn't even a real species of dinosaur.

In this chapter, we're donning our safari suit to bring you all the tales of fantastic beasts and where to find them among the written works of your favourite players. This is where Packham meets Beckham, Attenborough meets Middlesbrough and Michaela Strachan meets Gordon Strachan. Come with us down the rabbit hole.

Let's cut to the chase – Greavsie killed a horse. He didn't mean to, but he did. After missing out on the 1970 World Cup squad, Jimmy took part in the World Cup rally instead. This took him from London to Mexico via South America in a Ford Escort as co-driver to professional rally man Tony Fall. The pair finished in a very creditable sixth place, but not before reducing the horse population of Panama by one. Greavsie takes up the tail, er, tale at 100mph: 'Tony couldn't possibly avoid it. He tried, using every bit of his enormous driving skill but we collided head on. The poor horse's head was ripped clean off and its hooves smashed through our windscreen as it bounced against the bonnet of the car.'

Keep it light, Jim. This is horrific, and Greavsie perhaps shares more detail than we'd like, but there it is. You can have that in your nightmares too now. RIP Dobbin.

If that leaves you looking for a more heart-warming horse story, then Bobby Gould is like the cavalry to the rescue, bringing us news that while at Coventry City, Jimmy Hill 'once brought a horse down the corridor at Highfield Road for treatment from the physio Norman Pilgrim'. This feels like it's above and beyond the call of duty really, but it does the job of balancing out the football/equine life balance at least. Strangely, Gould doesn't elaborate on where the horse came from. Was it Jimmy's own? Was it a passing police horse? Or did he just find it, on the pitch perhaps? And Norman Pilgrim by the way? Good name, sir.

Bobby Gould continues as our wildlife correspondent as he brings us a tale of pigeons, also at Coventry. Gould claims that as a nipper his 'Granddad would take his pigeons to the games in baskets and send them back to his brother (my Uncle Harry) in Walsgrave Road, bearing the score.'

You have got to have a system, but we have so many questions about this. How many pigeons did he take to the game? Did he have to pay to get them all in? Or did just one fly back and forth? And most importantly, what on earth was he playing at? We're no sticklers for the rules but it seems to us that if you let one person bring a cage full of pigeons into a stadium, then you have to let everyone bring cages full of pigeons into a stadium, and before you know it there are pigeons everywhere and the ground will be coated in poo.

This sort of thing would never have stood at Charlton in the early 80s where club legend Derek Hales could do pretty much whatever he wanted it seems. Early on in Alan Mullery's spell as boss at The Valley, he went out on to the pitch to find Hales brandishing a shotgun, with Maurice the groundsman as his accomplice, scaring the birds out of the rafters: 'as the pigeons flew out, Derek was shooting them. He had a pile of dead birds at his feet. "Derek, what are you doing?" Ask a silly question … "I'm shooting pigeons, boss," he replied. "I do it twice a week." "Why?" "I like pigeon pie," said Halesy. "And," added Maurice with feeling, "it stops them shitting all over the seats!" They had logic on their side. I laughed all the way back to the Portakabin.'

Sly dig at Charlton's facilities aside, Mullers would have sucked a thoughtful tooth as he sat in his draughty office reminiscing about his time as a Fulham apprentice where he was on his own pest control duty, whacking poisoned rats with shovels. Being right on the river, Craven Cottage must have been running alive with the things, but Mullery was clearly less enthusiastic than his colleague Jack, who kept shouting encouragement like: 'Kill it!' and 'Smash the bastard'. A reluctant Mullers says he didn't like killing anything but dutifully 'clouted the rat and threw it in the wheelbarrow', because of course it was an essential part of his apprenticeship.

As we've seen, the life of an apprentice is a strange one at the best of times, but it clearly involves more animal cruelty than you'd think. Splitting the difference between the two previous tales is Kevin Sheedy as a youngster at Hereford, who tells us that his manager John Sillett, like Charlton sharp-shooter Hales, also kept a shotgun handy: 'Sillett suddenly appeared from his manager's office with a double-barrel shotgun – for which I presume he had a licence – took aim at a pigeon on the newly re-seeded pitch but managed only to wing it. He then gave me a stick and said to me: "Here son, you go and finish it off." So I had to put the poor creature out of its misery.' The sound of gunfire that constantly surrounded the Hereford manager is actually where 'Cillit Bang' got its name – possibly.

At least this type of roping in of the apprentices to destroy animals feels off the cuff, on the fly, improvised. But according to Sheffield Wednesday legend Mel Sterland, if you played for Jack Charlton it was part of the routine: 'Jack Charlton used to take us out into the woods to do some beating while he was shooting. We had to make bird noises and beat the undergrowth so that pheasants would fly up for him and his friends to shoot.'

It will come as no surprise to football fans that Jack Charlton is responsible for the deaths of more animals than CJD and myxomatosis put together, probably, but we didn't realise he got the youngsters involved in his dirty work. We would complain bitterly that this incident scarred the young Mel Sterland for life and forever tainted his relationship with the animal kingdom – if there wasn't already such compelling evidence from his earlier life that it was already a bit skew-whiff, to say the least.

Sterland has written a very entertaining autobiography, *Boozing, Betting & Brawling*, and it's fair to say it contains plenty of examples of all three. However, it's little Mel we're concerned with here. Little Mel, you see, reacted to being nipped by his pet budgie by putting the family cat into the budgie's cage to administer nature's justice, like something out of a Tweetie Pie and Sylvester cartoon. Luckily for the budgie, Mel was caught in the act that time, but the goldfish his elder sister Sheila won for him at the fairground wasn't so fortunate. Sheila was no doubt relaxing in the warm glow of her good deed when the family sat down to eat that evening. With young Mel nowhere to be seen and suspiciously quiet, she went into the garden to see what he was up to.

Now, a quick personality quiz for you here. What do you think Mel was up to with the goldfish? Was it:

a. Cleaning out a bowl in readiness for the new fish.
b. Happily watching the fish swim in a bucket as the evening sun danced on its golden scales.
c. Chopping it to bits because it couldn't walk.

If you answered a, you are the practical type.

If you answered b, you are one of life's dreamers.

If you answered c, you are Mel Sterland.

There was understandable uproar and recrimination when he was discovered, with Mel explaining himself by saying that he'd taken the fish out of its water-filled plastic bag with high hopes that it might walk: 'When it just flapped about, I decided to chop it up for some reason.'

It's a scene that an army of child psychologists would have their work cut out with. We've all met people with unreasonable expectations, but we're not sure we've ever met anybody, even a child, that expected their fish to walk. Nor have we met a critic so harsh that they met their disappointment by cutting that fish to bits.

Sterland's adolescent animal cruelty throws all the other such incidents into stark relief. Certainly Ralph Milne may have killed more creatures when his teenage budgie club business hit a storage problem, resulting in multiple avian deaths, but his plea that 'we didn't realise that an overnight temperature of minus six in the middle of

December would have an adverse effect on our little flock!' rings true, and it feels more like entrepreneurial ineptitude than genuine malice.

Elsewhere, Perry Groves admits to putting itching powder on his landlady's cats as a Colchester apprentice because they 'crapped on my pillow'. Their hair may have fallen out, but at least he didn't kill them, so Sterland remains top of the shop on this score. Interesting to note, however, that Groves didn't show the same zero tolerance policy for people defecating on pillows when Paul Merson was getting up to similar a few years later. Brave enough when it's a cat, Grovesy. Brave enough when it's a cat.

Others who may be up against the wall when the animals surely take over the world include Gazza, who apparently once fed a mustard sandwich to a gorilla at a zoo, and Kieron Dyer whose spider policy is to 'get a towel and whack the crap out of it'. Ron Yeats is another. His fearsome hard-man reputation seems to have stemmed at least in part from a time when he worked at an abattoir and apparently killed a bull with his bare hands. How did he even do that? Lock his huge arms around its neck from behind and strangle it? Or punch it square in the head from the front? Both seem unlikely, but begrudgingly impressive if true. Emlyn Hughes brought us that last story, after detailing a training ground row in which Yeats told him: 'Don't you ever call me silly again or I'll rip your arm out.' Gulp. This is the kind of thing that some football fans lament the passing of isn't it? The current Liverpool side may be hugely impressive, but can they boast a squad member that has killed a bull with his bare hands? Seems unlikely, though Andrew Robertson is our best bet if push comes to shove.

It's not all bad news for our furry friends, however. Chris Sutton loves animals and has kept a whole menagerie of pets at times, declaring with perhaps a pang of bitter experience that: 'Animals don't let you down – they are very loyal!' However, even that doesn't stop him going off grouse shooting with the local high society knobs, grateful for the invitation. We'd have to put Sutton in the 'It's complicated' column, then, along with Stuart Pearce. Pearce has first-hand views on elephants having been to Zimbabwe and seen the damage one can do to a village: 'Travelling gives us both sides of the argument and the opportunity to make up our own minds. It doesn't mean that I now believe all elephants should be shot but I can see someone else's point of view.' Stuart 'Psycho' Pearce there. On the fence when it comes to culling Dumbo and his mates.

Inevitably, perhaps, it feels like we need to turn to goalkeepers to find the true animal lovers in the football community. Perhaps it's something to do with their roles as guardians or something – protecting goal, penalty areas and half-time leads maybe extends to caring for animals. We don't know, we're not psychologists, but there is almost certainly something in that.

Andy Goram tells us of his Noah-like existence, living with goats called 'Gin and Tonic', cows called 'Ice and Lemon' and cats who remain anonymous for some reason. He also tells us of his Great Dane called Lauders, after Brian Laudrup. David Seaman, meanwhile, seems to have grown up with a fascination for birds' eggs, which may not be considered strictly right-on these days, but, in the largely bleak context of footballers and animals, is something we're choosing to view as being born from love. 'I kept my collection in a big box in my room. The one I prized most was a kingfisher, because it was such a good-looking bird and such a hard one to get. But the hardest to get was a starling.' It truly is like an early prototype for Pokemon Go, isn't it?

Also, Big Dave risked his life to save a pigeon: 'One day down by the canal, we spotted a bird in the weed. It was flapping about and it was obviously a pigeon, not a swimming bird, so I swam across and rescued it.' Hats off to David Seaman then, who may be the animal kingdom's best friend in football. We're so impressed that we're not even going to do any jokes about David failing to save other things that flew over his head. Nope.

You might suppose that one place players wouldn't have to worry about animals is on the pitch itself, but that simply isn't the case. There's that famous incident of horse-killer Jimmy Greaves picking up an encroaching dog during a World Cup match against Brazil and getting widdled on for his trouble. And that's not the half of it.

Former England defender Paul Parker went so far as to call his book *Tackles Like a Ferret*, but that's not why we're here. Instead, we want to focus on that time that Parker was chasing promotion with Fulham, and travelled to Derby's Baseball Ground towards the end of the season. It was a lively affair in which he tells us: 'a Fulham team-mate was punched and kicked attempting to take a throw and I think the referee panicked by calling a halt some 78 seconds early. As players from both sides rushed for the tunnel, it became apparent that the referee was not alone in panicking.' Now you might be ahead of us here. What is Derby's nickname? And what did Derby have as a mascot at the Baseball Ground? You know it – a ram. 'The poor creature obviously became frightened in the mayhem as fans poured forward hysterically and everyone on the team benches fled for their safety. I was among those trying to get to the sanctuary of the dressing room when the ram did what all rams do in moments of crisis and charged head first at the nearest object. In this case, it was me.'

Poor little Paul Parker took the wallop and sustained some cuts and grazes. However, if there's a terrifying story to be had at a football ground, it seems there's always something more terrifying to be had at The Den. Alan Mullery visited Millwall's old home for a cup tie with Spurs in 1967, and recalls, no doubt with a faraway look in his eye, that no sooner were the players in the centre circle, than two Millwall fans jumped the wall and came at them: 'One had a live cockerel under his arm and the other was carrying a miniature gallows. When they got to us, they rung the cockerel's neck, stuck the gallows in the mud and hung the bird from a noose.'

Good grief. That poor bird. The centre circle at Cold Blow Lane is no place to die. That is next level intimidation. Although, it's one thing ritually sacrificing the club symbol of Spurs – or Norwich, or Swindon come to that. But did the same lads ever try it for a game with Hereford, Wolves or, most challengingly, Hull? It's all right acting the big man with a mangy cockerel in your hands, but smuggling a tiger through the turnstiles can be a messy business. Believe us.

When it comes to traumatic dog stories we came across, there was clearly one in particular that took the doggy biscuit. In *Mental*, Jermaine tells many lurid and enjoyable stories, but none more shocking than the time his dog killed his girlfriend's cat. Now that's the sort of thing that can really test a relationship.

Pennant had an Akita (us neither) called Shadow. Nothing cute and cuddly has ever been called Shadow has it? Even Jermaine, who presumably loved the mutt more than anybody and shared tender moments with it, admits 'He was a very scary guy!' Once Shadow had done the deed, Jermaine's thoughts understandably turned to self-preservation and getting the crime scene squared away. He enlisted the help of his friend Sam, who seems to be some kind of Winston Wolf[47] character, and the pair settled on the story that the cat had escaped through a 'window in the wardrobe room'. Clever. 'We had

47 Winston Wolf – from *Pulp Fiction* if you're of a certain age, or those insurance ads if you're a bit younger, maybe.

to organise a professional carpet cleaner to come round and a painter and decorator, because we needed to completely repaint the walls and get new wallpaper. They were a write-off – it was the full works.'

Leaving aside the fact that his wardrobe has external windows, which we're guessing is a rich thing, Jermaine and Sam seem to act here with the skill and precision of contract killers. Sam even buried the cat very deep and far away to cover their tracks. Maybe this wasn't their first rodeo. The relationship with *Hollyoaks* actress Jennifer Metcalfe didn't last. It's unclear if the affair foundered once Jennifer found out about her cat, or if she didn't find out at all until she read *Mental*; or maybe she didn't find out until this very moment, reading this. Imagine that.

Let's not leave on a sad note, though. Instead, let's go back to the old black and white, knockabout fun, more innocent times – the seafaring days of former safe-cracker and Darlington owner George Reynolds. A man whom the tabloids would surely have called 'larger than life' in his time.

George's book *Cracked It!* is a romp, taking in his days as a criminal, his rollercoaster ride at Darlington, and most pertinently to this chapter, his time in the Merchant Navy. George, always with an eye for making a couple of quid, had a friend on his boat who had an interest in exotic pets and 'once tried to smuggle an eight-foot-long snake, but it caused such pandemonium on board it had to be killed and thrown overboard. He successfully smuggled canary birds and a chimpanzee the size of a gorilla.' We're not ape experts, but is it possible this was actually a gorilla? And could they not have given that snake a fighting chance? Did they have to kill it AND throw it overboard? Surely just lobbing it into the briny would have been sufficient? By the way, that snakes on a boat story isn't half as entertaining as that film about snakes on a plane – whatever that was called. The monkey fun didn't stop on the boat though, as George continues: 'We picked up a grass monkey[48] each and mine proved to be a bit of a handful. My mother adored the monkey, but it was so mischievous we had to get rid of it. First, I sold it for £10 to a pal, who brought it back because it was always trying to mate with his cat. Then I sold it to a donkey owner at Seaburn beach, and it would sit on the head of the donkey as children were taken on rides across the sand.'

48 We're no Steve Backshall, but us neither

This story has everything. Putting aside a bit of potential inter-species sex, which might not be advisable, it's a feel-good story we can all enjoy. But wait – it doesn't end there. If you're like us then you will very much enjoy any sentence that begins with the phrase 'the incident involving the monkey which landed me in the cells', in which case you're going to love this. 'The incident involving the monkey which landed me in the cells happened in Cooper Street, when it broke free from its chain on the front wall outside the house, picked up a ball-bearing and hopped along the street, smashing windows as it went.'

They say never work with children or animals, and George may have reflected on that during his time in chokey for monkey trouble, but we say good on the monkey. He was chained up, he escaped, he damaged property by making holes, and he ended up working on a beach. Why that's practically *The Shawshank Redemption*, but with monkeys. And who wouldn't watch that?

DONE DEAL

'Don't buy those carpets'

At times, these days, it can appear that actual football matches have been reduced to a mere sideshow next to the headline act of transfer speculation that drives newspapers and websites and provides the necessary globs of glue to keep Sky Sports News from catastrophically tumbling down around Jim and Natalie's ears.

Today, we're a long way from the sort of situation Graeme Souness experienced at Newcastle, where his assistant Dean Saunders informed him that the purchase of Michael Owen had been completed at 1am by 'throwing stones at my window to wake me up'. No, what with countless gossip columns, gossip column compilations, websites, 24-hour sports news channels, social media and iPhone push notifications, we couldn't avoid receiving news of Shrewsbury taking a 17-year-old on loan from Brighton even if we wanted to. DONE DEAL!

To be honest, all that hyperbole leaves us a little cold, but because it has become such a huge part of the game, we've been left with no choice but to hold our noses and dive in to the murky Transferic Ocean. To be fair, once you're in, the water's fine. There's loads of fun to be had – like Bryan Robson's delicious nugget that had Liverpool offered the same amount of money as Manchester United when he was at West Brom, 'I would probably have gone to Anfield.' Face facts, United fans: for one of your biggest legends, you were second choice.

It's important to remember, though, that transfers are life-changing events for the players involved. Have a read of this pure poetry from Neil Redfearn: 'For the first ten years of my professional career, I followed the golden rule – never fall in love with a football club. Then, on 6 September 1991, I walked through the players' entrance at Barnsley to start a month's loan and that was me for the next seven years.' No, you're crying.

Stay at a club for that length of time and not only do you generate an affinity, but it feels like home, like family. When Patrick Vieira left Arsenal after nine glittering years and went to Juventus, the poor lad didn't know if he was coming or going. In his book he explains that he began rooming with Lilian Thuram, but after their first night together he woke up all discombobulated when he looked over and saw Thuram rather than his Arsenal roomie Thierry Henry: 'Where was he? "Oh, OK" I told myself, "I'm with Lilian because we are about to play an international" (that's who I shared with when the France team got together). It took me quite a while to work out where I was, and why it was that Lilian was in the room with me. Not only that, but for the next couple of days, whenever I saw him in the room, I had this instinctive feeling that we were about to play for France, not for Juventus. I just couldn't get my head round the fact that I was no longer with Arsenal!' It's like he was institutionalised, like an ex-con struggling to come to terms with life on the outside. Just with better hotels.

That is the life of the footballer – your special talent means you can be plucked from one location and dropped in another almost without warning. It must take some getting used to. They say moving home and getting married are two of the most stressful things to happen in your life, but when footballers change club, it's like they're doing both at once. Yet rarely do we stop to take this in. Think of poor Shaun Goater, for example, and his state of mind when a dodgy fax machine almost ruined his big move to Manchester City: 'I was losing control, panicking and shouting, "It's broken! I can't send it, sort it out, sort it out!"' Luckily it was all fine, but the poor guy must've nearly spilled his Hooch all over his Shed Seven CDs in the panic (it was the 90s, you see).

But before we get carried too far down the raging river of transfer gossip, let us pause for a moment and spare a thought for those on the wrong end of a transfer. How, for instance, did a poor, unnamed Kettering player feel when Ron Atkinson flogged him 'for a lawnmower'?[49] Yes, it's exciting when your club makes a new signing; they look all bright and happy as they pose with a pen at a desk while the director of football bends down and puts an arm round them and grins at the camera. But people forget there's another club involved –

49 Mind you, if it was one of those proper ones you can drive, who can blame him? We'd all love a go on one of them, right?

the club they have left. And there are people at that club. Real people. Real people that have to deal with their loss. As Alan Curbishley notes, 'The player gets his move and good luck to him, but it's the people left behind who have to try and cope without them.' No one ever thinks of them, do they, Curbs? In full agreement is Kevin Keegan, who writes: 'I suppose in that respect football is a lot like life: when one door closes another one slams in your face.' Not quite sure that's how the phrase goes, Kev.

Now we've made the required acknowledgement to the poor saps on the sad end of a transfer, hopefully it's safe to move on and have a proper dig about in what Mark Walters charmingly refers to as the 'jiggery-pokery' of the world of transfers.

END OF THE AFFAIR

The first stages of a transfer can begin in different ways but perhaps the most entertaining for neutrals is when a player moves from being a mere 'player' to a 'want-away player'. The record time for a player to become a want-away player is held, we're fairly sure, by Tino Asprilla. Former Darlington owner George Reynolds famously paraded Asprilla about as an imminent new signing before a game with Carlisle to general astonishment back in 2002, but Reynolds recalls: 'He spent 35 minutes on his mobile telephone to his agent during the second half. Before the second half kicked off, he spent an extra 15 or so minutes in the chairman's lounge. That showed a lack of commitment.' Tino Asprilla there, quite literally trying to engineer a move away before he had even signed a contract – and indeed he soon hopped it, allegedly to follow up some interest in the Middle East.

The more time-honoured and conventional way to get a transfer is to hand in a transfer request. That little phrase has been bandied about for years and we all talk about them and speculate about whether one has been 'handed in' (they are always handed in, never emailed, posted or faxed – like breaking up with a partner, it's very much seen as something you should do face to face, although obviously with a partner you wouldn't normally turn up with a hard copy of your message).

Despite this, none of us really know what's written in the average transfer request letter. What we do know, however, is that whilst at Nottingham Forest, Steve Hodge got his mum to type up his request for him, as if he was asking her for a note to get him out of PE. Hodge had the added problem of having to hand in his request to the fearsome Brian Clough, who wasn't best pleased: 'He opened it and slowly read it to the end. "Who typed this?" "My mum." "Tell her not to give up the fucking day job!"' All right, Cloughie, don't have a go at his mum.

When Lee McCulloch was trying to get his dream move from Wigan to Rangers he at least managed to give Paul Jewell the right bit of paper, it's just that he produced it from an odd place: his pants. His weak explanation was: 'I didn't want any of my teammates or other members of staff to see it, so I walked around the training ground with it inside my shorts for half an hour.' Oh, right. But they would see it if it was in a pocket? This makes no sense, Lee. Jewell made the exact same point in a press conference where he made his displeasure with McCulloch known, and Lee admits: 'It was a fair point he made. But, I was all over the place that morning.' So was your transfer request, mate.

McCulloch wasn't finished though, and took his campaign to leave to the next level when Chris Hutchings took over as boss: 'I phoned the day before we were due to report back for pre-season and told him I was going to be his worst nightmare, that I would boot every single ball over the fence at training so that no work could get done. And I told him I would happily fight him if he wanted to confront me.' He even resorted to hiding weights about his person for the new season weigh-in to make it look as though 'I had chucked it'. You can understand McCulloch's wish to play for Rangers, but these are some remarkable actions. Who would've had to retrieve all those balls from over the fence? Who's he punishing here? It can't have gone down well with the Chester de Zeeuws and Paul Scharners of this world.

Alistair Robertson reports that Mickey Thomas also took drastic measures to accelerate a transfer. He'd been signed for West Brom by Johnny Giles, who then promptly left, leaving Thomas under the less enthusiastic Ron Saunders: 'Mickey used to wait for Saunders to get out of his car at training, then jump on his back as if he were a jump jockey and smack the top of his bald head,' says Robertson. Well, you have to give points for creativity. Also, if he did this every day, why didn't Saunders take steps to avoid it? Wear a spiky backpack, paint his clothes with that anti-climb paint, something like that?

Footballers want to leave for pastures new for a number of reasons – the money, to get first-team football, the money – but apart from the money, sometimes they seem to simply really like playing for a particular manager. Ron Atkinson tells a story in his first book about trying to complete the signing of Frank Stapleton for Manchester United soon after he had moved from West Brom. The meeting in a hotel room was supposed to be secret, but at some stage there was a knock at the door and Ron found his old West Brom midfielder Remi Moses standing there: 'I ushered Remi out of the way, and pressed him: "What the hell are you doing here?" As I shoved him into my own room, he explained: "I want to sign for Man U."' Unbelievable. Peter Odemwingie gets stick to this day for turning up at QPR's ground on deadline day hoping for a move from Albion, but at least Rangers were actively trying to get that deal done. Moses, meanwhile, stalked Big Ron to a secret location and then just brazenly strolled in asking if he'd mind buying him. It worked, though – Big Ron completed that deal a few weeks later.

Moses wasn't the only one who liked the cut of Mr Bojangles's jewellery-laden jib, either. When Atkinson was still at the Hawthorns there had been interest from Old Trafford for Bryan Robson, but Ron said: '"There is only one way, Robbo, you are going there," I promised him, "and that's if I am there as manager."' Later, when he did move to United, Atkinson says that Robbo immediately called him from England duty to say: 'If you are definitely going to quit and go there, just keep that promise.' Although, obviously, he was secretly hoping Bob Paisley would come in and gazump United at the last minute.

Managers do have that penchant for taking a player from their previous club to their current club, either because they trust them and know exactly what they'll bring to the team, or maybe just because it's nice to have a familiar face at training in the mornings. But one story that surprised us was the news from Norman Hunter that in the early 1970s legendary Leeds boss Don Revie was pretty close to leaving them for Everton, and told Hunter he'd take him with him should the move happen. Hunter was excited enough to immediately call his wife: '"Sue," I said, "don't buy those carpets. We could be on the move!"' We can only hope Sue was allowed her new carpets when Revie and Hunter both remained at Elland Road to win all those trophies.

Few can match the sly scheming of TV's Robbie Savage during his famously protracted transfer from Birmingham to Blackburn. He says: 'I phoned a mate at Sky and told him, "Listen, I'm going to go into the training ground on the lads' day off. I'll be there on my own, training on my own. Film it, and it will look like I've been banned from the first team."' Outrageously, just like Moses's hare-brained scheme, it worked. As sneaky as this was, in a way you have to admire him understanding the power of the media to create the perception of truth out of obvious fiction. He probably didn't mean it, but his mastery of the media was a blueprint for Donald Trump's rise to power in America. Nice one, Sav.

More impressive, however, is David Platt, who moved to Italy from Aston Villa and very quickly became a kind of Machiavellian figure, constantly scheming behind the scenes to get himself moves to different clubs. He started out at Bari and was there for a year before he was looking to move, ideally to Sampdoria, and he had been secretly talking to Roberto Mancini, who was playing there, about the possibility. But then Gianluca Vialli, also at Sampdoria, called him up: 'The question he had asked was whether I was going to play my football with him. I started to tell him that I had been speaking to Mancini and there was a chance I would be joining Sampdoria but he stopped me in mid-sentence. "Not at Sampdoria, with Juventus."' Vialli, there, tapping him up for a different move in a scene that you can imagine ending an episode of one of those Latin American soap operas.

Platty did go to Juve, but almost immediately regretted it and started angling for that Sampdoria transfer once more. When Juventus played Sampdoria away he decided to travel even though he was injured 'in the hope that I would see Roberto Mancini, the Sampdoria skipper'. It's ingenious, really. No direct phone call for Platty; just turn up innocently at the game, bump into Mancini and say 'Roberto! I didn't know you'd be here! Well, this is a happy coincidence …'

Platt's 'in' was that he was mates with Des Walker, also at Sampdoria at that time, which gave him an excuse to hang around outside the home team's dressing room. Mancini did appear at one stage, but Platt was disappointed that he 'made no mention of the possibility of me moving there'. Seeing as Platt had only been at Juve for half a season, you could hardly blame him. Still, Platt did at least get his message to Samp boss Sven-Göran Eriksson who passed by and 'smilingly said to Des in perfect English, "Ask him if he wants to come here." I laughed at his comment, then realised that here was an opportunity to let him know my feelings. I called out "Magari" ("I'd love to") as he went back to the dressing room. It brought the response of "vedremo" ("we will see").' He later also admits to resorting to calling Mancini at his home while away on England duty, but didn't get a response.

Whispered conversations, faux-accidental meetings, secret phone calls. There must be easier ways, surely? Still, it worked eventually and he played for Samp for two seasons before coming back to Arsenal, possibly after 'accidentally' bumping into Tony Adams in London one evening and telling him he wouldn't mind playing at Highbury in a joking-not-joking sort of way.

A lot of this seems underhanded and a bit disrespectful to the clubs paying their wages, but as is often pointed out, it wasn't so long ago that it was the clubs who held all the power and would act just as badly. Take Danny Blanchflower, who in the 1950s was a star at Barnsley and looking to move to the next level. The club repeatedly told him that there had been no enquiries for him, and he only found out otherwise because he met a friendly chap from the telephone exchange at an evening class. Apparently in those days, such workers could simply listen in to private conversations and, keen to spill the beans, Danny's earwigging new mate told him: 'So-and-so offered two players in part-exchange for you today. Barnsley said no. They want a straight cash deal.' It's like a beautifully primitive version of phone hacking, and eventually Blanchflower got his move.

Then there's the other side of the coin, where clubs decide they want to be rid of players. Fans often say of a player they'd like to see the back of that they'd 'drive them to *insert destination* myself', but West Ham boss John Lyall once went a step further to complete Neil Orr's move to Hibernian. He flew up with Orr to an Edinburgh hotel to finalise the deal but late on they were, and bear with us here, almost scuppered when the typist from the 'hotel secretarial service' (us neither) had gone home by the time they needed her expertise. Lyall explains: 'Without the typist there were no forms, and without the forms Neil Orr couldn't play for Hibs the next day. At this point I remembered the days in the office at West Ham, when I had painstakingly learned to type with two fingers. "Bring me a typewriter," I said. "I'll have a go"', which may be the most heroic sentence involving the word 'typewriter' ever uttered. After 'a dozen attempts' Lyall managed to complete the forms and Orr played the next day. Imagine how long it took John to type out his autobiography.

This act of selfless heroism wasn't the only one Lyall managed in his career, either. Mark Ward, who he signed for West Ham from

Oldham, remembers him visiting with his assistant and gallantly charming his partner Jane, who didn't want to leave the north for London: 'I instantly left for the kitchen to start making tea for our two guests. By the time I returned to the living room, Jane was much happier, laughing even, and in deep conversation with John.' Later on, when they had moved down, Jane didn't settle and wanted to move back, so once more Lyall stepped in and over a cup of tea talked her down, sweetening the deal with an extra £100 a week. Lyall's style was indeed pleasingly tea-based. We suspect he had a strong brew on when he was typing up Neil Orr's contract in Edinburgh too.

The most bizarre attempt we found to get rid of a player once more involves Brian Clough and comes courtesy of Viv Anderson's book, *First Among Unequals*. Brian Clough and his long-time assistant Peter Taylor famously fell out when Taylor left Clough at Forest and then took the reins at Derby. The accepted story is that they didn't speak for years, but Viv Anderson claims 'it was far more complex than that', and they did still communicate at times.

That communication led to one of the oddest situations we have read about, not just in transfers, but in all aspects of football. The story was this: Taylor wanted to loan both Anderson and Mark Proctor from Forest. Neither was keen, but out of respect for Clough they agreed to meet Taylor. Clough drove them to Taylor's house, which was in a remote part of the countryside and after some talks, Anderson and Proctor rejected the offer. Clough was initially angry, but then said: 'Could you give us a couple of minutes? I want a quick word with Pete. Go and have a cup of tea in the kitchen.' Tea playing its part again, here. 'While we were doing this, Clough and Taylor secretly left the house. Like two naughty boys, they scuttled off to do who knows what and left us out in the sticks with no transport.'

Luckily, Mrs Taylor kindly let them have another cup of tea (of course) and order a cab. Only, the cab never came, and Anderson reckons that somehow Clough might have ordered the cab company to not make the pickup. Finally, mid-evening, the Forest pair bolted: 'Over styles and fields we went, cutting ourselves on the undergrowth and tearing our clothes. Eventually we reached a village pub where we had a couple of drinks to calm us down. From there, we managed to get a taxi home to Nottingham, arriving about midnight, exhausted and bemused.' Startling stuff, like a scene from the start of *An American Werewolf in London*. Anderson reckons Clough and Taylor cooked up

Danny Blanchflower – told you he wasn't allowed to train with a ball.

Les 'Chappy' Chapman – aka Billy Swift and William Macswift.

George Graham – Sexy Arsenal Person #1.

Perry Groves – Sexy Arsenal Person #2.

Mrs Moore, Mrs Hurst, Mrs Peters, Mrs Bonetti. Probably not waving to grumpy Sir Alf.

A partially-severed arm didn't stop Hope Solo winning this giant medal.

Kevin Keegan finds solace in his dogs after the sad news about Santa.

Vince Hilaire – showing off everything he learned from Frank Lord, in a spiffing Palace kit.

John 'Budgie' Burridge with his best photo face.

Bobby Gould, moments away from another circle, probably, possibly about that shirt.

Mick Channon takes aim, possibly at the reeesseeeeerrrrrrves.

Greavsie and his death trap.

Mel Sterland celebrates another win for his sister at the fair.

Robbie Savage quickly tries to remember who the PM is.

Boris Johnson has done a bad thing. And Reidy already hated him.

Jim Smith coaches Frank Worthington on his relationship with Mandy Rice-Davies.

Carlton Palmer. Do not sit next to this man on a plane.

Gentle Joe Corrigan at the back, some random kids in the middle, Elton John down the front – Don Revie capped a lot of people.

Steve Hodge – it's not that stripey, is it?

New Order with the finalists for the 'World In Motion' rap (presumably Bernard Sumner is taking the photo).

Robbo: suit, shorts, no boots – inventing player-manager chic.

the whole ordeal, casting huge doubt over the rift between the pair of them that has passed into football legend.

This brings us to transfer deals that never happened. David Batty, for example, says Real Madrid were in for him when he returned from Newcastle to Leeds, but he had no interest in joining arguably the world's largest club. Of course he didn't – Haven Holidays don't operate in Spain.

Elsewhere, Trevor Brooking reveals he had an offer from Chelsea after retirement at West Ham – can you imagine? Typical wisdom from Sir Tricky for turning that one down. Zlatan Ibrahimović says that as a young player looking for a dream move to Italy or Spain his agent once told him Southampton quite liked the look of him. Zlatan's response, particularly for any Pompey readers, was a beauty: 'What the fuck! Southampton! Is that my level? Southampton!' To be so angry about even the idea of playing for Southampton does seem a little unfair though. Kevin Keegan played for Southampton for goodness sake. And Rory Delap.

Jermaine Pennant could've signed for Spurs from Notts County before he joined Arsenal, but his dad put a stop to that idea because 'he thought the manager at the time, George Graham, was a "cunt". They were his exact words. "He's a cunt, so I don't want my son to sign for him." That's what he said.' Well, it's good to have a reason and, to be fair, it's a better reason than Charlie Nicholas could muster – he turned down Bobby Robson and Ipswich early in his career, despite enjoying a trial for the Tractor Boys: 'The one thing that held me back was the fact that they played in blue, the same colour as Rangers. There was no way I could play in blue.' This possibly goes some way to explaining how such a tremendous player only managed 20 caps for Scotland – maybe he'd only play if they wore the away kit.

Steven Gerrard makes a big thing in his book of all the clubs he turned down to stay at his beloved Liverpool: Chelsea, Real Madrid and Barcelona amongst them. He claims, 'I knew I could never leave Liverpool. I would remain a one-club man as long as I played football in Europe.' Woah there, Stevie. That is some caveat you nonchalantly slipped in at the end, almost under your breath, hoping no one would notice. As you played for LA Galaxy, that means you were not a one-club man. It doesn't matter that they didn't play football in Europe. You can't make that distinction. It's like saying, 'I only cheated on my wife when I was away on business, not in real life.' You're only trying to kid yourself.

TAPPING UP

Sensitive souls get very upset about 'tapping up' don't they? Half the problem, it seems to us, is the term 'tapping up' itself. If it were called something softer, like 'sounding out', it would seem far more reasonable. And in the end, is there really anything wrong with it? We doubt clubs are too slow in putting about the names of players that they want rid of, after all. Besides which, it seems everybody is at it.

Self-styled one-club man Steven Gerrard, for a start, seems to have spent half his career at Liverpool acting as some kind of pimp: 'The club would let me know which long-shot target they had in mind and then ask me to contact him,' says Gerro. Brendan Rodgers once asked him to contact Tony Kroos, for example, and although Stevie G did as he was told, he writes that Rodgers 'just smiled when I said we'd be pissing into the wind with this one', and indeed Kroos soon signed for Real Madrid, despite a friendly text exchange. Gerrard doesn't explain, however, how he got Kroos's number in the first place, although we like to think he's a member of an exclusive international WhatsApp group for world-class cultured midfielders, possibly established by Andres Iniesta, new additions strictly on a unanimous vote amongst existing members only.

Sometimes it's not the timing but the conduit that's strange. Kevin Sheedy was largely in Liverpool's reserves when Howard Kendall shrewdly bought him for Everton, but the way in which that happened seems unnecessarily cloak and dagger. It started when he received a call from local journalist Colin Wood who asked if he'd be interested in joining the Toffees. Sheedy warily said yes: '"Okay," said Colin. "If you put the phone down it will ring again shortly and it will be Howard Kendall on the line." And, sure enough, the phone did ring almost immediately and it was Howard calling.' Kendall told him he was going to watch him in a game and of course the rest is history. But for this to be true, surely Kendall must have been literally sitting next to Wood? Why didn't Wood just pass him the phone? Or why didn't Kendall just make the initial call? They seem to be playing Secret Squirrel just for the fun of it.

Along similar lines, Terry Yorath says that his move to Coventry from Leeds began with a phone call from none other than BBC commentator John Motson, moonlighting as some kind of middleman for his BBC Sport colleague and then Cov chairman Jimmy Hill. The intrigue didn't stop there either. Yorath and Hill arranged a secret meeting at a Birmingham hotel. When he arrived, Yorath took a call at reception telling him to go outside and to 'look out for a yellow Jaguar'. Terry remembers: 'Sure enough, the yellow Jag soon arrived with a girl wearing a skirt up to her backside at the wheel. I couldn't take my eyes off her legs. She drove the car around a roundabout and then up a lane before pulling up near a churchyard.' This story has certainly taken a turn. Is this what is known in the transfer biz as 'add-ons'? 'Suddenly, out of the back of the car stepped Jimmy – he'd been lying down on the back seat so that he wouldn't be recognised.' We'd question how on earth Hill had remained undetected – was he covered by a few coats? – but we're more surprised that Terry didn't spot Jimmy's chin poking out of the sunroof. Naturally, charmed by Hill's proficiency at hide-and-seek, Yorath duly agreed to sign.

These sorts of covert operations seem to be more common than we thought. When they wanted to sign Aberdeen keeper Jim Leighton, Alex Ferguson and Martin Edwards at Man United were so keen to avoid getting into trouble with the FA that they concocted a plan so fiendishly complex it might have been drawn up by Danny Ocean himself. First, Leighton had to drive from Aberdeen to Cumbernauld 'just off the motorway' in a friend's car, because he had a personalised number plate that would easily give him away (hopefully it was J1M L8N). From there, all three of them drove to a car park, where Leighton parked his car and got in with Edwards: 'The plan was for us to follow the manager's car to the home of one of his relatives. He was to indicate the house at which we were to stop and where the back door would be left open for us. Ferguson would drive past the house but return later. Car telephones ensured that the manoeuvre was completed without a hitch.' Remarkable. All that's missing is a fourth car to provide some kind of diversion, the best safe-cracker in the game and a femme fatale to keep the FA's dogged private detective otherwise engaged. Why couldn't they have used the time they must have spent hatching this plan on the phone to just discuss some contract details? You can't escape the notion that they did all this less to keep out of trouble than to just have a great time pretending to be spies.

None of this, however, compares with the deranged behaviour of Llewellyn 'Alan' Curbishley when he was attempting to sign free agent Paolo Di Canio for Charlton. Curbs writes that he knew he'd have to contact Di Canio's agent for any deal, but that he first wanted 'to make personal contact with the player'. Now, admittedly this was in the days before social media, so he couldn't just slide into Paolo's DMs, but still, the sensible thing would have been to try and get a phone number for him – you know, like Stevie G would have done. Instead, Curbs had a different idea: 'When the PFA issued their annual list of players who were free transfers, I saw that Di Canio lived in Loughton, which was only a few miles away from my own home.' Yes. Curbs decided, unannounced, to just turn up at Paolo's pad. And if you think that sounds a tiny bit stalky, this is what happened next: 'When I got to the house it looked deserted and it was pretty obvious nobody was in, so I climbed over the gates, ran to the front door and scribbled a message on a piece of paper which I stuffed through his letter box. It simply said, "Paolo please call me I want to talk to you. Alan Curbishley."' That's right. Had you happened to be out walking near Paolo Di Canio's mansion (sounds like it was a mansion, doesn't it?) you might have seen the besuited manager of *Premier League Charlton Athletic* scrabbling over some giant wrought-iron gates (without a mate about to even give him a boost to get him started), then pegging it down the drive to shove a grubby bit of paper through the letterbox, before completing the return journey and driving off.

Even if Di Canio found the note, what was he supposed to think? Surely it could have been written by anyone. Plus, it doesn't even give a *reason* for him to call. It all sounds incredibly needy, like a last throw of the dice by a desperate teenager trying to convince the hottest girl in school to go on a date with them by being unconvincingly mysterious. We also imagine that Di Canio had security cameras at his property, meaning perhaps he was once even shown the grainy footage of this intruder: 'Signor Di Canio, sir, here's the footage – he doesn't seem to have taken anything, but obviously he may have just been casing the joint, so we'll be extra vigilant for the next few weeks.' Di Canio: 'Fine, good work – hang on a minute … can you zoom in there? Great. Can you clean that up? Perfect. Wait … is … is that … *Alan Curbishley*?' Amazingly, it worked and Di Canio turned out for Charlton anyway, rather than take out a restraining order, like we might have done.

Fortunately, not all meetings between player and prospective manager are quite so disturbing. Adebayo Akinfenwa says he knew Neal Ardley really wanted to sign him for AFC Wimbledon, 'because he even agreed to meet me in Nando's'. Well, who wouldn't be seduced by some of that lip-smacking Peri-Peri chicken? Wycombe boss Gareth Ainsworth may have taken note of Ardley's success, as he later plied

Bayo with ice cream while chatting him up on a farm owned by the chairman. Akinfenwa was hesitant at first, worrying it might be a test, but in the end: 'I took the ice cream. Of course I did. It was free ice cream.' Can't argue with that. Never turning down free ice cream is a rule we live our own lives by, and it's served us well.

If food doesn't work, managers aren't averse to trying booze. Stoke legend Terry Conroy played over 250 times for the Potters, but originally his big move from Glentoran was going to be to Fulham. That was before Stoke boss Tony Waddington flew over to hijack the transfer: 'He proceeded to clinch the deal by accompanying me home, ingratiating himself with my father, with whom he spent that night knocking back half a bottle of whiskey. By the time that was done he had my father eating out of his hand. "Whatever Terry wants to do is fine by me," he slurred.' And that was that. History altered by the grog.

Even better was Peter Reid, who convinced Lee Clark to commit the mortal sin of leaving Newcastle for Sunderland by simply getting him royally pissed. It's a story pleasingly corroborated by both manager and player in their books. For his part, Reid says he understood Clark's reluctance to make the switch, but six bottles of champers served to relax his moral code somewhat.

Clark's memory is similar: 'We met about lunch-time and I was with him until about tea-time. He got me absolutely shitfaced.' Sounds like a fabulous afternoon. But if Clark felt Reid's tactics had been slightly underhand, he soon got his own back quite spectacularly. Just before he was about to sign the deal, he heard that he was going to be in Glenn Hoddle's next England squad. So Clark and his agent made sure a clause was inserted saying he'd get a bonus if he ever got an England call-up. Obviously, Sunderland didn't mind this as, if he was playing well enough for a first call-up, they'd be delighted. According to Clark, the news appeared on Sky Sports News only moments after the press conference unveiling him as a Sunderland player: 'Reidy's face was a picture. He turns to me and says, "You little fucker!" I tried to play it all innocent and replied, "What you on about?" "You knew about that, you little fucker!"' All's fair in love, war and football contract negotiations.

AGENTS AND CONTRACTS

That splendid bit of business from Clark brings us nicely to the next stage of the transfer process – once the furtive meetings and covert texts and notes pushed through letterboxes have been completed and a fee is subsequently accepted, there comes the contract negotiations.

Once upon a time these were probably reasonably straightforward without too much in the way of shenanigans, but those were the days before agents, of course. Fast forward a couple of decades and you have things like Stan Collymore's agent Paul Stretford confirming to Liverpool boss Roy Evans that his client had agreed to sign by leaving this voicemail: 'The man from Del Monte says yes.' Stan reports this without comment, but you can't help thinking Stretford may have once managed a paper company in Slough.

The most notorious dialogue between player and agent must be that of Ashley Cole and Jonathan Barnett during negotiations of Cole's potential new weekly wage with Arsenal. It's one of the most famous lines ever written in a footballer autobiography and it's one Cole has never lived down: 'When I heard Jonathan repeat the figure of £55k, I nearly swerved off the road. "He is taking the piss Jonathan!"' Fans were right, of course, to mercilessly mock him for being so angry about being offered nearly three million quid a year to play football, but we're of the opinion that despite Cole's lack of self-awareness, Arsenal should have paid him. He was the best left-back in the world and they were crazy not to offer him more to stay – he went on to win eight more trophies at Chelsea after all. There. An unpopular opinion, but we stand by it.

The truth is that while agents are often portrayed as the big bad bogeymen of the game, they do provide a necessary service, often to young players with no real idea of their worth. Take Kieron Dyer when he was breaking through at Ipswich. Manager George Burley had made a new contract offer, saying it was the best he could do, but when Dyer, at his mum's behest, got his agent involved (coincidentally, it was Barnett once more), 'Hey presto, I was given a much higher wage of about £900 a week and a signing-on fee that was somewhere in the region of £100k … it all changed when an agent rang them.' You can't help but get the impression that clubs don't want agents involved because they want – understandably – to pay their players as little as possible.

As money began to flow into English football in the 90s, though, negotiations for the really big names became more lavish affairs. Alan Sugar writes in his memoirs about how he completed the signings of both Jürgen Klinsmann and David Ginola while on board his yacht in Monaco. Interestingly, it turns out that Klinsy pursued Tottenham rather than the other way around. Sugar, like the rest of us, was bemused as to why he chose Spurs over, say, a big club:[50] 'He would probably deny it, but I'm convinced that he had mapped out in his mind that he wanted to play in England, he wanted to be in London and he wanted to live in Highgate – and the nearest club to it was Tottenham.' Barnet probably had no idea how close they could have been to pulling off the transfer coup of the century.

In the days before football agents were more widespread, 1970s maverick Stan Bowles once tried to take on a kind of unofficial agent role himself. Towards the end of his career he played for Orient and was a bit of a mentor to a young John Chiedozie (who is now, we are contractually obliged to mention, the bouncy castle king of Hampshire). Stan reckons his tuition helped 'Cheddar' improve and get a move to Notts County: 'I told Chiedozie that he should look after me from the transfer proceeds because of the help I had given him, and he offered me an embarrassing amount of money: £100. I declined, saying: "Don't insult my intelligence!"' Now, at least one of your authors[51] holds the opinion that Stan was the greatest player in the history of the world, but even that author has to admit this was Stan's worst money-making idea since he wore odd boots made by two different companies to try and coin in sponsorship fees from both.[52]

Transfer negotiations are one of the areas of football about which we know least. We all talk about clauses, add-ons, image rights and all that, but few of us have ever actually been privy to the finer points of a proper contract. What is clear, though, is that club representatives, whether they be manager, chairman or CEO, can have very different negotiation methods.

Former Manchester United and Everton forward Norman Whiteside, for example, confirms the highly believable rumour that Ron Atkinson had a sunbed in his United office and even used it during contract discussions 'dressed only in his briefs and a pair of red goggles. It was probably quite a good negotiating tactic when I think about it, as it had the effect of unsettling you.' Well, it would, wouldn't it? It's unsettled us now, and we haven't even physically seen

—

50 Relax Spurs fans, we kid.

51 OK, only one.

52 Or the 2.45 at Haydock.

it. It's in our mind's eye, though. It's burnt in there, as deep as Ron's tan, for sure. Forever.

The strangest of all though, comes from Torquay chairman Mike Bateson. Neil Warnock writes that Bateson was a keen ventriloquist: 'He had this dummy called Algernon that he used to put on his arm. He'd get Algernon to talk to visiting directors, apparently. He had him dressed up in a tie, a blazer and a smart shirt.' This seemed pretty incredible to us, so we asked former lower-league striker Martin Gritton about it, as Grits was a popular striker for Torquay (as well as for most other lower-league clubs you care to name[53]). And Grits told us that not only was this true, but that Bateson would get Algernon to deal with contract negotiations for the Torquay players: 'We don't want to give him that, do we, Mr Chairman?' and all that. Yet, as terrifying as that sounds, we'd still prefer it to even a glimpse of Big Ron in his budgie smugglers.

A lovely subsection of contractual gossip is some of the unusual sweeteners that players have received when joining their new club:

NEIL REDFEARN: Upon signing for Watford, boss Steve Harrison apologised that chairman Elton John wasn't around to meet him as he usually would be for a new signing: 'Steve opened a drawer in his desk and said, "You'd better have these instead." He produced a couple of LPs, signed by the man himself.' Well, this is lovely. Like a segment from *Going Live!*

TED MACDOUGALL: On signing for Freddie Cox at Bournemouth: 'He offered me a wage of £28 per week, plus an extra £7 for each appearance and finally a set of curtains as a signing-on fee. Well it was a done deal.' That's very nice, but why curtains? Why not a TV or a sofa? Gives the impression Freddie just had some spare curtains lying about and had been trying to palm them off to new signings for months. We wouldn't have been quite as keen as Ted, mind – we'd have wanted to know a pelmet was included before sealing the deal.

53 While we're here, let's plug our Spotify podcast, *Football Legends*, based on our books and which features us, Grits and his amazing stories from his career, and former *Soccer AM* star turned YouTube sensation Robbie Knox.

RALPH MILNE: Given the above sweeteners, you'd be forgiven for thinking Ralph Milne would have been delighted to have been offered a choice between two cars when he joined Man United – a Ford Escort XR3i Cabriolet and a Ford Escort RS Turbo. But no: 'In my opinion, [they were] two of the worst cars you can imagine. I didn't want either of them.' Ungrateful sod, Ralphie. Still, he changed his tune eventually – to a sort of Alan Partridge tune: 'In the end I took the RS Turbo which went like shit off a shovel!' Jurassic Park.

Before we all start feeling sorry for the players faced with vent acts, desperate prospective managers breaching your home security and offers of home furnishings, though, it's worth noting that some players have some pretty swish tricks of their own. Tony Woodcock, for example, says he took the advice of Kevin Keegan when he got his move to Cologne: '"If they ask you what religion you are, say nothing", because you have to pay five per cent of your earnings to the Church.' Keegan and Woodcock, there, prepared to renounce God for the sake of a couple of extra quid.

Tony Cascarino was far more subtle in his tactics, believing that how you looked made a huge difference when negotiating a contract, even to the point of regularly dyeing his hair: 'You wouldn't believe the difference a dye makes. Present yourself to the chairman in your naturally greying state and you're asking for trouble: "Oh no, I'm not sure about this one. I don't think we'll get a year out of him." But add a bit of colour to your roots and the contract is in the bag: "Look at him, he's in great nick, I can't believe he's thirty-six! He must really look after himself." It's just an illusion but the illusion works.' Makes you wonder what on earth Sergio Agüero thought he was doing with that recent silver-grey dye he had going on. It's liable to shave a year off his next deal, minimum.

For Tony it was a bit of clever smoke and mirrors, a wily veteran using all his experience to win himself an extra yard, or an extra year. All perfectly legal. Unlike the actions of another former Villa striker, Andy Gray, who happily committed some kind of fraud to ensure his move from Wolves to Everton went through without a hitch. Basically, his boss at Wolves, Graham Turner, gave him his medical file to take to his potential new club, with Gray saying he 'handed me a folder that was as thick as my thigh'. Worried this could scupper the move, he says: 'I had a big open fire in my house and that night I sat in front of it sifting through this folder and chucking documents into flames.' We like to think he did a maniacal supervillain laugh as the flames licked at the evidence of his injury problems that were, it must be said, common knowledge anyway.

THE FINAL HURDLE

Finally, after everything is agreed, the signing happens. Many decisions will have been made to get to this stage, some more expected than others. When Don Revie nicked John Giles from Manchester United, he told Giles that Matt Busby had 'happily accepted the Leeds deal rather than rival offers from Blackburn and Manchester City, because he had a policy of selling a player to the lesser club – that way the player was less likely to embarrass him'. A policy that backfired pretty spectacularly on that occasion.

Ian Holloway 'jokingly' asked his wife to consult her tarot cards when considering signing an injury-troubled Paul Furlong for QPR: 'She dealt the cards and I have to admit, it was unnervingly accurate of his situation! The cards summed him up as being someone who had money around him and played at a higher level, but his main card showed an unbelievable desire to prove himself and Kim said, "If I was going on these cards, I should sign him."' You can laugh, but over 50 goals from just over 160 appearances proved Kim, and her cards, spot on. Shame she wasn't about when Rangers were spaffing millions in wages on Júlio César and José Bosingwa, really.

If Ollie had solid reasons for believing in Furlong, Simon Jordan had less evidence when sanctioning Peter Taylor's purchase of Stuart Green from Hull: 'Peter's daughter was dating Green and he wanted him down in London to make his daughter happy. So, to support Peter, I did it.' He must've been gutted she wasn't dating Michael Owen.

Our absolute favourite reason for finally deciding on the signing of a player comes from Stan Ternent, when he took the plunge to sign Chris Lucketti 'because he had built his own house from scratch, brick by brick. That told me far more about his strength of character than 1,000 words of bullshit on a poxy agent's CV.' Yeah, but surely that's exactly the sort of information you would find on a CV? Feels like Stan's being harsh on CVs there. It's not the CV's fault, Stan.

Once the contract has been 'inked', there's always the unveiling. But even that can go wrong. Before his glory days at Everton, Kevin Sheedy was at Liverpool, although mostly in the reserves. He should have seen the writing on the wall, really, because just after he signed on the dotted line, his new boss Bob Paisley uttered the immortal phrase: 'Congratulations and good luck, Philip.'

BOX TO BALLOT BOX

'Sediment of Guilt'

Do you remember Brexit? The one before the virus came? It was truly the political issue of our times, splitting the country in two like a Kevin De Bruyne through ball. It caused division up and down the land, tearing people apart across families, classes, communities and political parties. Unforgettably, nowhere was this division and rancour more keenly felt than among the personnel of the 1986 England World Cup squad. Peter Shilton and Chris Waddle took one side of the argument, Gary Lineker and Peter Reid the other, and it's fair to say that they all got plenty of stick from Twitter folk for sharing their views on the matter.

Footballers and politics, then – it's a minefield. Not a literal minefield, of the kind a vested and helmeted David Ginola campaigned to rid the world of in between shampoo ads in the 1990s, but a metaphorical minefield, you understand. Players should be grateful that their political actions didn't come under quite such scrutiny in the past, as one or two of them might have found themselves on the receiving end of stinging rebukes from people with long numbers at the end of their Twitter or Instagram handles.

Politics isn't a subject that comes up too much in a footballer's autobiography. Many of them are far too busy telling us about that time they hit the post at Pittodrie to get involved in telling us their views on Trident. And yet sometimes it pokes through, and we're here to round them all up for you, just in case you ever need to know where Mick Channon stands on the issue of apartheid – perhaps as part of a very niche pub quiz.

The main interaction between football and politics is in meetings with political figures. These players can be international superstars and that means that the great and the good and the politically motivated are often queuing up to be seen with them. Who can forget those images of Kevin Keegan playing head tennis with Tony Blair? Or a questionably braided David Beckham taking his England squad to meet Nelson Mandela? These things aren't always heavily orchestrated photo opportunities, however. A prime minister once appeared to Gareth Southgate, out of nowhere, in precisely his hour of need, a bit like Gandalf, only even more grey.

Before he became the waistcoated superhero and mum's favourite we know him as today, Southgate was of course once upon a time a very useful defender for England. Unfortunately, his international career will always be remembered for a certain penalty he missed to help send England out of Euro 96. You remember? Yeah, that one. However, what you might not have known is that after the match, as Gareth was dragging himself up the Wembley steps to the players' bar, presumably to drink himself daft, he bumped into Edwina Currie's fancy piece John Major: 'On the next flight of stairs, someone was calling. "Gareth, Gareth." When I looked behind me it was Mr Major running after me. "Gareth, you mustn't blame yourself for this, it's been an incredible tournament for the country. You will feel terrible for a while, but it's not your fault."'

John Major, there, giving it the full *Good Will Hunting*, and arguably setting Gareth back on the long road to the England redemption he currently enjoys. Although, let's face facts, it really was Gareth's fault. But then that's why John Major is a statesman, and we're not.

Major's far more, shall we say, divisive predecessor, Margaret Thatcher, is much more prolific in the lives and books we've studied. She's upsetting and inspiring people in equal measure, and meeting footballers, left, right and, centre – though mostly, of course, very, very right of centre.

At this point you must indulge us with a personal story. Years ago one of your authors saw Trevor Brooking on a train into Waterloo. After giddily chasing him up the platform and asking for his autograph, he was only too willing to oblige. Of course he was; he's Trevor Brooking. He's a lovely man. We wanted him to sign what we were carrying at the time, as we thought it would be funny to have a copy of J.G. Ballard's *Empire of The Sun*, which we were reading, signed by Tricky Trev. Instead Trevor offered a photograph to sign. He said he had some with him because he was off to the Conservative Party Conference, and the heart sank a bit if we're honest. For all these years since, we've tried to give him a pass and convince ourselves that he was going in an official Sport England capacity and that he wasn't really a Tory, but the pleasant memories he has here of meeting Thatcher on Downing Street with the England squad in 1980 throw considerable doubt on that idea.

'It was a wonderful occasion enjoyed by all the players and coaching staff.' See what we mean? A wonderful occasion, he says. 'Afterwards, we posed for photographs on the steps of No. 10 with the prime minister. One of the Fleet Street photographers produced a football and handed it to Mrs Thatcher. Ron said to her: "Be careful, Prime Minister or you'll be heading that ball down the street." She replied: "If I'm not mistaken, Trevor Brooking does the heading round here, doesn't he?" I was impressed by her knowledge. A week or so earlier I'd headed the only goal in West Ham's FA Cup Final win over Arsenal.' We can't know for certain whether the Prime Minister took her own avid interest in the beautiful game, or made an exception for that particular FA Cup Final as she knew she had guests coming, or if she was simply briefed by a subordinate, like they do when they give politicians *EastEnders* clips and Lewis Capaldi videos so that they can seem in touch if a real person asks them a question. What we do know for sure, however, is that neither Trevor Brooking, nor Margaret Thatcher, got many with their head.

Less thrilled to meet Thatcher was Mark Walters and many of his Rangers teammates, when she paid a visit to Ibrox: 'I remember quite a few of the players weren't that keen on her – me included – but the most vocal against the visit was Stuart Munro. He was furious to see her at Ibrox, and insisted politics shouldn't be mixed with sport. I've still got a photograph of Stuart looking the other way while she's talking to a couple of the dignitaries at the stadium. A lot of my teammates used to call me the 'left-wing left-winger', as my roots were steeped in Labour. It would be easier to tell you who liked Thatcher in the Rangers team at that time. I know Souey and Terry [Butcher] were fans, but there weren't many more.'

Well you can colour us shocked that Terry Butcher was a fan of Thatcher. We did not see that coming. And presumably nor did Stuart Munro, because he was looking the other way.

That all sounds like a very awkward afternoon at Ibrox. However, it may have been yet more awkward for Maggie if she'd paid a visit to Colchester's Layer Road in her 80s pomp, when she may have bumped into an old flame. Perry Groves, who began his career there, says that kit man Albert Danzy's favourite boast was that 'when he was a lad he'd gone out with' Thatch 'when she was just a grocer's daughter from Grantham'.

We don't appreciate the 'just' there, Perry. Nothing wrong with being a grocer's daughter. In fact we imagine there would be perks of going out with one. Free bread and milk, with the odd packet of biscuits thrown in, and you always know her dad's working till late. But we digress.

Groves tells us that this was at the height of Thatcher's power, with the Falklands War raging, and meanwhile this kit man was kissing and telling about her love life as a younger woman. Perry was wondering what some of the muckier-minded among you were no doubt wondering as well: 'I wonder if she was a goer. At least it would have shut her up for a while.'

We're not sure what to make of this from Perry. Everyday sexism aside, we shouldn't be surprised that he's gone straight below the waist here, given the sexual exploits he details throughout his book; but we simply don't want to think of Thatcher in that way. She had two children so, as far as we're concerned, it happened just the twice. And not even Gillian Anderson playing her in *The Crown* will change that and make us think of the former prime minister in a sexy way. No way. No sir. Nope. Not even … a little bit.

What were we saying? Ah, yes, the Falklands. While we're in the South Atlantic for a moment, let's clear something up. The memory of the 1982 war hung heavily over the England v Argentina clash at the World Cup four years later – you know the one, Hand of God, the greatest World Cup goal of all time, that weird shadow like a dandelion clock near the halfway line. In a bid to defuse the tension in the build-up to the match, both governments, both football associations, both managers and all the players were at great pains to say that the game had nothing to do with the war. As Diego Maradona writes: 'Of course before the match, we said that football had nothing to do with the Malvinas War'. See, told you. That clears that up, right? Well, maybe not: 'but we knew a lot of Argentinian kids died there, shot down like little birds. This was revenge. It was like recovering a little bit of the Malvinas.' Oh well, you can only try. As we say, sometimes the politics just slips out.

One of the men trailing in Maradona's wake as he was on his way to recovering a little bit of the Malvinas that day was Peter Reid, and that man is for sure no fan of Thatcher. With a tenacity that we can only wish was on display that afternoon in the Azteca Stadium, Reidy goes in with both feet on her famous assertion that 'there is no such thing as society'. The former Everton midfielder leaves no room for doubt about where he stands on the old politics, describing himself as a proud socialist. On Terry Butcher's mate he says 'most, if not all, of what Thatcher did at that time repulsed me because it went against everything that I stand for'. In particular he cites Hillsborough and Orgreave as moments that 'highlighted her indifference to ordinary people'.

Strong, stirring stuff. The following anecdote will come as no real surprise then, but is enjoyable all the same. Reid seemingly never met Margaret Thatcher face to face, but he did meet Boris Johnson once, and that will do just nicely for the following lovely bit of business.

The pair met when Peter Reid was asked to take charge of a celebrity England XI to play some German counterparts at the Madejski Stadium in 2006, and Boris Johnson was in the England squad. Trust us when we say this did not seem as unusual then as it sounds now. Some of you might even remember Johnson's involvement for a rugby tackle he performed on Maurizio Gaudino soon after coming on. He clattered head first into the former Man City midfielder in an act that gave an early warning of his attitude to Europe, and either reaffirms why you love our current Prime Minister, or confirms that you were right to be suspicious of him all this time (delete as appropriate).[54]

Reidy reminds us that the axe he quite rightly had to grind with Johnson concerned an article that appeared in *The Spectator* magazine, of which Johnson was then editor, which blamed drunken Liverpool fans for the Hillsborough disaster and claimed the city was 'consumed by self-pity'. Reid clarifies that Simon Heffer had actually written the piece, but Johnson had commissioned and ran it as editor. Peter says the 'thought of having him in my dressing room was offensive' and that his first instinct was for one of them not to take part, before realising the situation presented an opportunity.

Many managers must have longed for an excuse to tear a strip off a player as soon as they walked into their dressing room, but perhaps not that often at a charity match. Reid took full advantage of the meeting

54 The clip of this tackle is on YouTube and is worth a look for all its incompetent glory. You'll see the calm head of the much-missed Ray Wilkins leading Johnson away from his fallen opponent, as well as the future Prime Minister ominously/presciently wearing a no. 10 shirt.

in these star-studded surroundings, though: '"I've been meaning to have a word with you, you twat; having a go at Scousers, who the fuck do you think you are?" You could hear a pin drop and the likes of John Barnes, Richard Ashcroft, Nigel Benn and Sean Bean were all open-mouthed.' As a man who hasn't been told 'You are a fucking disgrace' nearly enough, Reid says Johnson was 'half-smirking' at first before realising his gaffer for the day was serious and 'shit himself'. Well you would. Peter Reid isn't somebody we'd want to upset even on just a personal level (perhaps over a parking space or a post office queue-jumping dispute). When he's coming out swinging on behalf of the people of an entire city, he must be formidable. This confrontation is one we'd love to have seen. Quite telling that none of the assembled Hollywood hard men, world-champion boxers, tiny indie frontmen or greatest rappers of all time were prepared to step in on Johnson's behalf here.

Reidy, if not quite alone in keeping the red flag flying, is certainly in the minority among his fellow professionals. Not particularly surprising in a profession that rewards individual talents so richly, but Joey Barton backs up the idea that most footballers are right wing, while himself railing against 'the imbalance between the accumulation of obscene wealth and the wider benefits of social progress'. Right-on, brother.

Wordy worthiness aside, Barton appears to be correct, certainly across the books we've read anyway. Terry Dyson, from the old days, inserts a Q&A in his own book in which he's happy to assert both that he doesn't 'think this country is firm enough on immigration', and 'I follow my parents and vote Conservative.' Dyson wouldn't be the first or last to follow his parents' voting pattern, but one young man struck out on his own, shook off those family ties, kicked against the expectations and advice of his father and ploughed his own furrow … and voted Conservative. Neil Warnock grew up proudly working class and tells us that 'Dad was Labour through and through. Like I said, the *Daily Mirror* was the only paper he'd ever have. He used to talk about Labour all the time. "This party's for the workers, son," he said, "just remember that, because no one else will help us but them."'

We can imagine the young Neil, gazing admiringly up at his dad from his Subbuteo, where he'd set up his solid 4-4-2 formation to defend deep, hit on the break and kick every bastard that moved, as he said this. 'So the first time I was eligible to vote, he took me down to the polling station', and his dad even told him where to put his cross, ensuring that nothing could go wrong now. 'Then he went outside and I scrawled my cross opposite the Conservative.' Far from being a mistake by the young Warnock, he says, 'It was my first act of rebellion against him. That'll teach you, I thought.'

Always best to vote with your heart we say, even if that heart is full of spite. He says that it will teach his dad a lesson but that's only the case if he told him what he'd done. That's how rebellion works. It's never clear in this instance whether or not his family ever found out what the teenage Warnock was up to. It would certainly have raised a few eyebrows if they had.

Although Joey Barton's truism that most footballers are right wing does seem to hold up, it wouldn't be fair to lump them all in together. Sure there are plenty of Conservative voters and supporters among their ranks, but as far as we can tell, there aren't that many dedicated followers of fascism. There is one, however, who will take your right wing, and raise you some more right wing – one who pleaded the following case after he felt he was misquoted in an interview:

'I told the interviewer that politically I was right wing. I'm not ashamed of it, the Right embodies values and ideals I believe in. This does not mean I'm a Nazi or a racist, it just means I identify with the Right.'

Fair enough you might think, let's not go around tarring every right-wing thinker with the brush of fascism. It's not as though this guy is fascinated by Benito Mussolini or anything like that now is it? 'Perhaps precisely because I am right wing, I am fascinated by Benito Mussolini.' Oh. 'Remember those mobile phone advertisements where they asked people who they most would like to have a one-to-one with? Ian Wright picked Dr Martin Luther King, my choice would have been Mussolini. I own dozens of Mussolini biographies. I think he was a deeply misunderstood individual.'

This, in case anyone is in doubt, is from the autobiography of Paolo Di Canio – gifted genius on the pitch, problematic views off it. Paolo bloody loves Mussolini, and devotes a lot of time to his own nationalist leanings in the latter stages of his book, alongside the odd recipe here and there. Now, as we say, we're prepared to be balanced and all that, but we do draw a line at calling Mussolini misunderstood. The reference to the 'One-to-One' ad is a funny one though. In case you don't remember that campaign, it was for a mobile phone company and whimsically asked celebrities of the day who their dream phone call would be with if time and, you know, people being dead wasn't a barrier to them picking up. Kate Moss picked Elvis Presley for example, and as Paolo remembers above, Ian Wright picked Martin Luther King. We'd like to think they asked Paolo before they settled on the more palatable Wrighty and Kingy version, just to imagine their faces when he said Mussolini. This is perhaps why Paolo was restricted to saucily stripping to his undies for a bubble bath ad, rather than trying to have a one-to-one chat with a fascist dictator who ended up swinging from a lamp post. It perhaps wasn't exactly the sort of thing they were looking for to punt their phones.

Some players aren't so opinionated, and prefer to act as social commentators, giving us their take on the issues of the day. For example, Jimmy Greaves feels moved in his memoirs to speak on a couple of infamous scandals in the swinging 60s: 'The Kim Philby Affair and in particular the Profumo Affair changed the attitude of the general public towards the Establishment. When we heard about the exploits of Christine Keeler and Mandy Rice-Davies in high society, including government circles, we suddenly saw the Establishment as being no purer than the rest of us. Respect, in all its forms, had begun to be diluted.'

Incredibly eloquent, erudite and incisive from Greavsie here, and we can no doubt draw a straight line from this take on the feet of clay found among the upper echelons in society and the anarchic approach to telly and football on *Saint and Greavsie*. Those spy and sex scandals are indeed a funny old game, after all.[55]

Gordon Banks was also rocked to his clogs by the Profumo affair. As a brief historical recap, the scandal involved an affair between John Profumo, Secretary of State for War under Harold Macmillan, and the 19-year-old Christine Keeler, Profumo's denial of said affair in Parliament, and the subsequent revelation that he was fibbing to the house. The whole thing, says Gordon, 'had shown the Establishment to be no purer than any other stratum of society'. Banks goes further and tells us that 'Macmillan gave way to Sir Alec Douglas-Home as prime minister, but the stigma of snobbery and aristocratic values lived on, in sharp contrast to what was happening elsewhere in society. In 1964

55 See our 'Christmas with the lads' chapter for a first-hand, and second-hand, account of a brush with Mandy Rice-Davies, when Frank Worthington takes her along to meet manager Jim Smith at a do.

when the nation took to the polls, Harold Wilson's Labour Party swept home on his promise of a new, modern society built on the fruits of the "white heat" of technology.' You don't get this from Jamie Vardy.

It's all there from Gordon and Greavsie. These World Cup heroes were there on the scene in the swinging 60s and are calling it as they see it. It's easy to see them simply as part of the same colourful wallpaper of that decade along with the scandals and governments they speak of, but here they are giving their take on how society was changing around them while we all thought they just cared about scoring goals or keeping them out. It's great, and we'd love to hear more insight into the political turmoil of the last few years from current footballers. Maybe we'll get it in good time, but as we've outlined above, players making political statements leave themselves open to all sorts of criticism and abuse. You only need to look at James McClean in the build-up to Poppy Day every year to see that. Only once their last ball is kicked can the current crop of players speak freely in some memoirs and let the public rebukes roll off them in the way older guys like Lineker and Shilton clearly do. Until then, we can only speculate as to the views of Bong on Brexit, Tarkowski on Trump, Mane on #MeToo or Danny Ings on all sorts of things.

* * *

The apartheid era in South Africa was a generation-spanning political issue that crops up several times in the written works of footballers. For a number of years while the oppressive regime enforcing white minority rule was in place, there was a sporting ban, which meant that the country could not take part in international sport. Unfortunately, this also meant there were lucrative opportunities for sports stars to ply their trade in South Africa on rebel tours, or simply by invitation – thus putting many players in something of a moral quandary. The hot takes on the political situation there are manifold and varied.

Malcolm Allison, for example, talks about taking a team to South Africa but maintains that they played against teams featuring both black and white players, and is vehemently anti-apartheid. However, the visit clearly left him with mixed feelings and some regret: 'Certainly it would be nice to take again a glass of wine on the slopes of Table Mountain. Without tasting the sediment of guilt.' Putting aside our own internal struggle with whether 'Sediment of Guilt' is a better name for a band halfway down the bill at the Download

Festival, or a Liam Neeson revenge thriller, it's interesting to see that Allison felt that conflict of earning money from a trip to South Africa quite keenly.

Mick Channon seems to have no such doubts on his conscience, saying, 'I know that many people believe sportsmen shouldn't go to South Africa because of their apartheid rules, but I was there to work.' Hmm, trying not to judge, trying not to judge. Channon does say, 'I'm most definitely opposed to apartheid, but I don't think it would help matters by Mick Channon refusing to go to South Africa.' Maybe not, Mick, but if everybody thought the same then where would we be? In fairness, Channon does say he has 'the same repulsion about South Africa's repressive measure as everyone else' and is at pains to stress he has no prejudice of his own; however, this last statement leaves us scratching our heads a bit. 'All I know is that you don't find starving black people in South Africa like there are in their millions in Ethiopia, the Sudan and Uganda for instance. That doesn't make apartheid right – but you've got to have a base to work from.' You can take that how you like, but it sort of sounds a bit like he thinks black South Africans living under a brutal apartheid regime should be grateful for what they have and put up with it, doesn't it?

A lot more casual about the whole thing entirely is, of course, Frank Worthington. A man who is seemingly a lot more casual about almost everything entirely, whether it's signing for Liverpool, playing for England or having sex in an aeroplane toilet. His take on time spent in the shadow of Table Mountain is this: 'After leaving Stockport I spent the summer of that year playing in South Africa for Cape Town Spurs and have to say that while I was no lover of apartheid, which was in force at the time, I loved the lifestyle.' So that's okay then. We've got Malcolm Allison choking on his sediment of guilt and Mick Channon tying himself in knots trying to justify earning a few tainted rand notes; meanwhile Frank's keeping it breezy and is able to completely separate the political issues from the drinking and dancing and vibing and that. Nice to be untroubled by such matters if you can be I suppose. 'No lover of apartheid' – that should cover it. It's a total cop out from Worthington, but it works. He's made the same decisions and taken the same money as Mick Channon, hasn't he? And yet, because he doesn't spend as much energy trying to justify himself, we feel less judgemental towards him. Maybe when it comes to politics you're better off staying well out of it.

And yet, let's finish with a story that shows that blissful political ignorance might not always be the best policy. Here comes Robbie Savage to tell us about that time being as thick as mince and drawing a blank on current affairs cost him a trip to the hospital. Savage tells us about a game in which he took a ball full in the face and was knocked out: 'I was lying on the pitch, and the club doctor came out to see if I was concussed. "Who is the Prime Minister?" he asked.

"I don't know," I replied.

"Robbie's got concussion. Get him off." I was carried off to hospital. They kept me in overnight too. The next morning they asked me the same question, and I still didn't know! I was young, I wasn't interested in politics, and it was a stupid question.'

Yes Robbie, it's the question that's stupid. 'Who is the Prime Minister?' is a perfectly fine question in our view. You don't need to be Kirsty Wark to know it, or indeed to be interested in politics. In fact, so basic is it, that you'd expect it to be asked by a time traveller in a film to establish their whereabouts in history. They'd be in a right mess if the first person they met was Robbie.

Leicester, Wales and *Strictly Come Dancing* legend Robbie Savage there, going to hospital for not being very bright. It's political correctness gone mad.

CHRISTMAS WITH THE LADS

'A real gun'

In the immortal words of Noddy Holder, It's Chriiiiiiisssstttmmaaaassss! That's right, it's time to talk about the most wonderful time of the year for football fans. Loads of games, loads of potential points, plus mince pies and grog waiting for us when we get home.

We need those Boxing Day games in particular. We emerge from our over-heated home, with its fug of sprouts, feeling bloated and mildly hungover, and we slog to the match, eager to draw in a deep lungful of football air, to sniff that unique blend of stale cigarette smoke laced with the sweet scent of thrice-boiled hot dogs, augmented by the whiff of misplaced hope. Nothing beats it.

But players and managers, it seems, are less keen. There are even dark rumours that some players try to ensure they serve a suspension that conveniently rules them out of the Boxing Day fixture. We've all had our suspicions about the pre-Christmas shirt tug or lazy trip, haven't we? Well, Neil Ruddock confesses this ruse in his autobiography, so it's real, and you need to deal with it.

Every year, managers complain about the Christmas rush of fixtures, and how it's not fair on families. But you don't hear panto dames moaning about their festive workload and asking the show to be moved to the summer months do you? Man up, lads. At least they do recognise, however, that there is nothing better at Christmas than seeing someone's little face glow with excitement as they unwrap the present you've just given them, shaking with anticipation at the goodies inside.

GIFTS

Well, at least until they find a sheep's heart nestled carefully amidst the crumpled crepe paper.

Yes, it's Secret Santa time. Where most people would play it safe with chocolates or booze or one of those quirky nostalgia books available from next to the till in Oliver Bonas, for footballers this is yet another area ripe for some top-quality banter.

Stuart Pearce was an early adopter of the Secret Santa, and credits himself with importing it from Forest to Newcastle. If you're not familiar with the sheep's heart reference, this was the gift given by Shay Given to Newcastle teammate Alessandro Pistone (Pearce adds that it was bought 'from the butcher' – you know, just in case we were concerned that the national goalkeeper of Ireland may have, by dead of night, driven out to the country, found a field of sheep, selected one, cornered it, slaughtered it, hacked its heart from its lifeless body, took it home, put it on ice, then wrapped it up the next morning to give to a teammate who he felt maybe didn't try hard enough in games sometimes).

A similar thing happened at Forest when Kingsley Black gave Bryan Roy a puppet with a pea for a heart, but if that makes it seem like the British and Irish may have targeted 'the foreigns' a bit (coming over here with their silky skills but an unwillingness to 'put a foot in'), rest easy. As Pearce explains: 'The foreign boys really made an effort.' And it is true. Nobby Solano gave Alan Shearer a Mary Poppins doll and Andreas Andersson, who must surely have had access to some kind of witness relocation programme (in which you'd hope they'd try a bit harder with his name), made Duncan Ferguson a convict costume, with upward arrows and all that.

Pearce doesn't report on how Ferguson reacted – or Pistone, or Roy, come to that and no one took nasty revenge in the Friday five-a-sides. In fact, the only person he pinpoints as not quite getting into the festive spirit is the very English Warren Barton. Apparently, the Newcastle boys called him Oompa Loompa ('he had a long body and short legs'), which he didn't appreciate, and Pearce made it worse one Christmas by giving him a pot of something he labelled 'Dwarf Growing Cream'.

Perhaps the best gift was one that didn't quite happen: Duncan Ferguson travelled all over the North East trying to buy a llama for Solano (he's from Peru, where they like llamas) but couldn't find one.[56]

56 It's all alpacas these days, isn't it? We'd never heard of an alpaca till our 30s, now they're everywhere, like salted caramel and pulled pork. Dame Kelly Holmes actually owns six of them (one of them is even called Crème Caramel) to help her keep her fields well trimmed. If only Duncan had known.

Shay Given might have been able to source him a sheep, had he asked. In many ways, they're the llamas of the Pennines.

We had always thought that Secret Santa was a fairly modern invention, but John Sitton has memories of it going back as far as 1980, when he received a pair of boxing gloves: '[It] raised a laugh and tormented me, but I like to think I took it in good heart. It probably came as a consequence of me having to attend court again on a second charge of Actual Bodily Harm.' Yeah, it was probably that.

Sitton's uncertain phrasing about taking the joke suggests even he thinks maybe he didn't, and it is true that Secret Santa can be a minefield. Yes, you're covered by the safety of anonymity, but if you're a good-hearted person like, say, Peter Crouch, there can be feelings of regret if a present is accidentally misjudged.

In Crouchy's *How to be a Footballer*, he tells of how one year he drew Liverpool boss Rafa Benítez out of the hat. At that time, Rafa was swanning about in a leather jacket and the players reckoned he was trying to compete with José Mourinho in the style stakes. It was a tough ask, really, because whatever you think of Mourinho and his often deathly football, the man at that time was pouty-faced sex on a stick in a cool raincoat, while Benítez was … not. Crouch thought he'd play on this a little, so his gift for Rafa was a new leather jacket and Mourinho's autobiography. 'You should have seen his expression when he opened the gifts. His face just fell. Oh no, I thought. I've actually offended him.' Peter finishes by saying: 'I never told him it was from me. Until now. Sorry Rafa.' Well, best to get these things out in the open.

In the olden days (the 1960s) the banter was at least much kinder – even sweet. Terry Dyson, part of the Spurs double-winning side of 1961, says one year the lads gave him the novel *Little Women*: 'The joke was, of course, that I was only 5ft 4in, single and on the lookout for a little lady!' We absolutely love literary banter, a form of banter that has sadly largely died out in the intervening years (give or take the odd German player being left *Mein Kampf* under the Weihnachtsbaum). The Spurs lads didn't stop there, either, as they clubbed together to buy chairman Fred Bearman, then 88 years old, a copy of *Lady Chatterley's Lover*, which had only recently had its ban overturned for all the sex with gardeners and that. Dyson says: 'Dear old Fred had told the gathering, '"After I've read it I'll tell all you boys about it."' Before adding, 'Now, who gave Dave Mackay the massive bull bollocks? Fair play, lad, whoever that was. Did you slice them off yourself or go to a butcher?'[57]

The apprentices of yore would probably be excluded from Secret Santa duty, probably because they'd be too busy recovering from whatever form of ritualised humiliation they'd been forced to endure. Still, their pain would at least be soothed by a Christmas bonus from the pro whose boots they had diligently scrubbed all year.

Yet there does not seem to be a standard amount for these tips. At Norwich, Chris Sutton says two pros, Paul Blades and Tim Sherwood, gave him £20 each, while club captain Ian Butterworth only coughed up a tenner. Poor form, Butters. All of those rewards seem low, however, when you consider that Steve Hodge reckons Charlie George gave him £50 one year, and that was a decade earlier. Down the road at Ipswich, Kieron Dyer, who was only four or five years behind Sutton in coming through the ranks, says that Gus Uhlenbeek gave him a massive £200, 'which I was over the moon about. That seemed like a fortune in those days.' Elsewhere, Julian Dicks gave a young Frank Lampard a hefty £100, making Lee Chapman's £20 the same year look a bit tight.

The interesting thing is that while a fair few players report on what they were given as apprentices, not many are as open about the tips they give to their equivalents once they've made it. The exception is Alan Shearer, who had Brett Ormerod in his employ at Blackburn. In his diary, Shearer writes: 'I give him the choice of £30 in his hand or a bit of a gamble. He can choose to pick one of three cups containing £1, £25 or £50. He decided to go for the cups and pockets the £50.' Ormerod deserves that for taking the gamble, and it seems like a great bit of fun, but did Shearer fancy himself as a bit of a Jim Bowen back then?[58] Had Brett chosen the £1, would Al have given it the big 'here's what you could've won', before folding the £50 note up and tucking it into his top pocket? Also, if Gus Uhlenbeek was chucking about £200 around that sort of era, £50 seems a little short for England's top striker, does it not?

THE CHRISTMAS PARTY

The footballers' Christmas party has become notorious over the years for scenes of drunken disgrace as much as joyful merrymaking. No

—

57 He did not say this.

58 Bowen was a Blackburn fan, of course. He'd have been proud.

wonder Mick Quinn proclaims it to be the footballer's best night of the year. Their parties, though, are a bit different to ours. Keith Gillespie hints at just why this is towards the end of his book, when he's struggling with his new life working a 9–5 job:

> I remember sitting at a Christmas party, listening to a guy complaining about the fact that he was paying his secretary £32,000 a year, and all I could think about was the contrast in the discussion from my old Christmas bashes. Some of the flashier lads might have spent £32,000 on a round of drinks. It wasn't the life for me; I was a duck out of water.

Thirty-two grand! Leaving aside the perplexing thing about ducks and water (ducks are quite happy out of water, Keith. They migrate by flying and everything. He means fish, right?), Gillespie's remarks are revealing. Footballers' parties may have superficial similarities to ones we may experience: they go out, they might do fancy dress, they drink, they have a good time. But somehow it's all just very … *different*.

FANCY DRESS

Footballers love a Christmas fancy dress party. Many understandably opt for the safe costume options: your Mr Incredibles, your Power Rangers, your Batmans. Especially your Batmans. It is a statistical fact[59] that no footballer Christmas fancy dress event has ever passed without at least one Batman showing up. According to Jamie Vardy, even Leicester centre-back Robert Huth went as Batman one year, which seems an unfathomable choice considering he would make an outstanding Herman Munster given just a small amount of make-up. Others to indulge in some Dark Knight action include Carl Cort, Robbie Savage, Niall Quinn (in his City days) and Lee Howey, who adds: 'This was proper Batman too with latex body armour and a cool mask. None of your Fathers For Justice rubbish.' Fair play, although we bow to no one in our love for Adam West's glorious Caped Crusader and this dig at his timeless outfit feels uncalled for.

59 Caution: fact not checked.

Howey's turn as Batman came at Sunderland's 1996 Christmas party, which seems to have been something of a vintage year for the Black Cats. Niall Quinn went as Friar Tuck, the injured Tony Coton was Long John Silver, Alex Rae was Madonna and there were assorted Nazis, 'including Martin Scott who was tastefully decked out as Adolf himself'. Different times (they weren't).

If that seems edgy, let us usher you to Merseyside for news of what goes on at Liverpool during the festive season. And we're doing this despite Jamie Carragher's words in the foreword to Michael Owen's recent book: 'My only hope in reading it is he doesn't go into too much detail about the Liverpool FC Christmas parties!' Sorry Carra, no room for the squeamish here, and as Michael didn't, we will. There's just too much gold not to.

The place to start is not a quote but a picture from Bruce Grobbelaar's book, *More Than Somewhat*, that has the most astounding squad photo we've ever laid eyes on. It's the 80s. It's Christmas. And it's the all-conquering Red Machine in full fun mode, done up as Nazis, comedy Arabs and with enough blacking up to make Justin Trudeau blush. Less pushing boundaries than setting fire to them before urinating on the cinders. Even John Barnes turned up dressed as a member of the Ku Klux Klan one year. He stands by it in his book, saying the KKK *should* be laughed at and perhaps he has a point. Meanwhile, John Aldridge remembers Kenny Dalglish cheekily wearing a judge's costume just after Jan Molby had been released from jail following his *hilarious* dangerous driving conviction.

King Kenny, it seems, saw the Christmas party as prime banter season, because, according to John Wark, another year he wore a Liverpool shirt with a hump in the back, a bit like Quasimodo. The players couldn't guess who he'd come as, so eventually he had to reveal all: he was Peter Beardsley.

'No one laughed louder than Peter,' Wark says. Is that true? Or did Peter laugh on the outside, cry on the inside and suppress all his rage for years until he was in a position where the boot could be on the other foot. Or the hunch could be on the other … er, back?

But let's just pause there for a moment. Little is really known about the enigma that is Kenny Dalglish. He's rightly revered, of course, for his achievements as a player and as a manager. But beyond that, what do we really know? Chiefly, it's that he's a decent man, he's a strong character and he speaks at lightning speed while barely moving his lips. He was undoubtedly a great manager – for one thing, he needed to replace himself in the great Liverpool 80s side and did it by signing Beardsley himself. A masterstroke. Apart from all that, the one thing we know for sure, because it's what everyone who knows him says about him, is that he has a fast and dry wit.

So what happened that Christmas? Dalglish's teams played tremendous football, but that night he went full-on classic Wimbledon: it was absolute route one stuff. Maybe he was so busy he forgot to sort a costume and, panicking, he finally thought, 'I know, I'll just stick a Liverpool shirt on and shove a cushion up the back: instant Beardsley! I bet no one will laugh louder than Pedro.'

Imagine this happening at your place of work, though. Your boss, a hard man but one loved and respected by probably all of you, agrees to a Christmas party. A colleague, say Kevin from accounts, who's perhaps not blessed with the looks of Ryan Gosling, but is a vital member of your team, will be there, hoping for a fun night out with his mates. It's all going well, and then suddenly in comes the boss, dressed as the Hunchback of Notre Dame – a deaf, half-blind, lovelorn, bell-ringing grotesque – and challenges everyone to guess who he is. When everyone fails, he points at the aforementioned colleague and says: 'It's him! Because he is *proper* ugly, amirite lads?!' HR would get involved first thing in the morning.

They enjoyed dressing up at Leeds in the 1980s, too. Ian Snodin remembers one Christmas when teammate Brendan Ormsby opted for a classic Roman costume (it's unclear if it was centurion or toga, sadly). After many drinks, the squad went to a club, where it became clear that Ormsby had gone commando: 'He was lifting the dress up and the women present were very excited. His manhood was a fair size, so he had every reason to flaunt it.'

Yes, it is generally accepted that indecent exposure is absolutely fine as long as you possess a large penis. Had Ormsby's organ been undersized, however, he would have been arrested immediately and women would have run, screaming, from the club. Don't blame us, blame the Magna Carta. It's all there.

The appearance of Brendan's bone has left us with no choice but to disqualify him from our Top 10 Favourite Christmas Party Outfits Worn by Footballers list, which you can find, well, here:

	Name	Costume	Notes
1.	Phil Thompson	Boy George	The stuff of nightmares. Imagine that looming up at you from the darkness. But maybe this is where John Motson got his otherwise meaningless 'Culture Club' reference from.
2.	Dale Gordon	A Tampon	Regular readers will know of this carefully crafted masterpiece, for which Dale bravely painted himself white and hung tampons about his person. Disco Dale loved a Christmas party – Harry Redknapp says at West Ham one year he wanted to cruise around London's trendy West End in an open-top bus. They were 15th(?) at the time.
3.	Jermaine Pennant	Osama bin Laden	Pennant augmented his bullet-festooned outfit at a Stoke City do with an AK-47 – 'a plastic one, obviously'. Obviously. But he reckons the furore surrounding this cost him a sweet transfer to the States.
4.	Craig Johnston	Fred Astaire from the front, Folies Bergère dancer from the back	Sounds hauntingly beautiful.
5.	John Aldridge	Cooperman from *Russ Abbot's Madhouse*	Aldo claims an Everton-supporting cabbie refused to take him home, suggesting he fly instead.
6.	Kevin Ball	Little Bo Peep	It's like he's daring people to laugh. Lee Howey says he wore a pair of 'fetching kitten heels'.

7.	Alex Rae	Madonna	The beauty of dressing as Madonna is that she's a Bowie-like chameleon with a raft of different images over time. We reckon Rae went full Blonde Ambition era.
8.	David Batty	A Russian Cossack	A fine choice, except the boots were too tight, causing 'a nasty gash down my big toe, which later became infected'. He needed pain injections to get through games for a while. A man truly suffering for his art.
9.	Richard Edghill	Billy Bunter	Says Edgy: 'I went as Billy Bunter, the fat schoolkid.' One for the teenagers. The following year he went as Just William. Maybe. Rich loved a school uniform, though; years later at QPR they all went to a school disco (not a real school, obviously).
10.	Jamie Carragher	Quasimodo	Proper Quasimodo this time, not pretending to be Peter Beardsley. In his book, Jamie remembers getting pictured cavorting with a stripper in the *News of the World*: 'And the hump wasn't just on my back, unfortunately.' The perils of men in tights.

ENTERTAINMENT

The clichés of the office Christmas party are nibbles, drinks, work clothes with Santa hats and some joker photocopying their arse. Those clichés may well be false these days – it seems unlikely anyone has photocopied their bottom cheeks since the 1990s, especially what with all the worry about climate change and paper waste these days – but whatever the truth is, the kind of entertainment laid on for footballer Christmas parties is a little different. The basics are probably the same:

booze, ill-advised snogging and some casual violence. But footballers being footballers turn it right up to 11. Most do anyway. Brian McClair says that while Man United were winning everything in sight, they'd content themselves with a quiet Italian meal at Christmas. It's almost as if the football was more important.

In his most recent autobiography, Alex Ferguson confirms the sweet innocence of United Christmas fun back then when he dishes out some high praise to one youngster in particular: 'Wee Paddy Lee was terrific at animal impressions. Every Christmas he would do ducks, cows, birds, lions, tigers – everything. Even ostriches. The players would be rolling about.'

What's particularly nice is that this seems to have developed into a kind of Christmas tradition. We imagine Paddy resolutely refusing all year to bust out his goose honk or cow moo, but come Christmas, there he stood, proudly belting out his quacks and bleats to his appreciative crowd. The Class of 92 really could have had a cracking Nativity: Becks as Joseph, Giggsy as Mary, Butty and the Nevilles as the Wise Men, Scholesy as the Baby Jesus and Paddy as all the animals in the stable.

The likes of Micky Quinn, however, would always long for something more hardcore, and that's probably the only reason he never played for United. Micky recalls that typically the dos he attended started with the basics – the hire of a room in a pub and the booking of strippers. Let's allow Mick to pick up the story once a few drinks have been taken and the lads have watched the show: 'Then the birds send the pint pots round and everyone puts in a few quid for "extras". This usually involves them shagging a couple of apprentices on stage with the rest of us gathered around and cheering them on. In those days lads would often be virgins. But you try getting a hard-on in front of 30 baying footballers. It ain't easy, but it all adds to the fun of the party.'

Apologies, there should have been a warning there. These lads are really putting the grot into Santa's grotto. We can't be sure that all footballer Christmas parties of Quinn's era, or any era, were like this, but at the same time we can only report on what we've read. And, as you can see, the impression Quinny gives is that, yes, this really *is* what *all* footballer Christmas parties are/were like. It's fairly well known that Brazilian legend Garrincha lost his virginity to a goat[60] – it's less

60 That's 'a' goat not THE G.O.A.T, you know, like the kids call Messi, or Ronaldo or Phil Jones.

well known that many a British footballer lost his to a stripper in front of dozens of leering, slightly older, very drunk men, possibly wearing tinsel or dressed as Boy George. It's an authentic vision of hell, and not an environment we feel we'd have thrived in to be honest. In a list of occupations where you are most likely to see your co-workers having sex in front of your own eyes, 'footballer' must be second only to 'porn star'.

Quinn's final line is a beauty, too: 'It all adds to the fun of the party.' Yes, quite often when we're at a party, with the music going, the drink flowing and the chat … er, chatting, we think to ourselves: 'This is really good. But what would make it *great* would be watching a teenager trying to achieve tumescence before having nervous sex with a lap dancer for our amusement.'

Backing him up, Lee Howey says they hired similar performers at Sunderland, and 'The younger members of our party were made to go on stage and "assist", which they did with an aplomb best left undescribed on the printed page.' Interestingly, this line is one of the few documented occasions of 'aplomb' being used other than to describe a well-taken goal.

Perhaps times changed, or maybe it was different from club to club, but Dwight Yorke didn't feel the need to hire professionals for Manchester United's Christmas do, and with 200 tickets to distribute, he felt he had only one sensible option: 'I went on the prowl around Manchester, firstly to clubs and then even into the Trafford Centre, to invite the girls. Any girl who made me go "wow" I would stop, introduce myself and simply hand them a ticket.' Yes, that is correct. One of the most famous and well-known football stars of his era stood around a mall handing out tickets to women with the virtual promise of meeting a load of wealthy, happy and likely sloshed footballers. Things had changed quickly since McClair's day. Of course, it worked: 'There must have been a 3–1 ratio of girls to boys and that's just how I wanted it!' Gotta play the percentages, right? Interestingly, 3-1 was almost exactly his games-to-goals ratio while at Aston Villa (annoyingly it was more like 2-1 at United).

Taking a partner to the Christmas party has its dangers, then, although you wouldn't expect that introducing her to the gaffer would hold too many risks. Well, not unless you're Frank Worthington, your partner is model Mandy Rice-Davies, of Profumo affair notoriety, and your Birmingham gaffer is Jim Smith, anyway. Over to Frank: 'Smithy was all charm. "Very pleased to meet you," he said, offering his hand before adding, "I can't believe it ... I used to w*** over you when I was a lad.' In any scenario, this would be an unexpected thing to say, but it seems even creepier when you learn that Smith was four years *older* than Rice-Davies, making us question exactly what he meant by 'when I was a lad'. Incredibly, Rice-Davies took it all in her stride: 'She just smiled, completely unphased, as I took her by the shoulders and ushered her away. Great woman,' wrote Frank, with a clear note of understandable triumph.

That's probably enough sexy chat for Christmas now – you're probably wondering where that other yuletide staple is – violence. Let's start at that aforementioned Sunderland party. That night, Richard Ord, dressed as a Mountie, became upset at a local gentleman's unwanted interest in Mrs Ord, and eventually decided to have a word. With his fists. This quickly spiralled into a spectacular Battle Royale between the gentleman's mates on one side, and the Sunderland squad, dressed, you will remember, as assorted superheroes, Robin Hood sidekicks and fascists, on the other. Howey remembers: 'Everyone was fisticuffing. Even Tony Coton was belting someone with his crutch.'

The police eventually brought an end to it, but later paid a visit to the squad, armed with CCTV footage of the melee. Howey says that instead of a straightforward dressing down, the sergeant took the opportunity to flex his comic chops by embarking on a deadpan commentary of the evidence on the tape, saying of Ord: 'We intend to contact our colleagues in the Royal Canadian Mounted Police to see which of their officers is currently visiting this area. He is clearly in contravention of his oath of office.' And of Batman Howey: 'And who was this caped crusader? The Northumbria constabulary has no need of vigilantism.' Apparently, the verbal mauling the squad had from Peter Reid was far worse, although Howey can't resist adding, just in case there was any doubt: 'We won the fight, too.' Well of course you did. You're Batman.

Vince Hilaire also tells of a night of chaos during a Portsmouth Christmas night out. The night began with a food fight between the players and some local 'builders and decorators' also out celebrating the festive season. That developed, vaguely, into a 'massive free-for-all'. Once they'd been booted out of that gaff, they (and the builders, it seems) bought a tonne of foam spray cans from a joke shop and went to a favoured club, where 'Things started playfully, but then got totally out of control. Punches were being thrown. Kevin O'Callaghan nearly lost an eye ... it was mayhem.' Before we all get carried away with the electrifying image of a fist fight shrouded in foam, let's spare a thought for O'Callaghan here, whose close shave with eye loss came hot on the heels of having his arm deliberately broken in *Escape to Victory* just so that Sylvester Stallone can play in goal. Still, there were lighter moments, such as when Hilaire noticed that 'someone had written in red ink on the wall of the club, "Noel Blake has got the biggest cock you've ever seen".' Was it in Noel Blake's handwriting by any chance?

Famously, it was at a Christmas party where Joey Barton stubbed out his cigar in youth player Jamie Tandy's eye. Barton's version of events in his book, *No Nonsense*, does qualify this horrible incident (a little), and it's well worth reading the whole breathless account, including how Tandy set fire to Barton's shirt first. But we can't help thinking about how different this incident might have been, though. Just three years later the smoking ban was in force, meaning it was unlikely anyone would have set fire to anyone's clothes, and Barton would not have had access to a lit cigar. In many ways, that whole incident was down to the slow pace of modern governance.

It's not like the powers that be hadn't had any warnings about mixing footballers, drink, Christmas and naked flames either. Flying Everton winger Mark Ward freely admits in his book that, years earlier, when Dave 'Waggy' Watson turned up dressed as a Hawaiian girl in a grass skirt, his immediate response was to think 'Are those skirts flammable?' Well he's only human, and there's only one way to find out, after all. 'One whoosh and his a*** was ablaze. That gave us both a bit of a fright but after putting out the flames, Waggy chased me around the reception area with no back to his skirt and his singed bum on display to all.' The most important thing, by the way, when relating a story about setting a human being on fire, is to asterisk any mildly naughty words – just in case any minors are reading. At least the incident did give Wardy a fright: who could've known that applying a naked flame to bone-dry plant matter would have had such a spectacular result?

Ward has time to note that there was an entrance fee of £25 to the party that year, explaining: 'It was good value, because that got you entry into the nightclub, a buffet, a stripper and a free bar until about 11pm.' Lovely detail. Almost wistful.

Astonishingly, igniting his teammate's clothing ranks only second on the list of Worst Things Mark Ward Did At A Christmas Party. Another time, Ward was dressed as Dennis the Menace and for some reason John Ebbrell, done up as Popeye, spent the night playfully punching Ward before running off. Well, fairly playfully. Ward says the last time he did it, it was 'quite hard actually'. Losing his patience, Ward gave chase, and accidentally bumped into a cowboy (who turned out to be Dave Watson's neighbour – sensibly not dressed as a Hawaiian woman). Seeing a chance of fun, Ward grabbed the realistic gun out of the cowboy's holster and continued to look for his prey.

He saw Barry Horne (dressed as the Pope) chatting to Neville Southall (costume unknown) at the bar and asked them if they'd seen Ebbrell, explaining that he was planning to shoot him with the toy gun he'd borrowed. These were the days of Pope John Paul II travelling about in his bulletproof popemobile, so understandably, Horne jokingly suggested Ward shoot the Pope instead.

> I raised the gun, aimed it straight at the centre of The Pope's chest and pulled the trigger. The noise was staggering, unbelievable. And as this bang reverberated around the bar, we were all stunned to see a massive flash of fire shoot from the barrel and Barry, who took a direct hit, was flung backwards. It was a real gun! There'd been a bullet in the chamber. I'd shot one of my team-mates at point blank range in the chest. The saving mercy – and thank God for it – was that the bullet was a blank, designed to crumple and ignite on impact rather than explode.

We've all had a night where we couldn't find Popeye so we shot the Pope instead, right? To be fair, there's only two letters difference between them. But yes. Mark Ward almost killed Barry Horne because some insane friend of Dave Watson's brought an actual gun to a Christmas party. And, yes, he does say the bullet was designed to 'ignite on impact'. Poor Horne's papal robes did catch fire and had to be put out by a quick-thinking mate who threw a pint of beer on him.[61] The one consolation was that Wardy had been wondering since

61 Thank goodness for that free bar.

Horne walked in that night whether his costume was flammable, so that was that question answered.

Tony Woodcock has an even more horrific story from his otherwise pedestrian diary of a season at Arsenal, *Inside Soccer*. Buried among many more prosaic entries comes this startling entry opener: 'The Christmas lunch ended badly. Sundy got stabbed.' As openings go, that is pretty strong. The follow-up sentence to a line like 'The Christmas lunch ended badly' should be about someone choking on the sixpence in the pudding, but no. There was an actual stabbing.

'Sundy' is Alan Sunderland and here's what happened. The Arsenal boys came across some Spurs fans during their celebrations. Obviously, this could have gone wrong, but Woodcock says everything seemed pretty friendly – until he went to the bathroom: 'This guy from the other table was in there. And he said, "Enjoying yourself?" and I said, "Yes, it's a really good do", and it all seemed perfectly amicable. But then he went to the basins to wash his hands, and when he had finished he snapped the glass shelf below the mirror and went out with it. I went out to discover he'd just gone up behind Sundy and stabbed him in the neck with the glass and run out.'

Awful stuff, but what did the Spurs-supporting culprit have against poor Sundy? Surely attacking Woodcock would have been more efficient? Not that we're suggesting he should have, obviously. Anyway, in the melee that inevitably ensued, one of the perpetrator's mates 'got his nose splattered', and began saying he was going to sue because his clothes had been ruined by the blood. So, while poor Sundy was nursing a punctured neck and probably wondering when someone might call an ambulance, the squad 'had a quick whip round to pay for the damage' to the brawler's clothes, 'which we shouldn't have done, because we then heard that he had been one of the people involved'. It was only after placating him that they took their poor teammate to the hospital, where he had seven stitches.

God bless us everyone!

OVER LAND AND SEA

'A scone with clotted cream'

Tennis great Arthur Ashe famously said that success was a journey, not a destination. What we think he meant by that, if we may speak for Arthur for a moment, is that getting there is half the fun. And having brushed up on the tales of travel and transport within the prose of our pros, we're inclined to agree. Here then, is what we've learnt about what happens when a group of footballers travel together.

The journey of a thousand miles begins with a single stepover, so let's begin – up where the air is clear, above the clouds, zipping through the blue. Come fly the occasionally friendly skies.

PLANES

Everything we've learned through our research tells us that almost anything can happen to our football heroes. And that's just on the ground. Thousands of feet up in the sky, all bets are off. There is fear, there is bad behaviour, but sometimes it's just nice.

When Leeds were flirting with the pinnacle of the English game in the era of David O'Leary's babies, their travel sounds comfy. O'Leary is full of praise for Peter Ridsdale and his 'use of a Swiss company called PrivatAir which provided luxury planes with spacious accommodation and excellent service'. O'Leary claims there's a 'false economy' in booking cheap flights because they can cause injuries. This is surely true. Peter Ridsdale has never been accused of spending way over the top on anything just for the sake of it.

Travelling with England sounds even nicer. Gareth Southgate says you get 'served a scone with clotted cream' for afternoon tea, which is delightful, while David Platt considers his England years well spent because he got to savour the comedy stylings of the man, the legend Steve Harrison. Platty remembers that 'the funniest man

I ever met' entertained the squad for an entire 'twenty-three hour flight to Australia' once. That sounds exhausting. Surely there are only so many impressions and pratfalls one man can do, but at least morale would have been sky-high even once they'd landed. We can only hope the other passengers enjoyed it as much, and that Harrison didn't pull out his showstopping party piece. You will all know by now about Harrison's trick of pooing into a cup from the top of a wardrobe or some bannisters (depending on who you believe) – and an in-flight version of that crowd-pleaser raises the tantalising prospect of Harrison sticking his bum out of the overhead lockers, but that's a very high-tariff manoeuvre, and not advisable, even for the talented Harrison.

Theo Walcott, who will always be a wide-eyed innocent teenager in our eyes, tells a lovely story about his finest moment on England duty. You may think it's his hat-trick in Croatia but Theo seems to have enjoyed the computer games they played on the flight back from it even more: 'We played a Socom game the whole way back. It was the SAS against terrorists, and we played five-a-side. Me, JT, Bridgey, Lamps, Rio, Wes, Wayne, Ashley and a couple of others. There was a real feeling of bonding on that journey.' Well it passes the time doesn't it? Good luck to them, as long as it doesn't startle the pilot. Rumours that John Terry was in full battle fatigues ready for an end-of-game presentation are completely without foundation.

Every opportunity to bond and build a team ethic on these journeys should be taken. Pity poor Alan Shearer, then, who was once put on his own plane away from the rest of the Newcastle squad 'because it took our insurance over the top', says Kevin Keegan. We'll question this if we may. Sure, Shearer was once the world's most expensive signing but there have been other expensive signings before and since. Do they always fly alone? Are we suggesting that Messi, Neymar and Suarez all had to travel separately for the insurance when they were together at Barcelona? Imagine the scenes for that Galactico-era Real Madrid side! It must have looked like the Red Arrows or *Stop The Pigeon*. We think somebody's having Kevin on here – or Alan. Given that the only Newcastle company Shearer was given for the duration of his 12-hour flight to the Far East was Peter Beardsley, we reckon it was Big Al.

One sure-fire way of rallying the troops when they do let you all fly together is getting the goalie to dress up. They're irrepressible, aren't they, goalies? What are they bloody like? Andy Goram decided to pep up a tense Hibernian squad on a journey to Hungary to play Videoton[62] in 1989 by convincing a stewardess to switch clothes with him – her into his Hibs tracksuit, and he into her uniform. 'I then went down the plane serving people. I had the scarf around my head, the make-up, the lipstick, the lot.' Andy says it went down a storm with players and fans alike: 'They loved it, and the plane was in uproar.' Plus, it worked, as the relaxed Hibs side won the game well. Of course, Goram was captain at the time. It takes the very best skippers to know when his players need an arm round the shoulder, when they need a kick up the backside, and when they need him to drag up and serve tiny packets of peanuts off a trolley.

The 'goalie dressing up' fun needn't stop when the wheels hit the tarmac, though. Legendary eccentric John Burridge once took it into the arrivals hall. Andy Gray, his Villa teammate and friend[63] says that 'Budgie was the biggest joker I ever met', and that's coming from someone who's worked extensively with Richard 'It was just banter' Keys. Gray well remembers one time when Villa were coming home from a European match and Burridge ran ahead of the group, 'managed to get hold of a custom officer's uniform and station himself at an unmanned passport-control desk. God knows how he did it.'

Budgie then waved his Villa buddies through and amused himself questioning the rest of the passengers and confiscating duty-free, until the real customs officers turned up and 'there was hell on'. Where were all the customs officers in the first place? How had Budgie got the uniform? Had he perhaps tied a customs officer up in a toilet somewhere, bound and gagged in just his underwear? It doesn't bear thinking about.

Steve Hodge says that on Forest European trips, the customs men were definitely at the forefront of somebody's mind. Players always

—

62 Very evocative name, Videoton. They have an exotic place in our childhood memories of UEFA Cup goals round-ups along with Fortuna Sittard, Grasshoppers and Dynamo Dresden.

63 Just how close the pair were is a matter of conjecture between them. Budgie emotionally tells us in his book that Gray 'will always be like a brother to me' – an enduring image, two tough titans of the game, forever standing shoulder to shoulder as they soldier through life. And indeed, it is Gray who writes the foreword for Budgie's book. Well, who else? They're comrades, virtually kin. So what does Gray say of their relationship? Well, he praises Budgie for welcoming him when he joined Villa, then, with a tear in his eye, adds: 'from that moment on we became pretty good friends'. Ah. It's the 'pretty' part that spoils it isn't it? That one word reduces their fraternal relationship to about one rung up from mere 'acquaintances'.

expected a tap on the shoulder from Brian Clough as the plane was about to land, asking, 'Are you carrying anything through?" If the answer was no, 'he'd give me a bottle of whiskey or 200 cigarettes to take through customs to ensure he got the maximum out of his "allowance".' Crafty old Cloughie. Fags and booze and no doubt a big Toblerone for Mrs Clough at home. Paul Sturrock tells us coyly that a Dundee United teammate, 'a certain pacy right-winger who has scored a lot of goals for us in Europe' no less, had his luggage inspected on a trip to Romania, and a load of dirty mags, 'such as *Mayfair*, *Fiesta* and *Penthouse*' (all the classics), were confiscated.

We're not happy with this fake coyness from Sturrock. There are enough clues here to make it obvious to somebody with a degree more Tangerines knowledge than us to discern who he's talking about. Bad form from 'Luggy', that. According to the code, surely what happens on tour should stay on tour. Which is, of course, a cue for some depraved behaviour on planes – an area in which we are spoilt for choice.

Let's start with that notoriously hard-drinking Everton side of the Kendall/Harvey management years, off on the jolly of all football jollies to Mauritius.[64] So good was the trip, in fact, that Aston Villa tagged along with them. Presumably a friendly was on the cards to promote the burgeoning game of football in Mauritius – or something. Anyway, it's a long flight and inevitably there was booze, with Mark Ward getting into an ill-advised drinking contest with Paul McGrath. However, that sideshow was just a decoy for the main carnage as Ward recalls being interrupted by 'Peter Beagrie spewing vomit all over the back of our seats'. Charming. At some point, Villa manager Ron Atkinson popped down from first class for a chat with Howard Kendall, who was of course sat with his lads already. Perhaps inspired by his prowess in necking tiny cans of lager with Mark Ward, Howard thought he'd chance his arm and asked Ron how much he'd want for Paul McGrath. Atkinson leaned in closer and 'placed his knee on a damp towel that was covering the remains of Beagrie's sick!' Taking it about as well as you'd expect amid frantic wiping, he began 'telling a fully relaxed Howard to control his players and returning upstairs to the sanctuary of his wife'. We're surprised they allowed him back into first class stinking of Beagrie Barf. Mrs

64 We've always wanted to go to Mauritius. Not least because it sounds like Scooby Doo trying to say 'delicious'.

Ron must have been fuming. Needless to say, the McGrath move didn't happen.

Worse Everton in-flight behaviour involved Pat Van Den Hauwe, with an incident seared deep enough on to Howard Kendall's brain that he decided to mention it in the otherwise glowing foreword to Pat's book. Ian Snodin remembers the incident simply as Van Den Hauwe causing 'a bit of a commotion with the stewardesses' but Kendall remembers it almost becoming a diplomatic incident, with police waiting for the players when they landed in America: 'Allegedly, one had exposed himself to a stewardess. Once we landed, no player would admit to being the culprit, and no player would point the guilty person out, so we were given a serious ticking off and warned about our future conduct.'

Kendall seems more annoyed because the in-flight bar on their connecting flight was withdrawn as a result than he was about one of his lads getting their lad out and traumatising the flight attendant. He also lived in blissful ignorance about who the culprit was until a reunion 20 years later when Pat admitted it. 'I was in no position to fine him so we had a beer and good laugh about it,' says Howard.

Remember, this is a foreword, a place where you are almost contractually obliged to wax lyrical about the author of the book, and Kendall has deemed this the perfect place to recount a fond memory about that time Pat exposed himself on a plane. Pat's account states that: 'It appears, although I can't remember the incident, that I had walked from the front of the aircraft to the back of it with my cock out. I won't argue with the people who said I did, as it was something I had done before at Birmingham.' Good grief. Not only did he do it, he had form for it. No plane was safe.

If Everton were a worse menace to have on a plane than motherflipping snakes, then the red half of Merseyside was never too far behind them. Nick Tanner recalls a Liverpool flight where a well-oiled Mike Hooper mistakenly grabbed a businessman in the belief that he was a journalist who had criticised him. Tanner says 'he had him by the tie and looked as if he was about to strangle him', before realising he had the wrong man, which must have made the rest of the flight very awkward indeed. Presumably Hoops offered to pay for his headset, all his drinks and an airline cuddly toy from the brochure to make up for it.

In the Spice Boy era at Anfield things were even worse because the fighting was internal. On a flight home from Vladikavkaz (another evocative Eastern European name), Robbie Fowler found that he had fallen victim to that footballer classic, the cut-up shoes. Well, perhaps he shouldn't have taken them off on a flight; bet he reclined his seat the whole way back as well. Fowler tried to brush it off and put on the spare pair in his bag, only to find that those had been cut up too. Along with the handles to his bag. How somebody had got scissors on to a flight we're not sure, but this was pre-9/11 and banter demanded scissors. Fowler decided that one of Razor Ruddock, Steve Harkness or John Barnes was responsible and decided that instead of working out which, he'd simply sort all three of them out: 'Problem was, I chose Razor first.' Robbie decided to cut up a pair of 'dead expensive Italian leather shoes that he was fond of showing off' in revenge, and Razor, either very attached to the shoes or vehemently protesting his innocence, 'had a proper cob on'. By now they had landed and were arguing on the runway: 'he told me again I'd have to pay. I just laughed at him, and I think that did it. Bam. He turned round and twatted me in the mouth. I had a cut nose and lip, and blood was pouring off me. There was a trail going from the tarmac right into the baggage reclaim.' A presumably barefoot Fowler must have cut quite a dash going through arrivals, bleeding everywhere, while Ruddock fumed, and either Harkness or Barnes did their best to keep a low profile.

One other nightmare Liverpool passenger is Jermaine Pennant. Fresh from the Champions League Final in 2007, Pennant flew off on holiday with his buddy, Charlton's Jon Fortune.[65] They doubtless had a nice time, but on the way back it all went puke-shaped: 'I was halfway down the aisle, saying, "I'm going to be sick, going to be sick." Next thing I knew I was waking up, on all fours like a dog, sweating my tits off in the middle of the aisle. The stewardess picked me up, put me at the front of the plane and gave me oxygen.'

It's difficult to maintain holidaying-football-superstar levels of cool when you're sat at the front of a plane wearing an oxygen mask and covered in sick.

Such behaviour would be enough to put us off flying completely, even before you factor in the possibility of plummeting to our death in a ball of flames. And we're not alone in worrying about that. Alan

65 Of that classic back four: Young-Fish-Costa-Fortune. Tremendous fun.

Curbishley tells tales on Scott Parker and Stephen Hughes at Charlton who 'used to sit at the back of the plane screaming whenever we hit the slightest bit of turbulence', while Jamie Carragher recounts flying back from the World Cup in bad weather to the sound of 'someone screeching in terror towards the back of the plane. I'd never heard howling like it before.' Carra assumed it was a child but 'When I looked myself, I noticed it wasn't an infant. Head in his hands, ducked into the safety position, was an inconsolable England and Manchester United superstar. It was Wayne Rooney.'

Not content with snitching on the very real fears of their colleagues, some people play on it for laughs. We've already established that John Burridge liked a prank; his boss at Villa, Ron Saunders, did not. Nor did he like flying. Nor, it seems, did he like Burridge much. The pair didn't get on and Budgie decided to put the wind up his manager as their plane into Birmingham was about to land: 'I decided it was time to go in for the kill and sock it to him. I got hold of my sick bag from the back of his seat, blew it up as far as it would go, then made a knot in the end.' Despite teammates urging him not to go through with it, Burridge 'leant over him with my bag all pumped up like a crisp packet and smashed it right behind his ear. It went BANG and Saunders went sliding down to the floor screaming. Roy McLaren turned round and punched me right in the face. The doctor turned round and said: "You idiot, you could have given him a heart attack!" I was full of adrenaline and started screaming back: "I wish I had given him one!"' Well this, in the words of Ron Burgundy, escalated quickly. Burridge reckons he lost his place in the team directly because of this prank. Well if you can't take a joke Ron, you shouldn't sit quietly on a plane minding your own business should you?

Beyond the paper bag tricks[66] there are a few of our football stars that have had good reason to fly in fear and fortunately lived to tell the tale. Ralph Milne describes a 'bordering on mental' landing in Hong Kong as he chased a late career bloom there. As the plane came in through the skyscrapers, he says, 'You could just about see folk scratching their arses in their offices.' Lovely image of Hong Kong there from Ralphie, putting him in the travelogue big league with the likes of Palin, James and Whicker.

66 Remember the bit where Budgie likened his inflated paper bag to another inflated paper bag, 'like a crisp packet'; that was a good bit wasn't it?

Even hairier than that is a tale told by Jimmy Greaves of an England trip to South America and a flight through the Andes to Lima. A nervy Greaves says that at one point they 'were so low you could actually see the pack horses on the high passes bringing the copper ore out of the mountains'. Jimmy then found out that the captain was taking a more dangerous route than they usually would because they were carrying the BBC's heavy camera equipment and needed to fly lower. This was before Greavsie became the TV colossus he became in retirement, so he had little time for such frivolities. Terrified, he told journalist John Camkin to 'tell Captain Biggles that the VIP passengers on board have had a vote and they have decided that the best thing he can do is chuck the f______ cameras overboard and fly a little higher...!' Decisive action here from Jim. There's no evidence that the captain took any notice of his advice, and the plane made it safely through the mountains, but it's telling that it was BBC cameras that Greavsie wanted to dash on the rocks below. It's an early indication that he was to become an ITV man from his head to his boots in the years to come.

We're all for this ability to admit your fears and try to cope with them. It all sounds healthier than the position a young Ally Robertson found himself in on an anxious flight with West Brom in the early 70s. On their way to a friendly with Feyenoord, the plane ran into trouble when an engine failed. Naturally, the Albion lads were the cool kids at the back of the plane and 'just thought it was a wind-up, but then the plane went into a dive. But because you had 20 young lads together, you couldn't let anything show. The people at the front of the plane were panicking like hell. And the players? Typical bravado: "What's all the fuss about?" Then you look out of the window and see flames!' You've got to love this. The plane is dropping like a stone, the best chance of the flames going out is that they might hit water, and yet here are the Albion boys all fronting up and trying to remain aloof in case they look daft in front of one another. It's no way to go out. Luckily, the plane managed an emergency landing at Heathrow with 'a couple of meaty thuds'. Nobody was hurt, and crucially for Robertson, nobody lost their cool either: 'A couple of dozen fire engines raced towards us along the runway with sirens wailing. We just didn't realise the magnitude of it all. We were just enjoying a beer.' Lads, lads, lads.

Before we land this thing, we feel we should finish with perhaps the ultimate players-on-a-plane story. It contains a dodgy flight, genuine fear, bravado, bad behaviour, and, above all else, Carlton Palmer.

After a Leeds v Southampton game, Saints players Egil Ostenstad and big Carlton stayed up for the weekend with different friends and then planned to travel back together on the Monday morning. It's nice to have a bit of company, after all. Well, not if that company is Carlton Palmer, it turns out. Carlton tells us that not long after take-off they heard a big bang 'like a muffled gunshot, and the plane lurched badly', which sounds very worrying indeed, more so when passengers were told to adopt crash positions. Ostenstad was clearly the more worried of the two men; his wife was expecting a baby and a crushing feeling of mortality was understandably sweeping over him as he placed his head between his legs, he supposed, for the last time. In such a moment we can all only hope that we have the soothing words of a travelling companion to put us at our ease. What poor 'whimpering' Egil got instead was Carlton: 'As we sat in the cabin, leaning forward with our hands clasped round our inclined heads, I started to talk to him. "You're going to die, Egil," I said. "We're all going to die. You don't drink. You don't shag about. You've had no fun and you're going to die. Here, in this plane, your life will end. I don't care, Egil. I've enjoyed my life. Have you had a good time? I've had a good time. But not you, Egil. Sober, serious, sensible Egil. The end."'

Jaw-dropping stuff this. But Egil needn't have worried about being taunted off into the great beyond with a frank assessment of his life choices ringing in his ears, because firstly, they managed a safe emergency landing, and secondly, Carlton was only kidding around. Or was he? '"Sorry about that, Egil," I chuckled. "Couldn't resist." "No problem," he managed to say, without being especially convincing. But I thought about what I'd said to him. And I kind of meant it.'

Bloody hell.

TRAINS

Think of the thrillers that have utilised the dramatic possibilities of a train: *Strangers on a Train*, *The Silver Streak*, *Murder on the Orient Express*, that James Bond one where Roger Moore scraps with the lad with the teeth. And while we can't quite promise you 'killers on the loose' levels of excitement on the journeys described here, we are not without incident.

Alan Mullery tells us that Fulham were big train drinkers at one time and that Bobby Moore, in a bid to maintain appearances at all times, paid the steward on the train to take away all his empties as he finished them. 'Mooro had twelve lagers in that time, but it was all done in such a stylish way, like a scene from a Steve McQueen film.' We don't remember that particular Steve McQueen film where he gets hammered on a train back from an away trip but we get the idea. Mooro's too cool for cans and naturally alighted the carriage looking bright-eyed and dapper. Of course he did. He was Bobby Moore.

Someone who fared less well at hiding the fact that he was all boozed up on the railways was the formidable Forest defender Kenny Burns. Travelling home from London with John Robertson one day, Robbo tells us that keeping a low profile was blown out of the water at Euston station, where a load of Man United fans 'spotted him and burst out into choruses of "Kenny Burns is pissed, Kenny Burns is pissed".' Rumbled, Burns decided to handle it as any half-cut centre-half with a propensity for aggro might as he 'boomed out, "I'll take any two of you on". Thankfully he had no takers and we were able to limp off like two men in a three-legged race and get on a sleeper heading up north.' A couple of things here – for a start, why is it 'any two of you'? That's hard. Not one of you, not all of you, but a specific number that even, or especially, in his bladdered state, Kenny has calculated he can comfortably take on. Fair play. Secondly, well done Robbo for getting his skipper home safely. He's gone above and beyond as a teammate here.

Another teammate who did what was necessary to give his team the aftercare they needed on a railway station was Ray 'Clem' Clemence. Phil Neal tells us about a dejected Liverpool squad heading home after losing the 1977 FA Cup Final, but having to pick themselves up once more for the European Cup Final a few days later. Busy boys.

Travelling back by train the players and staff were waiting in a huff at Watford station for a connection when 'Suddenly, for no reason at all, Clem began to dance and sing to himself. Some of us didn't notice, and those who did thought he had flipped. Suddenly a big grin spread over his face and he said "Let's dance, lads." And there and then, on Watford station, a bunch of guys who had nothing to be happy about began to dance, sing and snap their fingers.' Wonderful scenes. It's Liverpool FC's very own *La La Land* moment.[67] Neal says that a 'few beers on the journey added to the cure' and they were good to go

67 You know, 'La', like lad. Please yourselves.

again, seeing off Borussia Monchengladbach to lift the big pot for the first time. And look at them now. Is it a stretch to say that Liverpool's European success ever since is solely down to Clem's fandango? We don't think so. If the Battle of Waterloo was won on the playing fields of Eton as it's claimed the Duke of Wellington once said, then we can fairly say that all those European Cups were won on the platforms of Watford station.

It wasn't all peace and love in the age of the train, however. Despite Clem's finest work, you couldn't rely on all the other England goalkeepers to keep the peace. Both Terry Butcher and Kenny Sansom well remember an England trip to the continent that involved a train journey to Vienna and a bit of backfiring banter from Russell Osman. Osman, you see, fancied himself as a bit of a prankster and decided to squirt invisible ink all over goalie Joe Corrigan's shirt. Sansom tells us that 'Big Joe' reacted badly, ripping the shirt off and throwing it off the train.

Now this seems enough of an overreaction without what happened next. Butcher recalls, 'Joe was furious. "Right you lot," he boomed. "I want everyone to take off their socks and throw them out the window."' And here's the thing: everybody did it. All of them. Butcher says that 'Joe is a big and very strong man and not many people argue with him', which is quite something coming from Terry Butcher, while Sansom says, 'He was far from being aggressive, though. Joe was known as the Gentle Giant. We referred to him as "Gentle Joe with a heart to show".' Brushing over that adorable nickname, we have so many questions. Why did he throw his shirt out of the window? Why socks? And why did everybody do it, whether Joe was being scary or not? Were there no management, or adults, around to stop this thing escalating? However this played out, what we do know is that the Austrian countryside was suddenly strewn with one XXL shirt and a load of socks, and that the England squad arrived in Vienna wearing their shoes, but with not a sock between them. Actually, that's probably quite fashionable now.

AUTOMOBILES

Football stars in their football cars. This promised to be a very lengthy examination, but then we decided to leave out all the cases of drink-driving so we could fit it in. Instead, we bring you a rich tapestry of mostly booze-free road stories, such as:

- The Coventry City tour for which Bobby Gould tells us that Jimmy Hill 'fixed us up with a fleet of sky blue Rover 2000s from the Triumph factory in Coventry and we set off in convoy.' Lovely.

- Some road rage from Frank Worthington, who despite being a lover not a fighter insists: 'I once had to chase and whack a lorry driver who'd cut me up in Leicester.' Had to, mind.

- Vital, if dull, Spanish traffic news from Kevin Keegan on what used to be a particularly congested thoroughfare: 'Thankfully the road is not nearly as bad now that they have converted it to a proper dual carriageway with a central reservation.' Phew!

- Neville Southall being late for a Wales match and receiving a lift in a police car 'going 100 miles an hour down the dual carriageway; it was fucking brilliant to be honest'. Thrilling. It's lovely to see how giddy Nev got about it. We can only hope they let him put the blue light on as well.

However, what we really want to focus on here is footballers in cars together. What sort of things do they all get up to when they share a lift to the ground? Quite a lot as it turns out. Neil Redfearn is a big believer in it as a ritual, saying of his time at Bradford that 'the daily journey through the morning traffic played a big part in team bonding because, instead of driving into training on our own, we all had to muck in together', and suggests that the 'state of the carpets in the back' was a small price to pay for fostering such a brothers in arms mentality.

Wondering if that lovely sentiment is echoed around the grounds? Let's check in with Mel Sterland who used to give Carl Shutt a lift in: 'He used to stink of chip pan fat, which used to do my box in.' Oh well, we suppose it would, especially as no reason for this whiff coming off his passenger is given. We're left to speculate whether Carl Shutt had a part-time job on the side at a local chippy, or if the Shutt household was just running an around-the-clock chip pan in flagrant disregard for fire safety advice. Mel doesn't even tell us if he raised the issue with Shutty himself – he just mentions it in passing. Either way, Carl Shutt is not even Mel's most disrespected Sheffield Wednesday teammate in a car called Carl. For that dubious honour, step forward Carl Bradshaw.

The Wednesday youngster unfortunately couldn't read, and as you can imagine, this neither went unnoticed or unpunished in the Sterland's car: 'I remember seeing a white van with the word "maintenance" written on the side.' He asked Bradshaw what it said: '"Main entrance," he said. I was laughing that much that I nearly crashed the car!' Despite this, and plenty more ribbing about it, the twist in the tale is that Mel was best man at Carl's wedding. That's quite a pay-off, considering a relationship seemingly based on low-level meanness – maybe it was an honour bestowed in lieu of petrol money.

More in-car capers at Oldham where Joe McBride used to drive Micky Quinn and Mark Ward to training from Liverpool. Guess what this story involves? Chatting up women, you say? You're not wrong. According to insatiable Micky, he refused to let the road between them and 'a bit of a sort' in a passing car get the better of him and used all his subtle, charming ways to entice the opposite sex when he 'grabbed a piece of paper, wrote "Do you fuck?" on it in big letters and held it up against the window'. Now, to be fair, perhaps we've done Micky a disservice here. We've made it sound like this was his opening gambit, when in fact they were already 'giving it all the tongues and hand gestures and she was responding'. Who says romance is dead? Somewhat dangerously, the woman scribbled her own note while bombing along in the fast lane, improbably saying that she did indeed. Further communication hatched a plan to come off at the next exit to a car park where Quinn and Ward had their own cars, but once they had stopped and the thrill of the chase was over, they thought better of it, claiming 'she was a bit on the old side for us'. However, Quinn claims that as he pulled out in his own car 'I saw the blonde easing herself on to the back seat of Joe's GTI. Away win for McBridey.'[68] It's a tale as old as time isn't it? Brings a tear to the eye. To the best of our knowledge, McBridey and the woman went on to live happily ever after together. Although maybe that's about as believable as the idea

68 It's far from the most important thing here, but 'McBridey'? Surely Macca, or Bridey or Car Park Shagger are better?

that saucy Micky Quinn would drive away from such a scene without getting a good look.

There are many elements of the Quinn story that place it among the least erotic things we've ever heard, including the blatant disregard for road safety. Everyone involved is lucky they didn't end up in a pile up;[69] luckier than John Wark and his Ipswich buddies then. Wark tells of a horrific-sounding crash in a car with Dale Roberts, Glen Westley and driver Kevin Beattie on the 'windy coastal route' to a training session. The Ipswich legend says that Beat lost control of the car 'as he took a bend and it left the road, somersaulted three times and landed upside down'. As dramatic and *Casino Royale*-like as it sounds, miraculously nobody was hurt. Bobby Robson was in the car behind, first on the scene, and once he'd established that everybody was okay, he generously granted the lads the day off from training. It seems only fair.

Wark's thoughts quickly and practically turned to the Opel Manta's insurance cover, worrying that Beat 'only had third party, rather than fully comprehensive, insurance cover, he was unable to claim and lost £1,400'. It's commendable, given the situation, that Wark is still concerned here about his teammate's lack of cover, and it's remarkable that this took place in an age when footballers still had to count the pennies when considering which insurance they took out. So quick is Warky to mention these details that we like to think he was still hanging upside down when he first considered them. Hanging? Who are we kidding? As if any of them were wearing a seatbelt.

If keeping a car full of well-behaved footballers on the road is difficult enough, then having somebody dicking around in the back will only make it harder. Especially if that somebody is Dennis Wise, who knows no difference between a good-natured bit of back and forth to pass the time on a journey and a psychotic act that might kill everyone close by. Jones says that Wise was a good mate, but on this particular journey home from a game, little Dennis was taking some stick from Vinnie and two other unnamed and mercifully unharmed passengers, and he didn't take it too well: 'He completely lost it and got a wire coat hanger around my neck when I was going down the fast lane, and started pulling on it! He was sitting right behind me and all the rest of the lads tried to help me, but he wouldn't let go. We ended

69 Though in a sense McBridey did.

up on the hard shoulder rolling around inside the car having a scrap between the four of us.'

Jesus Crazy Gang Christ, this is awful. It's like a Mafia hit from a film, but a really stupid Mafia hit from a really stupid Mafia film. How would you come back from this when the 'scrap' came to its natural conclusion? Do you put Wisey out to thumb his own way back at the earliest opportunity? Or do you dust yourselves down and keep on trucking; maybe stopping for a Ginsters and a go on those massage chairs at the services to calm everyone down? At the very least we'd have moved Wisey to the front seat where we could see him. When Gary Numan sang 'Here in my car, I feel safest of all' we can only say good for him. He clearly didn't have Dennis Wise sitting behind him.

ON THE BUSES

The mode of transport we most associate with footballers, outside of Range Rovers of course, is the team coach. The coach is a club in microcosm – hierarchies in place, pecking orders established, free-flowing badinage – only now it's on wheels.

Given the amount of time players spend on the bus it's vital to get the blend of what's required right. And top of that list is grub. Keeping players correctly fuelled on the move is important stuff, but how do these meals on wheels happen? Well, we've learned from our extensive reading that there are adequate cooking facilities on board. Jimmy Case took pride in being the cook on the Southampton bus in his time there, and there was sufficient food on the Arsenal bus in the 1990s for Steve Bould to win an eating contest with nine dinners.

Once, while in charge at Bristol Rovers, Bobby Gould withheld the services of the bus microwave after a bad result at Plymouth, and even banned cold food. 'A bit of starvation, I reasoned, might concentrate their minds in reflecting on the drivel they had just served up.' Served up, you see? Like it, Bobby, like it. However, such draconian measures didn't take Rover Gary Mabbutt's famous diabetes into account, and Gould was soon sending biscuits up to the back before Gary went all queasy and cross-eyed like the girl in *Airplane!*. Bobby concedes that 'if one player was to be fed, they all had to be fed'. Hurrah for diabetic Gary getting everybody the meal that their basic human rights entitled them to.

Fish and chips seems to be a staple meal on the bus back from a game. We hear about this 'golden hour' after a match when players can eat what they want as their bodies are just burning calories like a furnace, and it would seem a chippy tea fits the bill perfectly; though Alan Curbishley moans that 'by the time we were ready to leave the chips would usually be cold and the fish would be sticking to the paper it was wrapped in'. And there was no vinegar, and we bet they forgot your gherkin too, didn't they Curbs? What a nightmare. Even for Liverpool in their 80s pomp, the chippy was the only option for the trip back to Merseyside. Steve Nicol remembers that 'Ronnie Moran used to go round with a bit of paper and a pen and ask each player what they wanted', the choice being anything you liked from 'pie and chips, fish and chips or chicken and chips'. One of Nicol's many nicknames was of course 'Chips', so it's unlikely he would have strayed outside of these boundaries anyway but he does add that 'any alternative request was met by a quizzical look from Ronnie and a straight-to-the-point reply: "That's all there is. Who the fuck do you think you are?"' It's important to know where you stand. And if you can know where you stand and get a pie and chips out of it, then so much the better.[70]

Once the food is sorted, thoughts turn to how else you're going to entertain yourselves. Brian 'Choccy' McClair gives us some lovely insight into the make-up of the all-conquering Man United coach of the 90s. He says it was full of creatures of habit who tended to stick to the same spots. McClair would sit up front with Brian Kidd 'talking nonsense', the Class of 92 tended to sit together, while curious Raimond van der Gouw 'plays flight simulators because he wants to be a pilot'. This really stood out to us from all of these bus tales as a useful way to spend time: learn a language, learn an instrument, learn to fly. McClair continues to say that when the individual pursuits failed, they would all watch a video together 'over and over again – some episodes of *Only Fools and Horses* and *The Bodyguard*'. The thought of Phil Neville guffawing every time Del Boy falls through the bar, or Peter Schmeichel sobbing gently when Whitney and Kevin Costner part goes a long way to humanising the machine-like efficiency of that United side.

What music goes on the stereo must have been a constant bone of contention on coaches up and down the land before mobile phones.

70 Nicol also brings us news that the bus driver that used to take Liverpool players from Anfield to Melwood was nicknamed 'SwallowMeKnob'. We don't know what else to do with that information other than share it with you in a footnote.

Eccentric gaffer Stan Ternent found a way to stop all the arguments about what they listened to – he just upset everybody. On trips home he would play his unpopular Joseph Locke cassette at full volume, telling his squad: 'It comes off when you win another fucking away game.' You see, there's no reason to stop motivating the troops just because you're on your way home.

It all seems a bit more harmonious at Leeds in the era of chairman Peter Ridsdale, even if the music is no better. Ridsdale goes all misty-eyed and recalls the 'unforgettable camaraderie' on the team bus: '"You're Still the One" by Shania Twain would belt out from the coach stereo, and players at the back would bellow along, disrupting the concentration of those playing cards. Then, more often than not, a few of them would burst into "Flying Without Wings" by Westlife.' How on earth did these songs get past the cooler[71] members of the squad? And did anybody ever tell Matt Le Tissier about the Leeds playlist? With the promise of Shania Twain and Westlife on the go he might have finally been prised away from Southampton with a transfer to Elland Road.

Obviously, the main pastime on a team coach is a good old game of cards – Snap, Twizzle, Rummy, Shithead, Pontoon and no doubt the odd bit of Poker. It's generally accepted that players are, in the words of Taylor Swift, gonna play, play, play.

The danger, of course, is that as the stakes get higher there's more chance that people will fall out. Paul Parker remembers Sir Alex Ferguson getting involved in the card school on the United bus but that he was a pretty bad loser. It strikes us that you'd be very brave to upset him. Billy Bonds tells us that tensions ran high on the West Ham bus a few times over a game of cards. Once Harry Redknapp was accused of cheating and he got so upset that he threw the cards out of the window and everyone sat there in silence, and another time Trevor Brooking hit someone. You read that right; genial, mild-mannered Tricky Trev was moved sufficiently to hit his teammate John McDowell. McDowell, you see, kept leaning over Trev's shoulder during a game and telling him what to do, until eventually 'the Brooking patience snapped, and he turned round and whacked John across the top of his head, giving him a most un-Brooking like volley'. We are shocked and appalled but it seems that McDowell had form for annoying people – Bonds also

71 Or Kewell-er.

says that on another occasion Frank Lampard Snr punched him on the chin. Popular bloke, John McDowell.

If you can't play cards then you've got to find alternative entertainment, and we did come across a few options. If you were at Ipswich in the heyday of their European sojourns, you could be led through a sing-song by Alan Brazil, whom Terry Butcher tells us has a great voice. If you were at Arsenal with Kenny Sansom then he would treat you to his many impersonations including the inevitable Norman Wisdom and Frank Spencer. And if you were at Everton in their mid-80s pomp, you had John Bailey and his pet monkey. Yeah, you did.

It's Peter Reid that brings us the revelations about Bailey and his sidekick, but calm down, it was a puppet. It does sound like pretty much anything went on those Everton trips, but a line was drawn before they let somebody bring an actual chimp on board. Bailey bought the puppet in Toronto, and Reid declares, 'I think he thinks it's real to hear him talking to it.' Now, when we started out down the road of researching football autobiographies, we were in blissful ignorance about the culture of puppetry that existed within the game. We've heard previously about Jim Smith's puppet-led cup final team talk, Mike Bateson of Torquay's contract negotiations alongside Algernon, and now this from John Bailey. Where will it all end? Does it still go on? Is Jürgen Klopp waiting to unleash Spucke ze Hund from under the desk at a press conference one day? Only time will tell.

Some of the larks and wheezes that people got up to on the bus strike us as genuinely pretty good though. There's Alan Shearer ringing the newspaper for crossword answers while his teammates are struggling away with it, before casually dropping them unexpectedly into conversation. And then there's this oddity brought to us by David Batty. It seems it wasn't all crosswords on the Blackburn coach; sometimes they would scrape out their meat pies and throw the contents at driver 'Stoney'. 'Another time we crept down the bus as it sped along the motorway and, using masking tape, bound Stoney's arms to his sides, from the shoulders to his elbows. He was steering God knows how many millions of pounds worth of Premiership talent in a strait-jacket! Even worse, for a few seconds he did it blind because one of the lads put his hands over his eyes.' Poor old Stoney. He shouldn't have to put up with this sort of thing while he's going about his job. Aside from being incredibly dangerous, it must have got really annoying. What's happened here is the players have dragged the driver into their shenanigans, when really they should keep most of that gentle ribbing/brutal bullying stuff amongst themselves. As most other clubs do.

In the 'bit of fun' file we have the pasting Charlie Nicholas took from his Arsenal teammates on the bus after appearing in some swimming trunks in full colour in the *Daily Star*. Absolutely fair enough. Tony Woodcock says of those Arsenal lads: 'They are all pretty sharp, but Sundy is undoubtedly the squad leader.' Well of course he was – he had the squadron leader's moustache.

In the 'only to be expected' file we have Ian Snodin telling us about those rascal Everton boys attacking his clothes after he fell asleep on the coach. 'I stood up and the sleeves on my jacket came off – the lads had shredded my suit, they'd cut my belt, all down my trousers, my tie, my shirt ... I looked like Robinson Crusoe.' There it is again. As sure as night follows day, if a footballer falls asleep, he's getting some of his clothes cut up. That's just the law, and if you don't like it, you can go and live in Venezuela.

And in the 'buses we'd rather never set foot on' file we have that Colchester bus ruled with an iron hand by Roy McDonough. Roy backs up our point about those lads that had the temerity to try to grab 40 winks on the bus back: 'they would wake up with cigars – which some of the lads smoked on the coach – up their nostrils, ashtrays emptied on their heads, Biro moustaches, or a new hairstyle'. Being drawn on while asleep also seems ubiquitous on these occasions, by the way. Again, that's just the way it is.

One time, on an overnight away trip to Blackpool, it fell upon Roy to deal out the justice when a young Perry Groves committed the heinous crime of bringing a bag with him. 'I couldn't believe it, a fucking bag – all I took away with me was the tracksuit I was sitting in, with a toothbrush and shaving razor in one of the pockets, plus my matchday suit.' Now your author once had a mate come to stay with him without a bag, with just a toothbrush and a clean pair of pants in his pocket, which feels odd; Roy's belongings don't even include a clean pair of pants, which feels like a gamble. When Grovesy stepped off the bus for a snack, McDonough says, 'I yanked everything out of his bag and found a horrible pair of green-and-white striped pyjamas, the sort of thing my grandad had slept in. I put them on, over my clothes, pulled up tightly around the crotch with my nuts poking through the bottoms and the waistband riding high around my chest.'

McDonough claims he was teaching the fledgling Groves a vital truth about showing weakness or giving people enough rope to hang you with or some such. Groves confirms this story, adding that Roy was still wearing them as they entered the hotel: 'At least I got them back by bedtime.' Yes, Perry, but did you want them back?

A journey that long shows an admirable commitment to a joke and it's thanks to Roy's principled stand that no footballer has ever taken a bag for an overnight stay again, probably. But here's the thing, we bet that McDonough sitting there with his nuts poking through Grovesy's pyjamas all the way from Colchester to Blackpool must have started to make everyone feel a bit awkward by the time they passed Spaghetti Junction. And we have a few more stops on the awkward bus for you before we park this chapter up for the night at the depot.

The Southampton bus during David Armstrong's day got totes awks before they'd even left the car park, with Saints superstars Mick Channon, Alan Ball and Kevin Keegan all vying for top dog status by getting on the bus last. Armstrong takes time out from combing his head to tell us that: 'If one got on and found he was not last he would get off again and wait. This rampant display of one-upmanship annoyed the rest of us sitting patiently in our seats because our departure was often unnecessarily delayed until such time as they were all in place.' Imagine winning the World Cup and still thinking someone's better than you if they board the coach after you. Dave does say that apart from this 'they all got along famously', but the other lads would have been fuming. The chips must have been stone cold by the time all three legends had climbed aboard.

You might expect diva behaviour such as this from the odd player but surely the gaffer would be above all that. Not if it's Martin O'Neill, who once left his Norwich charges waiting outside after an away game for a few hours. Eventually, skipper Jon Newsome went in to chase him up but it didn't help. Once O'Neill did appear he gave the starting 11 a hug each and thanked them for a great result and performance before laying down the law to his captain: 'Don't you ever come looking for me again. If you do, I will sack you. I say when you go. I say when we arrive. I say when we leave. I'm the manager.' Blimey.

It sometimes sounds to us like Martin has picked up some of his erratic boss man behaviour from his years spent under Brian Clough. And there was plenty of odd to go round when Clough was on a bus. Clough's duty-free mule, Steve Hodge, has a few tales to tell. He says that Clough always kept a curtain partition between management and players but occasionally 'The curtains would whoosh back' and Clough would say random things like 'Thanks for spoiling my weekend you shithouses.' However, it doesn't sound as if everything was rosy even if you were on the management side of the cloth. Erstwhile assistant Liam O'Kane had many responsibilities under Cloughie it seems, and paramount among them was making sure he packed the talcum powder for Clough's post-match post-bath routine. All well and good until one day Liam left it behind in Nottingham, and tentatively let the gaffer know of his mistake. 'Clough's response to this seemingly minor bit of news was swift and decisive. "Albert!" he called to our ever-present bus driver. "Stop at the next services would you. Liam's going to be getting off!" So we pulled up at Watford Gap and Liam O'Kane had to get off. The bus pulled away leaving him in the car park.' O'Kane then rang his wife to come down and collect him, find some talcum powder then drive him down to the capital before driving home. This is quite a commitment to talc. You don't see that so much anymore. But aside from being lost in a cloudy baby powder reverie, we have several issues with this:

- If talc is so important to Cloughie, surely he should bring his own?
- Why didn't Liam ask Mrs O'Kane to bring some talc with her once she was getting involved?
- Why didn't they buy talc when they got down to London, or even, and this is a wild idea, try the services they'd stopped at? This isn't *Treasure Hunt*. They're not looking for the Ark of the Covenant, they just need a bottle of talc. London's got both Boots and Superdrug – we've seen them.

Despite the loyalty and good toiletry-remembering habits that Clough inspired in his staff, eventually they have to go and spread their wings like O'Neill. Archie Gemmill was one of his former players, then one of his able deputies at Forest, before finding himself at Rotherham on a bus with a load of randy lads including Shaun Goater. Or a load of randy lads AND Shaun Goater, depending on who you believe.

Goater tells a story of the Rotherham coach getting stuck in traffic when 'a car drew alongside us with some girls inside. All the lads came across, ogling them and banging on the window.' So far, so men of a certain era, but 'Suddenly, Archie Gemmill marched up from the rear of the coach and heard one of the lads say something along the lines of, "Get your tits out!" to the girls. Gemmill looked at me and bawled me out in a personally insulting way, saying that the girl in the car was his daughter.'[72] Now that is an awkward and unfortunate situation. The Goat maintains his innocence and insists he'd merely fallen in with the wrong crowd on that side of the bus. He then made Gemmill apologise to him for the accusation, which he says 'was a pivotal moment in my life, a rite of passage if you like'. He might be right. Fair play to Goater for coming out of this with the moral high ground.

Similar bawdy and uncalled for language could inevitably be found on the Birmingham bus when Karren Brady was taking her first tentative steps in the football business. She was once invited to travel to an away game with the players by manager Terry Cooper – a kindly invite we're sure you'll agree. In practice, however, it wasn't quite so lovely. Brady says, 'Let me tell you, spending all those hours on a bus with 35 men and one small toilet is why I have never set foot on the team bus again. Then, as I walked back to my seat after one of my doomed toilet visits, one of the players said to me, "I can see your tits from here."' Come on mate, you've let yourself and everybody else down there. We're no fans of Karren Brady, but we'll side with her here against the patriarchy in all its leery entitlement. It shows remarkable restraint on Brady's[73] part that she doesn't name the player, but she did at least have the last laugh, telling the wrong 'un: 'Well, when I sell you to Crewe, you won't be able to see them from there.' Boom, as the kids say. Sick burn. Roasted. Mic drop – Brady out. No really, Brady out. That toilet does sound grim, though.

Perhaps our favourite of all the tour bus tales, however, involves Ron Saunders being so petty it's almost beautiful. The late Saunders was a good manager at several clubs, but most notably at Aston Villa where you'll remember him being startled half to death by John

72 Inappropriate behaviour aside here, what was Archie doing up the back of the bus if he was coaching staff? We thought there were rules to this sort of thing and he has to be down the front.

73 Baron Karren or Lady Brady or whatever title it is she's got now.

Burridge on that plane. Before his Villa days, however, he had a spell at Norwich, where he had fallen out with his chairman Sir Arthur South. South's Villa counterpart Doug Ellis tells us in his book, *Deadly*, that when the Midlands side secured promotion under Saunders, they happened to do so away at Norwich. Saunders clearly felt a personal vindication but managed to maintain a professional veneer while he was at the ground. Once they were on the bus, however, all bets were off. Ellis recalls: 'We arrived at a roundabout adjacent to Sir Arthur's business premises, a furrier's shop. Ron instructed the coach driver to go around that roundabout two or three times while all our players were asked to give the two-finger sign to Sir Arthur's place.' This is great – that'll show him. What says 'victory', what says 'I'm the better man', damn it, what says 'Britain' more than driving round and round a roundabout flicking the Vs? Surely this is the successful journey Arthur Ashe was talking about.

ALL WE WANT IS CONSISTENCY

'Single-minded chin'

Now for a chapter that, we don't mind admitting, might tell you more about your authors than the players. In short: it's not them, it's us. It's about the mistakes they make in their books you see. The tiny, inconsequential, forgivable ... no actually, really rather annoying mistakes they make from time to time. And then never stop making.

Let's put down an early marker. See if you can see what's wrong with this, from Mick Channon: 'It was just over a year after the 1970 World Cup in Mexico that I made my full England debut on 11 October 1972 at Wembley against Yugoslavia.' So well over two years later then, Mick? Seriously, what chance have we got if we're dealing with this?

As you're reading this, you are probably somewhere on the enjoying football spectrum – from liking a kickabout and glancing at the results, to forensically studying every detail of every match and career in a dark room full of old Rothmans Yearbooks, and being instantly able to recall those facts in any conversation should the need arise. And it will. Oh, it will. Placing ourselves somewhere between the two, the authors of this book like to think we've picked up a thing or two over the years of devotion, but wouldn't presume for one minute that we know more than those actually involved in the stories themselves. But here's the thing – and not to be dicks about it – *sometimes we do.*

One thing we've learned from reading as many of these books as we have is that often players don't know their own career. They will forget match details like who scored in which game, they will misremember who was at a club with them at any given time, and in some cases they will even forget which clubs they were sold to – we're looking at you, Neil Ruddock.

Sometimes the misinformation arises due to a bit of artistic licence. The tale is told and the yarn is spun and let the facts go hang. Maybe some feel that if the fiction is better than the truth, print the fiction. However, in football terms, that fiction may well be Steve Bruce's series of Steve Barnes novels, and therefore we know that not to be the case.

So in the words of Aaron Lennon, 'Gimme Some Truth'. Let's go deep, as your authors hit that sweet spot between Woodward and Bernstein and Saint and Greavsie, and uncover the half-truths, the fake news and the baffling oversights peddled by our heroes. A pain shared is a pain halved (or something), so we'll lay them out and can only hope you're made of sufficiently stern stuff that it doesn't keep you awake at night too. Let's start small with some numbers-based stuff and work up shall we? That way, you may start with a shrug, but by the end you might be every bit as frustrated as we are. And if nothing else, that's what we're here for.

It's easy to get numbers wrong isn't it? Sums are hard, phone numbers are too long, and contactless card payments have even done away with remembering your PIN, unless you're some kind of Jeff Bezos figure that spends more than £30 at a time. So we can almost look past this first batch of wrongness based around numbers if you can.

We should definitely forgive Gordon Banks because he won the bloody World Cup – a feat he puts down to an Alf Ramsey formation switch from 4-4-2 'to play 4-4-3'. Come on Gordon, you were behind them the whole time and must have had the odd quiet moment to count them all. You've got one too many in there. Maybe Greavsie could have played in that line-up after all.

Jason McAteer seems to think that you can take 24 players to a World Cup instead of the 23 everybody else takes, and Leroy Rosenior is another one who goes one louder a couple of times. Once he claims to have scored two in a West Ham win at Sheffield Wednesday in 1989 when he really only got one,[74] but he spreads the love by erroneously giving Paul Ince a hat-trick in a magnificent 4-1 win for the Hammers against Liverpool. He was indeed 'on fire' that night, but only got two in the finest claret and blue night of the baby

74 Alan Dickens can thank us later for getting him his goal back.

Guvnor's burgeoning career.[75] Paul Ince is not a man that requires such a confidence boost. He always struck us as having every faith in his considerable ability and even now he will occasionally rock up on *Match of the Day* in jeans and a jumper, killing the open-necked-shirt-last-knockings-of-a-wedding vibe that Shearer and the others usually have going on, and caring not a jot as he does it. Overly confident, if anything.

Derek Dougan talks proudly of fellow Northern Irish sporting royalty Mary Peters who 'had won the Gold in the Decathlon in Munich'. Derek's given Mary five more events there, the silly sausage. Mary Peters is a legend for winning the pentathlon, not the decathlon. The pentathlon was as much as athletics felt women could handle at that time, in its sexist dark past. In more recent years we've upgraded to the heptathlon of course, and we can only hope that one day women will achieve equality in this area and be considered daft enough to do ten athletics events in two days, just like the men.

Elsewhere Graham Roberts remembers playing alongside Diego Maradona for Spurs in a testimonial for Ossie Ardiles, saying that: 'Not many people remember, but the South American genius actually turned out for Spurs back in 1984.' Well you're right Graham; not that many people remember it being in 1984 – because it was actually in 1986. May 1986 to be precise, just before he knocked England out of the World Cup and put Peter Shilton in a bit of a mood for ever more. Not content with having the privilege of playing alongside El Diego, Graham seems to get a bit sniffy about Ossie having a Tottingham testimonial at all, saying it 'was staggering considering he had only been at the club for a few years and was the highest paid player at White Hart Lane'.

There might be something in what Roberts rather churlishly says, but then it turns out Ossie had been playing there for two years longer than he thought, so that fact, plus the promise of getting a crowd in to watch Maradona in a (really smart) Spurs shirt, might have helped a bit in the 'Can I have a testimonial, please?' chats.

Be honest – you think we're petty, don't you? Let it go, that's what you're thinking. Has Elsa from *Frozen* taught us nothing? What's a misremembered goal, a number slip, a wrong year or a pole vault

75 The other goals came from a highly comical own goal from a young Steve Staunton, and a Tony Gale free kick that was supposed to be indirect but he put it in anyway. It was that kind of night.

between friends? Well okay, if the numbers didn't get you then maybe the names will.

We all get names wrong though, don't we? We've all called an 'Archie' 'Alfie', a 'Rebecca' 'Rachel', a 'Les' 'Len', or just completely forgotten somebody's name and fudged it by forever calling them 'mate' every time we see them, but if you're writing the book of your life, surely it's worth spending at least a little time getting them right.

For example, Glenn Hoddle consistently refers to his Spurs manager Peter Shreeves as Peter Shreeve,[76] Mark Walters complains that Andy Hinton,[77] rather than Sinton, was pinching England caps in his position, and Frank McAvennie calls Ron Atkinson 'Roy'. You know, as in 'Big Roy'.

Perhaps most unforgivable of all is the time Carlton Palmer talks about meeting Harry Redknapp 'and his wife Janet' in Dubai.

Janet?

Janet?

Surely Trevor Morley if there is one football manager's wife's name in the world we all know it's *Sandra* Redknapp. He bloody loves that woman and doesn't shut up about her. He constantly mentions her in terms of getting under her feet if not in work, spoiling her Saturday night Italian if vexed after a defeat or her reluctance to move anywhere but Dorset preventing him taking jobs outside a 100-mile radius (apart from Jordan). Sandra was a much talked about, but never seen wife in the tradition of 'Er Indoors, Maris Crane or Mrs Mainwaring, until H became King of The Jungle on *I'm A Celebrity ... Get Me Out of Here*, and we all got to meet her. There's no other manager whose wife's name we know, whose journey to work we know, whose house we could pin down to one of about 20. Yet somehow Carlton forgot all of this and has probably been calling poor Sandra 'Janet' for years.

Though you wouldn't think it having watched him play, Carlton is less than accurate on more than one occasion. In *It is What it is* he talks about being suspended from the 1991 League Cup Final while at Sheffield Wednesday and hoping for a reprieve: 'The previous year, the same thing had happened to Gary Neville but he had asked the

76 We do remember a bit of this at the time but his name is definitely Shreeves. People used to lose the S off of poor Peter's name quite a lot. Probably the same troublemakers who gave an unwanted S to George Michael(s).

77 Unless he was deliberately getting his name wrong in a supreme act of shading.

F.A. to show leniency and they had postponed his suspension. Ron and I went down to London to see if we could cut the same deal. No dice, which pissed me off no end.' You'll remember, of course, that time 15-year-old Man Utd apprentice Gary Neville asked permission to play in the 1990 League Cup Final between Nottingham Forest and Oldham, because he was suspended two years before making his debut. Who could forget? It's worth mentioning also that the 'Ron' in that quote who went down to London with Carlton is, of course, Big Roy Atkinson.

In the same book Palmer also recounts his brief time at The City Ground playing under former England teammate David Platt. Platt didn't pick him, and therefore they didn't get on. It's a tale as old as time, but Palmer's reasoning is somewhat shaky: 'Platt took a similar line with me as George Graham had at Leeds (Graham was his manager at Arsenal … perhaps he had spoken to his protégé?), and I found myself not being selected to play.'

This is some weapons-grade paranoia from Carlton. George Graham was long gone from Highbury when Platt was bought by Bruce Rioch and never played under him anywhere else, so protégé might be stretching a point a little. As much as we enjoy the image of George Graham as some kind of Emperor Palpatine figure, pulling his dark strings in the background while former players of his all over the country do his bidding, there must have been another reason Platt didn't pick Carlton. Answers on a postcard, Forest fans.

Palmer definitely doesn't like Graham. He describes him very eloquently as 'a swaggering bully of a man, his debonair appearance never quite able to obscure the jutting, single-minded chin and resolute, unbending jaw'. Beautiful, powerful stuff, and we might even be on Carlton's side. However, he does say of Gorgeous George that 'Leeds was his last hurrah', and we can't let that slide because he went to Spurs afterwards and won the League Cup didn't he? That's a bit of a hurrah, surely? A 'yay!' at least, if not the full hurrah an FA Cup might merit.

By now you've either got a taste for this sort of stuff, in which case perhaps we should form a support group for one another – it's a kind of disease – or you've skipped on to find some saucier morsels elsewhere in the book. If it's the former, then gather round as we shine a light on a few more moments of wrong we encountered.

WHAT THEY SAY v	THE TRUTH
Billy Bonds tells us the closest he came to an England cap under Ron Greenwood was as an unused sub in a World Cup Qualifier v Italy in 1977 'while England made certain of reaching the finals with a 2-0 win'. He says friends never forgave the gaffer, 'but they don't understand Ron. His job that night was to ensure England won and went to Argentina …'	Someone's been lying to lovely Billy Bonds all these years. England didn't go to the World Cup in 1978, Bill. They didn't qualify after all.
That night in Turin. We all remember it. Every little detail of it as England crashed out of Italia 90. Parker's deflection, Lineker's equaliser and of course Gazza's tears. We can all picture the scene as Gary Lineker went to see if he was okay. In Peter Shilton's version of events, though, 'Gary Lineker signalled to Bobby Robson on the bench to 'watch the lad'.	No he didn't. The whole world saw Lineker say, 'Have a word with him', not 'watch the lad'. Indeed, it's probably what set him on the road to the *Match of the Day* gig he currently enjoys. How has Shilton got this wrong? It's burned as indelibly into the mind of England fans as Nobby dancing, 'Do I Not Like That' and David Nugent's outrageous goal against Andorra.
Jack Charlton calls Ireland's 1990 penalty shoot-out v Romania 'the first in the history of the competition' and claims that's why they hadn't prepared takers.	Penalties were introduced to the World Cup in 1978, two years after Panenka decided the Euros with that famous penalty we now call a … no, it's gone. There was then a pretty famous shoot-out between France and West Germany in 1982 in the Battiston semi-final, and three more at Mexico 86. Perhaps he means the first one in which David O'Leary scored a winner.

Zlatan Ibrahimović seems to be under the impression that Sweden lost a final group game against Germany at World Cup 2006, and didn't go any further.	We wouldn't want to tell Zlatan Ibrahimović he's wrong to his face, but Sweden definitely got out of England's group – then lost to Germany in the last 16. How good at football do you need to be to start forgetting details of World Cups you've played in? Elsewhere, Zlatan mixes up Bobby Robson and Bryan Robson, but to be fair even Bobby Robson did that occasionally.
This is in a similar bracket. Liverpool stalwart Phil Neal writes: 'My memories of the Cup Final clash with Manchester United in 1976 are also very vague.'	They're probably vague Phil, because that's 1977 you're thinking of. The 1976 final was Southampton v Man Utd and none of your business. Again, how many trophies do you need to win before you forget what cup finals you were in? A lot of trophies probably, and to be fair Phil's got them.
Brian Laws on transfers as Scunthorpe manager. 'Along the way we had to use the loan market and did well to bring in goalkeeper Lionel Perez (later to play in the top flight for Sunderland) from Newcastle.'	This must be the most niche of all these spots (and therefore the one we're both most proud and ashamed of), but he's wrong about Pérez. Pérez was at Sunderland in 'the top flight' from 1996 until 98, then went to Newcastle and loaned to Scunthorpe from there. Very much on his way down, rather than Laws spotting his potential. Sorry.
Norman Whiteside fondly recalls appearing at the 1982 World Cup for Northern Ireland 'when I broke Pele's fourteen-year-old record as the youngest player ever to play in the World Cup finals'.	Any fool knows that Pelé won the World Cup at 17 in 1958. That's 24 years, not 14, Norman. That's just quick maths, as the kids say.

Andy Goram is justifiably proud of becoming Rangers goalkeeper and ousting Chris Woods in doing so. Woods, who he describes as being, in 1986 mind you, 'England's number one'.	Andy is stretching the truth a little here. Shilton was still very much England's number one in 1986 and for another four years before Woods took over in earnest. Number two then? Shall we settle on number two? Yes let's. Sorry Gary Bailey.
Ruud Gullit overextends himself with the claim that 'the champions of Europe between 1975 and 1985 were English clubs such as Liverpool, Nottingham Forest, Aston Villa, Everton, Arsenal, Ipswich Town, West Ham United and Tottenham Hotspur. They won the big European prizes (European Cup, European Cup Winners Cup and UEFA Cup).'	Both West Ham and Arsenal can be flattered to be included in this list as they lost the finals they were in during this run. Ruud's word count goes up as he extends the list but our respect for him goes down.
Emlyn Hughes talks fondly about his *A Question of Sport* days and recalls a time when Tony Currie hilariously misidentified a game as being Ipswich v Norwich because 'One team were in green, the other in blue.' He goes on to say that he knew it was wrong because 'I recognized several East German players in blue. It was obvious that this was the classic, historical confrontation between the two Germanys in the 1974 World Cup.'	The beauty of this one, of course, is that Emlyn thinks he's correcting somebody else and is wrong in doing so. Delicious. First up surely Norwich play in yellow shirts and green shorts, not green shirts like Germany do away sometimes. Secondly, if that World Cup game is so classic and historic, why didn't Emlyn remember that West Germany played in white in that game? We'd be well good on *A Question of Sport*.
Chris Sutton says that during his time at Celtic, 'We always enjoyed beating Rangers at "Castle Grayskull" [sic], as we used to call it within the confines of our dressing room.'	We know he means Ibrox but Castle Grayskull was where the good guys were based in *Masters of the Universe*. Confusingly for a skeleton, Skeletor lived not at Castle Grayskull, but at Snake Mountain instead. So either Sutton thinks that Celtic were the baddies themselves, or they're all mistaken.

This one is also kind of quiz-based as it was the answer to a tremendous trivia question for a while in the 90s. When Teddy Sheringham[78] scored to equalise for Manchester United in the 1999 Champions League Final in Barcelona, and Clive Tyldesley's life peaked, a quiz question did the rounds that went something like, 'Who was the last Englishman before him to score in the Nou Camp'. The answer, somewhat trickily, was Carl Shutt who had scored for Leeds in an unusual neutral rematch there against Stuttgart in 1992 (look it up).

So we were surprised to see Sterland claim that Shutty notched 'at the San Siro'. And goes so far as to say that 'all the lads were taking the piss out of him because he kept saying, "I can't believe it, I can't believe it, I've scored in the San Siro."'

Mel freely admits that he missed the game in question due to injury and didn't travel. But surely he knows they travelled to Spain rather than Italy. Somebody must have told him. Sure enough, the game took place in the Nou Camp in Barcelona.

While at pains to say he was never frightened of Roy Keane, former Arsenal tough nut Patrick Vieira lets slip that the only player to ever truly put the wind up him was Vinnie Jones 'who I played against when he was at Aston Villa'. Vieira talks about the 'pure nastiness in his eyes and in the vibes he gave off. You could feel that you were not safe when you were playing against him.'

Vinnie Jones never played for Villa at all, so either Patrick is thinking of somebody else, or Vinnie rattled him so much that he was seeing him everywhere.

78 You know, off of *The Masked Singer*.

Ben Thornley talks about being an impressionable young player travelling with Man Utd to play at West Ham and says, 'To get to the ground you had to go past the notorious Boleyn pub on the corner, where they hung the effigy of Becks after the 1998 World Cup. So that was lively.'	This is a fib that has been allowed to take hold in the mists of time. The pub where that happened was The Pleasant Pheasant in South Norwood – deep in Crystal Palace country, and nowhere near West Ham. Admittedly, Beckham's first away game after the World Cup was at Upton Park and he received dog's abuse, but these two things have become conflated over time and it's simply not true. He's mistaken.
Steve Hodge talks about the infamous 'Hand of God' match between England and Argentina and remembers that after the game 'Maradona was running around celebrating in his shiny striped shirt.'	Of course, Argentina didn't wear their famous sky blue and white striped shirt against England. They wore a solid blue one. There's kind of a stripe in the design if you look closely enough but no more than the England shirt they were up against, and nobody claims that England wore stripes. All of which would be absolutely fine if Hodge's book wasn't called *The Man With Maradona's Shirt.* Even under normal circumstances somebody misremembering the Argentina strip from that day would be unusual. One of the greatest players of all time scored two of the most famous goals of all time while wearing it. But not only did Hodge play in that game, he facilitated one of the goals (the cheaty one), swapped his shirt with Maradona at the end, then named his entire book after that match. 'Shiny striped shirt', indeed.

Are you starting to see what we're up against? One more. Just one more.

WHAT THEY SAY	V	THE TRUTH
Neil Ruddock on his return to Spurs. 'Terry [Venables] reminded me of the conversation we'd had when he sold me to Southampton.'		The thing is, Terry didn't sell him to Southampton. He sold him to Millwall, and then he went from The Den to The Dell before returning to White Hart Lane.

It's a long and exhaustive, and indeed exhausting list. You must be coming round to our way of thinking now, surely? Even the most easy-oasy, laissez-faire, come-a-day-go-a-day, laidback types among you must be getting their gears ground a little bit by now.

Stories of Bobby Robson getting things a bit muddled with his players are not hard to find and some players are only too happy to line them up for us, but here's an example of Kenny Sansom swinging and missing.

Sansom evidently had a gift for impressions and tells us that he was trying to lift spirits on the plane back from Mexico and World Cup disappointment in 1986: 'I stood up at the front of the plane and in my best Columbo voice told Bobby Robson, "My wife thinks you're terrific, Mr Robson." He laughed and then called me Dave before turning to Luther Blissett and calling across, "What did you think of that Bluther?" I tell you: he may have been a great football manager but his memory was shit.'

Now then. This appears to be a case of the Steve Potts calling the kettle Kingsley Black. Sansom is trying to set this up as a confused Bobby Robson story but he's mugged himself here. He refers to Luther Blissett being on that plane. Well neither Luther, nor Bluther, were in that squad or on that flight and there is no way that the last part of this story happened. Now who's Columbo?[79]

Maybe we're being too harsh with all of this. After all these guys are top-level sportsmen and they've got other things to worry about. Emile Heskey is very good at illustrating that players can get caught in the moment and don't get bogged down in the detail while it's all going on. For example, he says of Liverpool's incredible 5-4 UEFA Cup Final victory over Alaves: 'I played in the game and honestly, I can't

79 It's us. We're Columbo.

remember a thing. I was exhausted and I was genuinely just playing on autopilot by then. I was mentally fucked.' Fair enough. Even in more general terms the former England striker is good on why the memory might not serve you well as a footballer: 'You are bouncing from one game to the next, hotel to stadium, training ground to home, airport to another city in another country.' Okay, okay, put like that it seems more understandable that some players might be hazy on the details.

Because being a footballer is our dream job we imagine that every game, goal and moment would stand out as a unique shining beacon in our minds if it were us out there. In reality, we can barely tell one day from another in our real jobs. Maybe it's the same for footballers. And maybe we shouldn't worry about it. We're only envious that we're not so good at football that we could casually forget the details of our glittering professional career. So let's wrap up the nitpicking, and move on to fresh pastures where nits will not be picked. In a minute.

Please allow us one final stop on the truth train. Harry 'Arry' Redknapp, The Grand Central Station of factual inaccuracies. There will be those among you who probably feel that his stories are not meant to be held under scrutiny any more than those of Hans Christian Andersen. That he's a dream weaver, a teller of tales. That to demand facts and evidence from him is like asking Peter Pan to explain the mechanics of flight. That he's a national treasure who should not be burdened with questions. In which case, in the words of every decent pre-*Match of the Day* news bulletin – look away now.

Let's start at the very beginning and Harry's account of his first game in charge at Bournemouth in 1982: 'They [Lincoln] were a very strong team in our league. They had John Fashanu and Neil Shipperley up front ...' Van wanker[80] Neil Shipperley was born in 1974 so would have been about eight had he trotted out for the Imps that day. His fantasy strike partner, Fash The Bash,[81] did at least play for Lincoln, but not until the following year. Instead, both Gordon Hobson and Derek Bell got hat-tricks that day in a 9-0 win for Lincoln that did little to indicate Harry's future success, but don't warrant a mention, bless them.

Remember when Harry did the South Coast unthinkable and defected from Portsmouth to Southampton as boss? He claims he had

80 Some say 'Vanker'.

81 Full name: John Bashanu Fashanu.

no idea how much the rival fans hated each other despite spending a large part of his life on the South Coast, and liking football. As we all know he later returned in glory, but not before he took his Saints to Fratton Park for an almighty hiding at the hands of his former charges. Pompey smashed them 4-1 on a day that you might think Harry would find awkward. Not so apparently.

'The Portsmouth players were fantastic. They all came up, wished me well and still called me gaffer.' Sounds lovely. No grudges then. Far from it according to Harry who claims that his former striker Lomana LuaLua 'took pity on me', and, Harry implies, came off injured when there wasn't too much wrong with him. He says, 'Portsmouth were soon 4-1 up and I think it was at that point Lualua decided enough was enough. We had always got on well and he didn't want to rub it in.'

This seems to us to be on a par with referee Jeff 'Good Guy' Winter believing the Anfield Kop rose to its collective feet to see him off on his last appearance there. Why didn't LuaLua just ease up if he thought that was the case? Why score two so quickly if he wanted to make his former gaffer's day easier? It doesn't make much sense. In fact, instead of feigning injury to get himself taken off, the official story was that he aggravated his hamstring doing his famous flipping celebration. So either he took himself off to spare Harry's blushes or celebrated scoring against him so hard that he pulled a hamstring doing it. You be the judge.

However, Redknapp's pièce de résistance is the shaggy dog story about Carl Richards, a striker he signed for Bournemouth from Enfield. Harry takes up the tale: 'Carl was terrible. After about four games of this he came to see me. "I've got a mate," he said: "He was asking if he could have a trial. He's a striker, like me."

"And is he as good as you, Carl?" I asked, suspiciously.

"No, he's not as good as me," he said, "but he's decent."

"Well. Tell him not to fucking bother then," I snapped.'

The mate, in Harry's story, turns out to be Ian Wright, who can be added to the list of those that have slipped through his fingers along with Marcelo Salas and Andriy Shevchenko. Wright, apparently, having been signed by Palace, scored a hat-trick 'the following Saturday'. The trouble is that Richards signed for Bournemouth in 1986/87. Ian Wright was already playing regularly in the Palace first team in 1985/86 so it's unlikely that he wanted a trial with Bournemouth, or that he was hanging around at Enfield when Harry was picking Richards up, as he suggests in the tale. Oh, and it doesn't look like Bournemouth even played Palace until the 1987/1988 season. Ian Wright may or may not have scored a hat-trick in the game – to be honest we went to look it up but we'd lost the will to live, but it's fair to say that Wrighty's own book is short on corroborating evidence for Harry. The two have clearly had their run-ins since this fictitious first meeting, with Redknapp's former West Ham striker putting it politely with: 'I don't find I've got that much to say to him.'

We simply don't know why he does it. Harry's is a life well lived and a career to be admired. Why he feels the need to make stuff up is beyond us. But maybe they're all just honest mistakes. What we do know is that should he ever get the call for a *Jackanory* reboot, or *CBeebies Bedtime*, we'd like to see him leaning out of his car window reading it.

We promise we'll stop now.

TACTICS, TANTRUMS & TEA CUPS

'Slipper bath'

What, exactly, do we know about that mysterious inner sanctum known as the dressing room?

Well, for starters we know that it's a complex place full of egos, testosterone, hierarchies and nudity. Nowhere else quite compares, as Marco Negri writes as he discusses settling in at Rangers: 'I quickly understood the rules of the dressing room and the balance I had to strike between enjoying the experience and knowing my place.' Negri may say he picked it all up quickly, but clearly this is a fragile ecosystem of rules, regulations and giant baths that would baffle an outsider.

'There's a special camaraderie about a football team's dressing room,' wrote Emlyn Hughes. 'The humour is rich and ripe.' We must not forget the humour – better known as ... well, let's go to Paul Parker: 'Even now, after years out of the game, the dressing room banter is the part of the game I miss most.' Course it is, Paul. All ex-footballers miss the banter; this has been established over many years of ex-footballers telling us that they miss the banter. As laymen, we can only speculate as to how magical the dressing-room banter must be to leave so many grown men in a constant state of melancholic longing for that sparkling changing room repartee. Paul adds that 'the smell of Deep Heat is the same in any dressing room', and he makes an excellent point there. It is a place that grabs all the senses – not just seeing and hearing, but taste (oranges? Do they still do oranges?), touch (massages, fights) and smell – chiefly, the unmistakable aroma of heat rub.

So this much we know. And yet, these places remain largely a mystery. Unlike in US sport, where cameras have been invading 'locker rooms' for years, access to football dressing rooms is still relatively rare. We might occasionally see steamy pictures of a lower-league side celebrating a giant-killing in the cup – with obligatory references to drinking beer instead of champagne and the reporter inevitably getting doused in Lucozade. And we have vivid memories of your Reids, your Warnocks, your Frys and your Sittons swearing with entertaining vigour at their charges in TV documentaries in ways that we haven't quite seen in the new era of swish docs about the Man Citys and Sunderlands of this world. But beyond that, we can't say we really have much knowledge of this forbidden place.

Fortunately, our research has helped us build up a picture as to what really goes on behind closed doors. So, let's all take our clothes off and slip into a big old bath together and discover the truth of what goes on in the dressing room.

RITUAL

So much of football is about ritual. We fear change, whether it's kick-off times, short goal kicks, or the dreaded hot button topic of VAR (Apologies for even mentioning it. Seriously.). We all have our rituals – the pubs we go to, the lucky socks we wear, or the jaguar's paw that must be in the right-hand inside pocket of our jacket (just us?). Anything that interferes could cost our team victory and ruin an entire week.

Players are no different; most like to repeat the same routine before every game. Stuart Pearce admits his programme was pretty much planned to the minute after 2.15pm, and involved regular stretching and kicking a ball against a wall. But, while we have no doubt that this rigmarole was the very personification of intensity, it doesn't sound particularly out of the ordinary, apart from the fact, noted by Joey Barton who would secretly watch him prepare while a youngster at City, that 'he wore nothing but his socks, shinpads and a pair of white pants … He'd be sweating, scary.' We can imagine.

Slightly stranger is the admission by several players – Terry Phelan, Paul Walsh, Sam Allardyce and Carlton Palmer amongst them – that they downed a shot of brandy just before taking the field to get the blood pumping. Palmer says of his Sheffield Wednesday days: 'I would wander into the lounge area in the main stand at Hillsborough, past the surprised sponsors and be-suited executives, jog to the bar where the bar staff had lined up my drink, swig it down, and run straight onto the pitch.' Superb. And we salute the use of 'be-suited' there. Lovely.

Viv Anderson reports that he once discovered Brazilian midfielder Emerson having a crafty fag in the toilets before a game at Middlesbrough, which probably isn't as unusual as fans may think – or wasn't. But the dressing room toilets are certainly a recurring theme. Chris Sutton says he used to eat tonnes of food the night before a game before plying himself with coffee before the match, 'in between frequent visits to the toilet'.

Lee Clark says legendary eccentric keeper John Burridge approached games at Newcastle in a similar way: 'His food intake before a game involved jars of Heinz baby food, with a tray full of nuts and raisins. His farts and shits were horrific! And he always went to the toilet with the bog door open so we could smell the aftermath.' Primal, isn't it? Like a lion marking its turf.

Even World Cup winners like to enjoy a big old poo before games, with Jack Charlton saying: 'I would take the programme and go and sit on the toilet for three or four minutes. I'd always leave the programme on the left hand side of the toilet before I went back to the dressing room.' Nice idea to leave something for Billy Bremner to read. Thoughtful. Others preferred to purge out of other orifices. These days, we see former Fulham and West Ham defender Tony Gale as a safe pair of hands in the Sky commentary booth, but Leroy Rosenior says he would show some signs of nerves in his playing days at the Boleyn: 'Tony was always vociferous before a game and his loud tone set me at ease. "You're gonna be great, Leroy," he said. "Just come short and get the ball from me, or spin round like we used to do at Fulham. I'll find you. I always did." To be fair, he was right. He then went off to the toilets to be sick. Again that put me at ease as Tony always did that.' Marvellous – we love the idea of Leroy being a bit nervous until he hears the soothing sounds of Galey fetching up his breakfast. Ah, the reassuring chuckle of half-digested scrambled eggs on toilet water.

Tone was in good company, mind. The great Sir Stanley Matthews admits that he chundered before every match he played. Given that Stan famously played until the age of 50, that's a whole lot of puking going on. No wonder they called him the Wizard of the Dribble: 'In a perverse way, I felt it did me good, ridding my stomach of partially digested food that might lie heavy and impair my performance. Eddie Clamp, my Stoke colleague of the sixties, used to call it "Stan's technicolour yawn".' We could have sworn that was a phrase from the 1980s. There's nothing new is there?

Urine is probably the least repulsive of the sick-faeces-pee triumvirate, and yet we can't help thinking that former Everton captain Kevin Ratcliffe's habit was the worst of the lot – it just seems more ... *calculated*. Norman Whiteside tells us that he 'used to pee in the tunnel before leading the team out'. Now, we don't particularly want to delve too deeply into this practice, but Whiteside's description does leave us with questions. Principally: how did he do this? You may assume it was surreptitious, with Little Kevin being poked out of the jockstrap and the stream allowed to flow freely out of a leg of his shorts. But this was the 1980s – there was precious little room for anything to escape the tiny tighties worn by players of that era.

Man City's VIP tunnel would today rule out that kind of behaviour. Think of the baffled diners looking up from their cheeseboard to be greeted by the sight of an Everton player – the Everton captain, mind you – splashing the windows at his leisure in front of a shocked Moonchester and a dismayed Moonbeam. Unacceptable.

Generally, we associate dressing rooms with players getting psyched up for games, and as we'll see, there's plenty of that. But relaxation is important too. In his World Cup diary of 1986, Peter Reid says that Glenn Hoddle was listening to some tunes to get him in the mood prior to the quarter-final with Argentina: 'Glenn Hoddle was sitting by the wall with ear-phones on. I asked him what he was listening to and he made a gesture like an eagle – he is a big fan of The Eagles, and that was his way of relaxing.' Absolutely fine. Except ... what gesture would clearly denote an eagle? Did he flap his arms? But that could have meant The Byrds. Or did he make talons with his hands and screw his mouth into something like a beak? But that might have been a bit rodentish and made Reidy think he was listening to the Boomtown Rats. Maybe it was an elaborate charade of both.

One thing we do know is that Glenn enjoys seeing others appreciate music before games. In his diary for the 1998 World Cup, he admits: 'Les Ferdinand's tapes were a big hit. Les certainly knows where it's at musically; Incey and I were watching him dancing as he was getting changed. He couldn't help it. It was great to watch.' Sounds a bit pervy to us, but at least one of your authors would watch the great Sir Les Ferdinand do much less interesting things than dancing.[82]

—

82 Such as shopping, gardening or playing crazy golf, if you ever fancy it, Les. Les?

At least the headphones kept it personal and stopped anyone falling out over musical tastes. Stuart Pearce remembers hearing Newcastle manager Ruud Gullit muttering, 'What thee fook is thees shit?' (Stu's phonetic spelling, not ours). Pearce adds, as if explaining why a Tinder date went wrong: 'Musically, Ruud and I were incompatible.' He says that he didn't even play his faves like The Clash, either: 'a lot of people don't like that music so I compromised with Big Country, Oasis and Spear of Destiny. I would never sell out with crap like garage.' Interestingly, Pearce's choice meant that the Newcastle dressing room was the only place you could still observe anyone listening to Spear of Destiny in 1998.

Stu adds that when he returned to Newcastle with West Ham, Alan Shearer pushed open the dressing-room door so he could hear what the lads were playing: 'It was soul and I looked at him in disgust. "You've sold out," I said.' OK, Boomer. For Pearce, music is a serious business, as tribal as football.

Terry Butcher takes us back to Mexico 86 again with word on how he relaxed before a game. Like you, we expected walls to be butted and iron nails to be crushed in his grinding teeth, but no. He preferred hypnotherapy tapes 'made especially for me by an Ipswich doctor, Doc Lewis ... Doc's taped message had told me that the sun would be hot but it would act as a stimulant. Despite the heat I would be cool inside and ooze authority.' Butcher says that the Ipswich team had been using it during the previous season, 'but I was the only England player to use the technique'. Probably with good reason, Tel: Ipswich had just been relegated. Moreover, he was listening to this tape prior to England's insipid 1-0 loss to Portugal.

More conventional – in a way – was Ted MacDougall who writes: 'My pre-match stretching exercise with Alan Ball at Southampton consisted of having a "slipper" bath – that's two of us in a single bath of hot water. The lads would go and get us a bar of chocolate each and we would eat that while in the bath.' How exactly did this develop? Did Bally say he fancied a pre-match bath one day, and Ted agreed, then one or the other murmured 'shall we get in together and put our feet up each other's armpits?' And then when they agreed to this, which one whispered 'Shall we have a Drifter while we're in here?' Well, it would be nice to have something shareable. Don't get us wrong, it sounds adorable, it's just that football seems to have changed awfully quickly between the era of Sir Stan yakking up his morning cornflakes and Ted and Alan blissfully scissoring under a cloud of Matey bubbles.

Players themselves have a whole spectrum of ways to get themselves wound up, with degrees of aggression. First, there's Terry Butcher who, presumably after the hypnosis tapes, liked to make himself heard in the standard manner: 'I normally shout encouragement such as, "First twenty minutes lads," or, "Early shout sorts it out," "Back each other up in tackles," and so on … It's important for a big beefy man to make a noise and it can also intimidate opponents. If he's quiet it gives the impression he's a wimp or easy meat.' Surely not all hard men are loud mouths, though. Football's had its fair share of silent assassins after all – Ole Gunnar Solskjaer, for one. No, wait, he was the Baby-Faced Assassin, that's different. Anyway, Butch adds, 'I always run on the pitch at full speed with my fists clenched and teeth gritted.' Fair's fair, that does sound terrifying. Particularly for the mascots. And especially if they're holding his hand, fingers slowly being crushed as they're dragged along in his wake like a teddy bear caught in the door of a moving train.

While Terry the Butch was all about the words and the noise, others are more about the action, like ex-Rangers midfielder Lee McCulloch, who, with keeper Allan McGregor, once found a tactile way to get the adrenaline flowing before an Old Firm game: 'We stared at each other, eyeball to eyeball, and kept pushing each other like we were about to fight. I told him to slap me to get me even more angry and he did so with his gloves on, then I just slapped him back right in the face. We didn't smile, we just kept on getting angrier and angrier.' Sadly, Lee's forgetting the first rule about Fight Club there, although the slapping with gloves on reminds us of a different kind of club.

Sitting at the top of the aggression tree is, as you'd expect, Andy Morrison. The former Manchester City bruiser admits in his relentlessly violent book that before games he'd 'go into the toilet and head butt a door'. Of course he did. Yet it must be said that John Fashanu seems to be playing a different game altogether. Dwight Yorke recalls a European tie with Inter Milan when they were both at Villa: 'the Italians did not know what to make of this glistening giant, stripped down to his shorts and all oiled up, going through a kung fu martial arts-style routine in the communal warm-up area before the players' tunnel', which comfortably demolishes Butcher's belief that being quiet makes you look like a 'wimp'. But then, who among us could carry off the oiled-up look quite like Fash?

TEAM TALKS

All of these rituals and superstitions are, however, merely the backdrop to the real drama of the dressing room: the manager's team talk. This, we are often told, is where the manager makes his corn, where a few well-placed words – the fabled arm round the shoulder, the metaphorical kick up the backside – can be the difference between winning and losing. Managers must keep their team motivated by whatever means necessary or they might suffer that classic prelude to losing their job – losing the dressing room.

Never. Lose. The. Dressing. Room.

As you'd expect, different coaches have different motivational styles. Lee Howey played under our old friend Terry Butcher when he was player-manager (remember them?) at Sunderland, and after reading this account of Tel's motivational methods, we are wondering just how those hypnosis tapes had evolved over the years, because he seems to have lost his mind. In this tale, he makes his entrance into the dressing room just 35 minutes before a crunch game during a particularly poor run of form: 'Quite the lad for a grand gesture, his head had been shaved down to the wood. For some reason he seemed to think this was inspirational and the stuff of leaders, rather than what it really was – bonkers. He bellowed: "We're fucking commandoes! I've had this haircut because I'm a commando and you're all going to be fucking commandoes too. We're gonna parachute in, get the victory, then fuck off out! NO SURRENDER!"' Howey says Butcher was well aware of the loaded nature of that final phrase and was hoping it might fire up the Catholics in the squad, but, perhaps not surprisingly, he didn't get the reaction he wanted, or expected. Not that we're quite sure what he expected: 'Everyone just stared at Butch in silence. It was truly bewildering.' What a journey: from quiet contemplation with hypnosis tapes, to sprinting into battle with jaw and fists clenched, to this apparent full-on breakdown. It's quite the metamorphosis.

These attempts at psychological mind games rarely seem to work. Neil Warnock laughs in his book about the fact that when he took over a QPR side struggling pathetically near the foot of the Championship table in 2010, there was a sign on the dressing-room door saying 'Winners Only'. He took the sign down and within 15 months they had won the league. Despite this, David Batty tells us that Howard Wilkinson absolutely loved to leave motivational phrases – 'cryptic daily messages' Batts calls them – on a whiteboard in the Leeds dressing room, along the lines of: '"Be professional" or "When the going gets tough, the tough get going"', which don't seem particularly cryptic – more like a sign that Wilko was a fan of Billy Ocean.[83] But once again, it didn't really work: 'Frankly, we thought it was a joke,' says Batty witheringly, although one thing they did inspire was a classic old-school classroom prank: 'One day, when we were waiting for Howard to come in, I erased every other letter from his daily slogan. I can't remember what the words said, but I do recall how visibly upset he was that they had been violated.' Once, when one of your authors was at school, a talented classmate drew an extremely accurate caricature of our form tutor, naked and masturbating, on the whiteboard. The look we saw on Mr Haddock's face that day when he strolled in to be confronted by that searing piece of satire was, we assume, very similar to that of Wilko's: disappointed. Resigned. Oh so tired.

When we imagine real, tub-thumping team talks, they're probably not far away from that delivered by Scotland boss Willie Ormond before a match in 1975 with the auld enemy, as described by Ted MacDougall: 'Right lads, I want you to get bloody stuck into them. Get right up their bloody arses. These Scotland fans will have walked eight miles to get to the game because the Underground's on bloody strike. Give them something to bloody shout about!' Yes, that's the stuff! Get those tartan hearts roaring with pride! This call to arms must've really resonated – it was basic, yes, but it was a match with England. This was exactly the kind of thing that was required. MacDougall says that Ormond then asked if there were any questions: 'Sandy Jardine, our captain, replied, "Yes boss, the lads would like to know when we are getting our expense sheets?"' Oh Scotland, you lovable shambles.

England won 5-1.

Yet, as fans, we often demand this sort of blood and thunder approach. We love to hear about things like Fergie's famous hairdryer treatment, while Neville Southall confirms the cliche that teacups do, or at least did, get thrown about by irate gaffers, in this case, Everton's

83 Rumours that other motivational messages included 'Red Light Spells Danger' and 'Get Outta My Dreams, Get Into My Car' sadly remain unconfirmed.

Mike Walker: 'When Spurs beat us at White Hart Lane he lobbed a teacup at the wall and covered my CD player with tea. I'm not one to lose my temper, but I told him he was a prick.'

But does using terror really work to win the hearts and minds of players? Here's Dwight Yorke remembering a truly sensational half-time team talk from Roy Keane in 2008 when his team were losing 2-0 to Northampton in the Carling Cup:

'We knew we were in for a tongue-lashing. We waited for the fireworks. Keano emerged from the washroom, quietly, calmly. He washed his hands, dried them and asks our kit manager if he can get the tactics board.' Christ. He takes his time. It's not blind rage. He plans it. And then delivers. 'The board goes up. And Keano's aura of calm completely disappears. He takes a running jump at the tactics board and smashes it over with a kung-fu kick. He screamed at Danny Collins, "Never come to me and ask for a contract again." And then the captain, Dean Whitehead, is next. "Captain? Captain? Some fuckin' captain you are," he rages, slapping Dean about the head in the process, before turning on us all. "I can't trust any of you ——. None of you. I'll rephrase that. The staff I can trust. But you lot? None of you."' Smashing the tactics board – which Jimmy Bullard reported he did at Ipswich too – screaming, slapping people about – absolutely terrifying stuff. Who among us has not wished to inflict that on our team when they're getting tonked at half-time? But the most impressive thing there is surely the words 'I'll rephrase that'. It's beautiful. Mid-rage. Angry enough to destroy equipment like an Irish Chuck Norris, and yet still, at the back of his mind, he's thought 'wait, Roy, you're being unfair on the physio there. And the kitman. It's not their fault.' And he corrects himself. And it worked, too. Two late goals from Anthony Stokes plus four successful penalties ensured that Dean Whitehead's head did not take a further beating at full time.

Such bursts of anger come with risks. Vince Hilaire remembers Howard Wilkinson, possibly still internally fuming about some disrespect shown to a whiteboard message featuring a quote from a Lionel Richie hit, was going mad at half-time after a complex free-kick routine had gone wrong. In his anger, he kicked the treatment table, but unluckily, it was screwed to the floor and did not budge an inch. Hilaire writes: 'So he said, "I want you to give me 50 per cent more effort than you did in the first half and then Alan Sutton can treat my fucking foot because I think I've broken it."'

Wilko would have done well to consider a more cerebral approach. Ruud Gullit reckons: 'Managers who throw a tantrum risk raising the issue of their expiry date. The first burst of anger makes an impression, but the effect soon begins to wear off.' To demonstrate the point he recalls an FA Cup tie where Chelsea were losing 2-0 to Liverpool and he was so disgusted with their display that he just sat in the dressing room reading the paper at half-time: 'There was a deathly silence. Just before the bell rang to signal the second half I made a slight tactical adjustment and I said to them calmly: "You have forty-five minutes to make up for that appalling display."' Chelsea won 4-2. If you look carefully, you can tell that Ruud is quite pleased with himself about this incident.

He's right about the tantrums though. Shout and bawl too much, and players simply stop responding – at least, they'll stop responding in the way the coach wants. Up at Dundee United, Ralph Milne had a delightful party piece: 'I had this daft trick inspired by Stan Laurel where I would fold my ears in on themselves. Then put my finger in my mouth and blow, which in turn made my ears pop back out.' He used to break it out behind boss Jim McLean's back when he was giving both barrels to some poor, under-performing teammate: 'The result was hilarious to watch as they struggled desperately not to smirk, or, worse still, burst out laughing in our irate gaffer's face.'

At least these pranks were done without the gaffer's knowledge. Andy Morrison, while on loan at Crystal Palace, was less worried about consequences. After one nasty defeat, he and the rest of the Palace squad were on the wrong end of a verbal lashing not just from boss Alan Smith, but also from chairman Simon Jordan. They took turns apparently, and neither of them was playing good cop. Morrison picks up the story: 'We had been in there for forty-five minutes and I was starting to get pissed off. I had had enough and so I lifted my left arse cheek up and let out an almighty fart. It was like a trumpet going off and it echoed around the room. Jamie Pollock started laughing and one or two of the other lads did, too. Jordan didn't find it amusing.' Soon after, Morrison's loan ended. But there was a lesson there: bang on too long, and you start to lose the room. Thank you for coming to our TED talk.

But we reserve the best tale of motivation we read for Harry Redknapp. It didn't come from him, though. It came from the visiting chairman of Wimbledon, Sam Hammam. Essentially, he got to Upton

Park early and covered the away dressing room with graffiti. Redknapp explains in *Always Managing*: 'Filthy insults aimed at the Wimbledon players: stuff about Vinnie Jones, stuff about John Fashanu, calling them wankers and worse. At that moment, Sam walked in. I was furious. "What have you done?" I asked him. "No, not me, you have done this," he said, standing there with pens in his hand.' You can keep Ruud Gullit and his *Daily Mail* (it was, wasn't it?), your mystical envelopes and your shattered tactics boards. Swearing all over the walls is the purest, most brilliant psychology we have ever read when it comes to understanding and motivating a particular group of players. Underhanded, of course. But utter genius.

DISPUTES

Clearly, dressing rooms can be heated places, where tensions can rise fast and tempers can get out of control. Paul Walsh writes that he and Brian Stein once had a particularly nasty row at Luton that started on the pitch and culminated in the dressing room when Stein threw a boot at the back of Walsh's head. This resulted in a ruck during which some of the very worst swears were thrown around with reckless abandon: 'There was some nasty stuff said by both of us and it was always going to be hard to rectify the situation after that,' says Walshy.

Pretty hardcore, but nothing compared to the kind of insult Arsenal keeper Jens Lehmann aimed at Emmanuel Eboué after a mistake he made during a game with Manchester United: 'My first target during the break was my pal Eboué: "You wimp!" I screamed, pretty much the worst thing you could say to a Premier League player.' Yes, take that Eboué, you weed, you weakling. Jens absolutely went for the jugular there.

Other rows quickly descend into a kind of enjoyable farce with insults thrown around that we previously had little knowledge of. For instance, Keith Gillespie did not get on at all well with boss Kevin Blackwell at Sheffield United and during one game when he was a sub, Blackwell decided to replace a winger with young full-back Kyle Naughton, rather than the more obvious choice of Gillespie. This sent Keith over the edge, and the simmering tensions boiled over back in the dressing room: 'Blackwell was shaking with rage. It got silly. "That cunt over there," he said, pointing at me. "Fuck off you cunt." "You're a fucking cunt." "You fucking egg." "You're a fucking egg."'

The 'egg' is a new insult on us. We're still not quite sure what it means, or why it's worse than the worst word they used earlier in their exchange. But when rage hits, sense can be the first casualty. Of all the disputes we read about, the most ludicrous concerned a cup of tea. This one requires a bit of back story from Derek Dougan: 'Since coming to the Midlands in 1961 I was surprised by a regional taste for sterilised milk, which I cannot drink. In my tea I always have pasteurised milk.' This seems fine – anyone's entitled to their particular taste for milk in their tea after all, and it's only a minor difference. It's not like today, when we have cow's, goat's, almond, soya, oat, hemp, rice, cashew and coconut milks all widely available for the discerning tea drinker. Doog explains that at half-time, he'd skip the tea rather than drink the brew with sterilised milk that was served, and then after the game he'd nip to the tea room next to the dressing room to get his usual cup with pasteurised milk.

Still with us on this milky odyssey? Anyway, all was fine until a poor performance against Burnley left boss Bill McGarry in a terrible mood. At the end of the game, trainer Jack Davis was kindly bringing in Doog's special brew when McGarry blew his top: '"Get that … tea out of here!" If the tea the rest of the players was drinking was not good enough, he went on, then … The rest of his words were lost in mutterings, as he gave us a verbal lashing.' Doog says in the showers afterwards all the players ignored the game and told him he should have argued back over his tea. Deciding they were right, Doog dressed and stormed up to McGarry's office to have it out with him. Fortunately, common sense prevailed and McGarry admitted he was in the wrong. And so the Big Tea Dispute came to a close. But, surely, people cannot have fallen out over something much more trivial than the type of milk dribbled into a nice, strong, post-match cuppa? As long as the milk doesn't go into the cup first, surely we're all okay? Doog also lets us know that Bill McBuzzkill banned sweets from coaches too, although in this case everyone ignored his rules and the gaffer had no idea what 'rebellious munching was going on behind him'.

If you're ever sitting around with friends and you've become bored of discussing literature, philosophy or politics, an always reliable subject matter is to decide who are the hardest managers currently working in the game. In recent years, the Premier League managers you'd avoid tussling with would probably be the Sean Dyches and

Nuno Espírito Santos of this world, or perhaps David Moyes, who, even as he edges into his late 50s, seems to be all sinews, elbows, knees and menace. Going further back, if you ever had suspicions that Martin Jol was a bit handy, he'd be ready to tell you that you're right. Ledley King says that once the then Spurs boss asked the squad which players they'd take to war with them. After a brief discussion, he chipped in: '"You should take me – I'm a lion!" He made it clear he could look after himself.' Well, we wouldn't tell him his brothers Dick and Cock have got daft names, that's for sure.

While plenty of managers can handle themselves, it hasn't always stopped players from having a proper pop when the occasion arises – mainly at Southampton, it seems. Lawrie McMenemy recalls with regret a scuffle he had with centre-back Mark Wright after he'd delivered a half-time dressing down following a poor showing. When Wright 'mouthed something derogatory' as they filed out to the tunnel, McMenemy lost it: 'I shouted at him to repeat what he had said and grabbed at him. It was beside the open door to the bath area. We were caught off-balance and ended stumbling through the door pushing and pulling at each other.' In a rare mea culpa for footballer autobiographies, Lawrie adds: 'I realised the seriousness of what happened, let go of him and told him to get out. I stood there on my own, appalled by my reaction.' So, we're led to believe that the fight sort of petered out and the boss, belatedly, took the high road.

Except, that doesn't seem to be the whole story. David Armstrong, the Saints' goal-getting midfielder, remembers a different ending to the dust-up, as he happened to be in the shower area at the time: 'Before I knew what was happening there was some shoving and Wright pushed Lawrie into the water.' Does this mean that when McMenemy was stood on his own, appalled at his reaction, he was actually doing so from within the communal bath, water dripping from his club suit? We can only hope so – not because we don't love Lawrie, because we do love Lawrie ('I don't believe it … I don't believe it … He's not even give us a fuckin' penalty'), but the image of Wright finishing the fight by shoving his boss in the bath is just too wonderful.[84]

In a later era at The Dell, Matt Le Tissier reports on what could have been a fight for the ages between boss Chris Nicholl, a bruising centre-half in his day, and left-back Mark Dennis, who, you know, did

84 Especially as Lawrie often favoured the long mac as his touchline attire, now sadly lost in an era festooned with pitch-side gilets and jardigans.

not take any prisoners, to put it politely. Tiss says Nicholl was furious to discover that Dennis had been playing snooker until the early hours before a League Cup semi-final, and was pretty eager to confront him about it: 'We were all listening outside the dressing room when it kicked off. Chris was absolutely boiling and hit out and cut Mark's eye with a right-hander. He thought Mark was going to hit him, so he got his retaliation in first.' Mark Wright, perhaps empathising with Dennis, took him to hospital for stitches, and, once repaired, Dennis sought revenge: 'He stormed back into the changing room to find Chris having a shower, naked in all his glory.' Just as we settle in for the details of an epic fight reminiscent of the wrestling-in-the-buff scene between Oliver Reed and Alan Bates in *Women in Love*, only without the roaring fire, Tiss says Mark Wright managed to calm things down. Shame.

If there's one manager we'd struggle to picture getting involved in a stramash, it has to be Sir Uncle Bobby Robson – yet even he could get drawn into a scrap if the conditions were right. This tale is from 1971, when Sir Bob was still a young gaffer, and comes from Kevin Beattie's autobiography *The Beat*. At the time, Beattie was a youngster on duty cleaning the dressing room after a match: 'All of a sudden there was a confrontation as Bill Baxter and Tommy Carroll, who were not playing in the Leeds match, had a go at the Gaffer. A punch was thrown, but in what seemed a matter of seconds, the Gaffer and Cyril Lea had sorted them out and pinned Baxter and Carroll to the floor.' Boom – sounds like Robson and Lea very efficiently double-teamed them, like it wasn't their first time, working together in unison like Starsky and Hutch in their pomp.

More common than player v manager fights are player v player fights. Adebayo Akinfenwa has had one or two, and has the whole thing down to a fine art, grading his assaults according to the severity of the provocation: 'throughout my career when I give beat-downs I've developed a level system. The higher the level, the harder I go at them. Because I'm right-handed, level one is a left-hand punch. Level two is a right-hander. Level three is a combo … Lyle Taylor is the first to push me all the way to level five. I unleashed!' Well, you've got to have a system. It's like the Nando's Peri-ometer. Bayo does at least say it's 'mostly playful', but the 'mostly' bit doesn't sound particularly reassuring. You can't really get 'playfully' mauled by a tiger, after all. Anyway, here are our picks for the best dressing-room bust-ups:

PAUL DEVLIN V MARCUS BENT

This one comes courtesy of Neil Warnock, who managed this pair at Sheffield United. He says they were not exactly best mates and on one occasion when Bent was trying something fancy and lost the ball instead of passing, Devlin got cross. They argued on the pitch and all the way back to the dressing room, until the discussion was finally ended, quite abruptly. The key thing here is to note how much Warnock relished the whole thing as the pair went nose to nose: 'Straight away, Devlin tilted his head back and head-butted him. Smashed his nose. Blood everywhere. It was brilliant.'[85]

Now you may not care for Neil, and at least one of your authors is not his biggest admirer, but you have to love this. Far too often when there's a scrap in a match some cliche-ridden ex-pro or some robotic commentator will say 'now, we don't like to see this sort of thing'. This is despite the roar of the crowd indicating that, yes, we absolutely *do* like this sort of thing – very much, in fact. At least Warnock admits that it was, indeed, brilliant. Just not necessarily for poor Marcus.

MALCOLM MACDONALD V TERRY HIBBITT

Dressing-room fights tend to be extensions of something that's happened on the pitch beforehand, and this was no exception as Supermac and Hibbitt got into it over a bad through ball. Malcy explains: 'I flew at Terry, got hold of him by his shirt, and lifted him up the wall with my left hand with the aim of hitting him with the right. As I drew my fist back, John Tudor grabbed hold of the top of my arm, and what happened was that I propelled John straight over my shoulder, as I went to smash Terry, and he hit Terry on the chin with the top of his head!'

Well, this is some sort of comic book combat, is it not? Malcolm Macdonald hurling an *entire person* from behind him over his shoulder and therefore converting a human body into some kind of rudimentary weapon? Incredible work. It's like something out of *Desperate Dan*.[86] Macdonald says things calmed down and later he approached Hibbitt on the coach home: 'I went and sat next to him, slapped him on the knee and said, "Forget it, Terry … both our points have been made." That was the end of it.' Supermac gallantly being the

---

85 Regular readers may remember that Devlin liked nothing more than to wrestle with Robbie Savage in hotel rooms for a bit of fun to pass the time.

86 Or Captain Hurricane for those requiring a deeper comic cut.

bigger man there, accepting an apology from Terry for having another human thrown in his face.

TED MACDOUGALL V BILLY BONDS

This occurred at West Ham and started, Ted says, with Billy Bonds 'having a right go at me' while in the bath: 'So I said to him, "Why don't you do something about it instead of talking about it all the time?" So he took one step forward and I really wellied him, I hit him straight across the chest and he fell back into the bath! Some of the players got hold of him, thank God, and in comes Ron Greenwood and assistant manager John Lyall and they've got hold of me with my arms pinned across my back and I said, "That's what's wrong with your so and so club, it's full of cliques."'

Now, while we're pleased to find another story of someone being pushed into a bath, we do have a few issues with this tale. Firstly, Clyde Best in his book remembers their tussle happening on the training ground, not in the dressing room. Secondly, we're fairly certain this would have been a fight Bonzo would have won handily. And thirdly, if Ted did have the presence of mind to summon up his comment about cliques, we can only applaud his clear thinking in such a heated moment.

PAUL CANOVILLE V KERRY DIXON

On a Chelsea pre-season trip to Aberystwyth (Roman Abramovich is thinking of a tour there next season, actually), Paul Canoville ran a nice bath for himself after training, went to get his toiletries, and came back to find that Dixon (no stranger to a bit of aggro, as is evident from his own memoirs) was about to take his spot.

'"Hold on, Kerry," I reasoned politely, "that's my bath." "Can't see your name on it," he sniffed, and stepped into it. That really annoyed me. I thought it was disrespectful and rude.' We have no argument there, Paul, although we're not totally sold on his solution, which was to jump in the bath with him: 'Wooah! You should have seen his face! So it all went off. Micky Droy came rushing in to be greeted by the sight of two naked angry men shouting and shoving each other. Just as Kerry landed a right-hander on me, and before I was able to retaliate, Micky, who was built like a Hummer, grabbed hold of me.'

If only Alan Ball and Ted MacDougall had been there to explain to them the pleasures of a slipper bath and a Double Decker each.

PAOLO DI CANIO V SHAKA HISLOP'S SUIT

This tale comes from Harry Redknapp's anecdote-packed book (which doesn't narrow it down much, admittedly) *Always Managing*. It's at West Ham and at half-time, goalie Hislop blames Di Canio for a set-piece goal because Paolo didn't set up the wall properly. Why that was his job and not Shaka's, we're not sure, but that's not the point. The point is Di Canio's incredible reaction. After yelling some expletives, he somehow managed to lift a giant barrel of Gatorade above his head: 'He was walking round the dressing room with it, shouting and screaming, his legs trembling with the strain. "Fuck you! My fault? Fuck you!" All the players were diving for cover under the benches; I had a brand new suit on, so I scarpered quicker than most, under the table in the middle of the room. And from there I heard it – whoosh. He threw it. We all watched it, as if in slow motion, sail through the air until it landed on Shaka's lovely white linen suit.'

Fortunately, Di Canio's version of a team talk worked and the Hammers went on to win in the second half. But still the question remains: why had Shaka Hislop been wearing a white linen suit?

A BIT OF BACK AND FORTH

And so we end where we began, with Paul Parker's lament about missing the camaraderie of the dressing room. It's not all broken noses, Gatorade showers and slipper baths – there are laughs, too.

Like at Rangers. When Andy Goram was there, the dressing room was full of gentle humour guaranteed to help welcome in any newcomers. Take the occasion when Dale Gordon signed and first arrived at Ibrox.

Goram recalls that Disco Dale turned up on his first day wearing a large crucifix, so Goram summoned John 'Bomber' Brown to (playfully) threaten him never to do such a thing again. The Goalie then warns us that 'this isn't a book about political correctness – it's the truth about dressing-room humour'. Well, same here, sort of. Brace yourselves: 'I turned to the boys and said, "That's all we need. Things are going well, and the gaffer has gone and signed a black English Catholic." A voice piped back, "Could have been worse. He could have been gay." That broke the ice with Disco Dale.' Less broken, more shattered. It's quite the feat to incorporate bigotry, racism and homophobia into about a dozen words. But, as Goalie says, that is the truth about dressing-room humour.

Examples of that abound, but we did find some gentler stuff, even in the Rangers dressing room. Goram reports that after Euro 96, Paul Gascoigne greeted him and Colin Hendry by assembling a makeshift goal, sticking a mop into a traffic cone to represent Hendry, before flicking a ball over the mop's head and volleying it home, in homage to his greatest England moment.

Elsewhere, Diego Maradona reveals that the teammate who provided that all-important assist for his legendary second goal v England in 1986 was keen to remind people after the game of his role in the move: 'Negro Enrique came up to us – he had been in the shower – and added: "I'm hearing a lot of praise for him, a lot of praise, but with the pass I gave him, how could he not score?"' He has a point. He surely would have deserved two Fantasy Football points for that magical assist.

And then, of course, there's Kevin Keegan. You wouldn't catch him making off-colour gags about his teammates – he had no need, because, as Emlyn Hughes reminisces, the man was simply a natural entertainer: 'One of his favourite tricks was to come into the dressing-room first thing in the morning clucking like a hen. And he would not stop. There was no conversation; just this infernal squawking which sounded like a hen that had laid an egg.' We particularly enjoy the fact that this was one of his 'favourite' tricks, strongly hinting that he performed this farmyard routine for his teammates' pleasure on a regular basis.

Naturally, there are plenty of other harmless stories about shoe destruction and eye-opening tales about penis shape or size (Muzzy Izzet on Leicester keeper Pegguy Arphexad's mythical member: 'The joke in the dressing room was that he used to feed it mice'), but in the end, the ultimate bit of dressing-room bantz comes not from a footballer, but from a comedian. We hardly need to tell you it was Freddie Starr – no other comedian has spent so much time blagging his way on to team coaches, into dugouts and inside dressing rooms as Starr. Then playing for Middlesbrough, David Armstrong tells us that once he even somehow inveigled his way into the most sacred of all areas: 'One day he jumped in the communal bath after training with the rest of us and then got out again. No one thought anything of it until, to our horror, we saw he had left a deposit floating in the water. You have never seen a group of men vacate a bath as quickly.' To be fair, we've never seen a group of men vacate a bath, so we have little to compare it to, but we accept we would move pretty fast when faced with the prospect of being contaminated by a log of Freddie's freshest faeces.

THE GREATEST SHOW

'Chas and Dave on *Blue Peter*'

Cup finals have always been the stuff that boyhood dreams are made of. Even if certain competitions might have lost a touch of their lustre in recent years, they are still undeniably special. When we were growing up and kicking around in parks, playgrounds and front rooms when our mums weren't looking, it was definitely cup finals we were dreaming of – not sneaking into the top four and securing a place in the Champions League qualifying rounds.

So it's nice when the pros agree and get all dewy-eyed about the big showcase occasions. Emlyn Hughes, who enjoyed a few, talks of 'a tingling in the bones, hope in the heart and shuddering in the pit of the stomach', while Stanley Matthews says, 'A Wembley FA Cup final is the school photograph of a footballer's career.' And that's Stanley Matthews, who's got a cup final named after him for goodness sake. Only three people have FA Cup finals named after them – Stanley Matthews, Steven Gerrard and Giorgio Armani. That's just facts.

Neil Warnock remembers when the FA Cup 'stood astride the fixture list like a Colossus' – a special day 'just below birthdays and Christmas'.[87] And that was just watching it at home. If you were lucky enough to get up close then it was even more special. Perry Groves was a ball boy at the 1980 FA Cup Final and got so giddy with it he forgot that his job was ostensibly to give the ball back. He was stationed behind a goal with another lad, and when the ball came bouncing between them, they started to scrap over it instead of firing it back, until Arsenal keeper Pat Jennings shouted at them. Perry won the scrap, naturally, showing the kind of killer instinct that helped make him a pro. Well we never heard of the other kid again, did we?

87 Official ranking of days is Christmas, Birthday, Cup Final, Easter, Pancake.

At that same FA Cup Final, while Grovesy was being a terrible ball boy, a young Howard Webb (already bald in our minds) was watching with his dad. Down from Yorkshire for the day he was, with dreams in his head and the magic of the cup in his heart. And his abiding memory of the day is needing a poo. Crammed in at the front, Howard's dad had to ask a friendly steward if he could take care of it: 'Luckily, this bloke obliged, leading me down oak-panelled corridors to some plush executive loos before delivering me back to a very grateful parent a few minutes later (and a few ounces lighter).' Ah, the romance of the cup. Now not every showpiece has a future World Cup Final referee getting caught short, but they do all seem to have a pattern to the day, indeed the week before. Let's take a stroll through it.

THE PREPARATIONS

If you've done well enough to get yourselves into a cup final, then know this: people are going to want tickets from you. A somewhat sceptical and not strictly right-on Danny Blanchflower says that when his Tottenham side made the 1961 FA Cup Final, 'Every cripple in the country must have written to me for a ticket. I never knew that so many people went to football matches who couldn't stand.' Language of the time aside, we think that Danny might be suggesting that not all of these letters were from the genuinely infirm. Whatever the truth of it, there's certainly a market for tickets, and money to be made, if you're so inclined.

Lawrie McMenemy took his Southampton team to FA Cup glory in 1976, and claims to be horrified that 'two tickets for the semi had been discovered in the wrong hands when a local butcher had put them up as a draw prize for anyone who bought from his shop. It was traced back to us.' Lawrie is shocked and appalled because of course nobody in their right mind that was involved with the club would be selling tickets on the black market would they? Here's Southampton's Mick Channon: 'Let me say straight away, I've sold match tickets to the black market – about half of my allocation went that way for the FA Cup Final in 1976, the rest I gave away to family friends.' Oh, okay. Are you sure? Because we were quite prepared to believe Lawrie clutching his pearls at the very idea of it. Channon goes on to say 'Of course, people squeal at the time, but you can't blame a player wanting to cash in on one of the very few assets he is ever likely to have', which probably successfully dates his book for you. We're now in a time when

Raheem Sterling has bought 500 tickets for a Wembley trip for kids at his old school. Back then, players were getting in touch with their inner Del Boy just to make ends meet. Kevin Beattie of Ipswich backs up Channon, saying that 'most of the players at Portman Road made more out of selling cup final tickets than they received in wages and bonuses for playing and winning at Wembley from the club'. When it's put like that it seems understandable that some players get involved in it. Not that we would, of course. Nope. Honest as the day is long, us. But if you do need any we might know someone.

Luckily it's not all shifty deals in underground car parks in the build-up to a cup final, because the media commitments will take up a lot of your time. Everybody wants a piece of you, with photo opportunities, radio interviews and TV profiles on the slate.

Steve Hodge got to Wembley with Spurs in 1987 and remembers a giddy whirl of a build-up week 'with a celebrity golf day (the celebrities being Cliff Thorburn and Russ Abbot), we sang our song ("Hotshot Tottenham") with Chas and Dave on *Blue Peter*, and had a press day which was centred around the final being Glenn Hoddle's last game for Spurs'. There are some big hitters in that sentence, and even though we're respectful of Glenn's hero status at Tottenham, and we're thrilled by the prospect of 18 holes with The Grinder and Basildon Bond, you'll forgive us if we zero in on the music.

You don't have to be a Tottenham fan to appreciate that Chas and Dave were the kings of that lost art – the cup final single. And it's fair to say that there was a time when Tottenham got to finals often enough to keep Hodges and Peacock busy. Not as busy as Manchester United of course, who got to so many cup finals in their pomp that they had to put somebody in charge of the singles they put out, and that man was Brian McClair. Choccy recalls being contacted by Status Quo for the 1994 single, saying, 'I can't say I'm their biggest fan, and they're not everyone's cup of tea, but no one can deny that they've been very successful at what they do. We met Rick Parfitt and Francis Rossi and had a good laugh in making the single, "Come on you Reds".' The song got to number one for two weeks, but before Choccy gets carried away it's worth remembering that 'Doop' by Doop went there for three weeks that same year.

Emboldened by their chart success it's possible that United overreached in the years that followed: 'The year after our first double saw us venture into rap, with the usual degree of success which accompanies football players when they attempt that style.' Well somebody doesn't remember Liverpool's banger 'The Anfield Rap'. 'It was called "We're gonna do it again!" but we didn't, that season anyway.' It seems to have been diminishing returns thereafter, and with the faintest of praise he says, 'Our last contribution to the genre, "Move, Move, Move" produced by Pete Waterman, was ... all right.' We're not sure we even remember that one. It's possible that things went downhill in the charts for the Reds in McClair's later years as music monitor due to the negative Eeyore energy brought into the studio by Paul Scholes. Wonderful player though Scholesy was, it's fair to say he lacked a certain spark when it came to the showbiz element of the job: 'The only thing I loathed about reaching Wembley was the whole sorry business of recording a cup final song. Ours was called "Lift it High" and we had to dance in the dressing room where the recording was done. The whole thing was so embarrassing, I detested it.' This was the 1999 single, so it didn't stop them winning the treble, it just stopped them winning the hearts and minds of the CD-buying public.

Peter Reid entered more into the spirit of the thing in his day, cursing the fact that United charted higher than them in 1985, but revealing a pattern around recording and performing the song. He says that recording the song involved a few cold drinks 'just to lubricate our vocal chords obviously'. Obviously. He then says of performing the song on *Wogan* 'We battered the ale on the way to the studio' and a fusspot producer 'told us we couldn't go on, unless we stopped drinking'. Now this sounds like an ultimatum from the producers, but somehow, persuasive and thirsty Andy Gray flipped things around 'telling the producers that we wouldn't be going on unless they gave us another bevvy', so they drank and they sang after all – then probably drank again. In the face of stiff competition from elsewhere, we think we might be safe in saying that the Everton team of the 80s put away more booze than just about any other football team of note. They were absolutely crackers for it.

Dennis Tueart got a bit starry-eyed when Sunderland recorded their own cup final song in 1973, 'Sunderland All The Way', very much enjoying the fact that he and a couple of teammates got invitations along to *Top of the Pops*. Tueart saw Suzi Quatro's debut appearance and had a lovely chat with Brian Connolly, lead singer with glam rockers The Sweet. 'Brian loved football, and it was clear to me having met Rod Stewart and Brian that many pop stars would have loved to have been footballers, and vice versa.' There's great truth in this, and Rod certainly backs it up himself. But even more important than that, he says 'if you can find a recording of the show, you'll see us dancing at the back'.

Once the song is sorted, suits for the day need to be sourced. Of course, the most infamous cup final suits are the white ones worn by the Liverpool 'Spice Boys' in 1996. McAteer claims that David James was arranging the whole thing and expected them to be brown but was told 'they didn't have enough material in the brown'. Now forgive us, but this is Armani we're talking about here. Not having enough material all seems rather unlikely. It's almost as if people are making excuses in light of the grief they got. That said, maybe, just maybe, the stick that Liverpool get for those suits is unwarranted. After all, two years earlier, Paul Parker reminds us that Chelsea 'wore a delicate shade of parma violet, which is a light sort of purple'. Parker then says his opponents' suits were made worse when the rains came and made them look all blotchy and 'faintly ridiculous'. So what's the big idea? We were never that upset about Liverpool's white suits anyway, but if the fashion police are out to make some arrests then why does nobody talk about Chelsea stepping out in violet before them like some kind of soggy Showaddywaddy?

So you've got to your final, you've flogged your tickets, you've made your record, and made a rash suit choice. All that remains before the big day is to settle on your best side. And that is best done, in our opinion, before you get to the ground. Garry Nelson says that Brighton boss Barry Lloyd dropped him in the toilet before their play-off final with Notts County. Well he didn't drop him *in* the toilet, obviously, we mean he told him in the toilet just before the game that he was dropped. Which seems a bit off, though not as bad as dropping him in the toilet.

Mind you, regardless of the when and where, people are still going to be upset when they receive the crushing blow of being denied their big moment. Steve Hodge complains bitterly that Brian Clough 'bottled it a bit' in 1991, when he simply marched up the team coach the day before 'threw a crumpled up bit of paper at Pearcey and said, "Skipper, here's the cup final team." And he was gone', leaving a man nicknamed Psycho to deliver delicate bad news as he scurried back behind his curtain. It's one way of doing it.

Even that other great managerial guru Alex Ferguson found it tough to leave players out, gently telling ageing skipper Bryan Robson '"You can have a drink tonight if you want," he said. "I've got to look after the young lads who are coming through and make them feel part of it, so I'll be leaving you out of the squad. Here's a few quid. Get yourself a drink."

"I don't want your money, I don't want a drink," I replied. I felt more angry than insulted.' It does sound like it went wonky between Fergie and his once great, but by then fringe player, Robbo. However, there are a few things to note about this incident.

Firstly, history tells us that Fergie was right to back his youngsters that were coming through.

Secondly, if this set Bryan Robson down the path to management and that wonderful picture where he's in a jacket and tie up town and football shorts and socks down below, then we're all for it.

Finally, this might be the only instance we've found where Robson turned down a drink.

THE NIGHT BEFORE

Having made it through the week in the glare of the media it's important to find a good hotel, have a quiet meal and get the team tucked up in bed for one last good night's sleep before the big game. Unless you're Brian Clough, of course. Viv Anderson and any number of Forest teammates tell us that the night before a League Cup Final Cloughie ordered his squad to neck a case of champagne together, and that 'not one of you leaves this room until you have all told us a joke.' Big Viv says, 'I finally made it to bed around midnight. Needless to say I woke up with a hangover, as did quite a few of the other players.' Well yes, of course they did. Clough was so adamant that it was a good idea, however, that even though Archie Gemmill had already gone to bed he dragged him up again to join in, while the conscientious midfielder protested bitterly, presumably in his jim-jams. Clough says 'he had a point, of course, but he was isolating himself and his mood offended me'. We're not sure that this counts as isolating himself[88] so much as simply going to bed, but we're sure Cloughie knows best.

It's not just eccentric tactical geniuses that can keep players awake in the pre-match hotel you know. Alan Mullery remembers a run-in

88 This was years before the coronavirus kicked in and isolating yourself became fashionable.

with some 'sexy neighbours' when he was trying to get some kip before a Tottenham cup final. 'It was a man and a woman fooling around together. The woman had the dirtiest laugh I'd ever heard.' Now we're not sure if Mullers was actually trying to ignore it or if he had a glass pressed up against the wall, because he seems to be across all the details. 'The man started to grunt and the woman started to moan. The banging got faster and faster. Their headboard was knocking against our wall and they were obviously enjoying themselves thoroughly!' It took Alan an hour to complain to reception about it and everyone agreed it would be too awkward to break it up. Instead, Alan and his room-mate simply turned up the telly and waited 'for the kinky couple to complete their steamy session. It was two hours of non-stop action.' Now nobody said they were kinky, Mullers, but your mind plays tricks after a while, we suppose. Extra points for Mullery's tale for saying that 'their performance was worthy of a gold medal in the Bedroom Bonking Olympics'. Nice to hear bonking again isn't it? The word that is, not the actual bonking that kept Mullers up all night.

When QPR reached the League Cup Final in 1967, they moved into a hotel in London's West End, which seems like an odd move as it's further away from Wembley than they would have started off at Loftus Road. Besides which, the plush surroundings did nothing for the nerves of a young Rodney Marsh who says he couldn't catch a wink all night. Up early next morning, he took a calming stroll through Hyde Park, had an omelette and watched a bit of telly before the coach arrived to whisk them away, 'an exciting moment for me because the drive to Wembley was one of the things to which I'd been looking forward. Faces and banners and pointing fingers seemed everywhere as we rolled through the crowds and the traffic.' This is really lovely stuff. What a charming and idyllic day for everyone involved, 'and we even saw a group of Rangers supporters who had marched from Loftus Road to Wembley carrying a coffin marked "West Bromwich Albion".'[89] Oh lads. You've let everyone down a bit there. A coffin? How did that seem like a good idea to at least four people at once? Would they even let you in the ground with a coffin? Not these days with rampant bloody health and safety rules we shouldn't wonder.

89 They were playing against West Brom; this wasn't just an arbitrary attack on the Baggies.

PRE-MATCH

Marshy's morning constitutional to calm the nerves seems very civilised to us and he's not alone. Bobby Gould tells us that Dennis Wise and Vinnie Jones went for a stroll on the morning of their cup final where they 'bumped into June Whitfield in the street', the universal sign of good luck. It's like magpies, only one June Whitfield is for joy. If you see two, you're in trouble; and you don't even want to know about three.[90] Best of all the strolls though is surely Bobby Charlton and Ray Wilson stretching their legs on the morning of the 1966 World Cup Final. It's always twisted our melons that just hours before the biggest match in English football history, Bobby popped down 'to Golders Green to replace a shirt I had bought earlier in the week'. We're surprised that famous disciplinarian Sir Alf didn't keep his lads wrapped in cotton wool all morning, let alone send them down the town to swap a top. We're fascinated by Bobby's thought process here. The shirt situation has clearly been bothering him. He'll have had a glance at the watch and eventually, possibly with a sigh, resolved to pop down there, 'then it's done'. Remarkable presence of mind.

Transactions and hotel business complete and it's on to the coach and off to the ground, and everyone it seems is looking for a moment to break the tension and lighten the mood. As we've learnt previously, some managers will invite a comedian on board (your Starrs, your Boardmans), or pull out a puppet,[91] while others let things happen more organically. Lawrie McMenemy remembers a semi-final where his Southampton side arrived at a junction near the neutral Stamford Bridge at the same time as their Crystal Palace opponents led by Malcolm Allison. 'We could see the players clearly with Malcolm sitting at the front wearing his fedora and that monster coat with the fur collar. Mel Blyth, who had played for Palace, shouted in his high-pitched voice: "Look at the f****** state of him."' That would do it.[92] Paul Parker says that Steve Bruce

90 And avoid Terry Scotts at all costs.

91 Please see *Booked!*, our first volume, which contains the full story of Jim Smith giving a cup final-bound coach load of QPR players a team talk with a monkey puppet. You won't regret it.

92 That Palace run was notable for the involvement of the showbiz hypnotist Romark. He said he'd inspired Palace along the way but he and Allison fell out before the semi and he placed a curse on the Eagles instead. We are not making this up. Football was different then.

had his own regular gag for such occasions. Like a dad with a car full of kids he would trot out his crowd-pleaser of '"We're nearly there now boys. I can smell the hot dogs." He said it every time without fail.' It's indicative of Man United's run of success that Bruce was able to have a running gag for all the times they got to Wembley. The commitment is admirable. It's easy to get blasé about such things. Take Patrick Vieira for example; he casually talks about traditional cup final hymn 'Abide With Me' as a song 'I soon learned to recognise and love' going on to say 'by the time I left Arsenal, believe me, I had heard it a few times!' Alright mate, we get the idea. Get to a few cup finals, did you?

Once all the preparation is done, it's finally time for the players to come face to face in the tunnel, where games can be won and lost. Rodney Marsh says that it gave him a chance to realise 'that nervousness was not my own special problem. I could see it in their eyes and in their manner', while Jan Molby brings us news of those charming Crazy Gang lads and their idiosyncratic ways. 'Vinnie Jones had written a newspaper article in which he said he was going to rip off Kenny's [Dalglish] ears and spit in the hole. As we were waiting to walk out, the Wimbledon players kept shouting, "In the hole! In the hole!"' A great bunch of lads.

Even more galling than those rough boys trying to unsettle the Liverpool 'Culture Club' is the fact that they then strolled out for the pre-match presentation and rubbed shoulder pads with the actual Queen of Hearts Princess 'Lady Di' Diana, as if butter wouldn't melt in their mouths. Boss Bobby Gould managed to keep it together while her Royalness 'flashed me that endearing coy look', but you can tell he was going a bit gooey inside.

Diana, naturally, was a bigger hit with the football lads than Prince Charles, with Jaap Stam dismissively saying 'I'm Dutch, so meeting England's future king is not a moment that will change my life forever', which is a shame because it's our understanding that since meeting Jaap Stam on that day, Prince Charles talks of little else.

THE BIG MATCH

Finally, the big moment arrives. Twenty-two players at the peak of their powers left to battle it out completely focused on the game at hand. Unless you're Jermaine Pennant and your family still need their tickets sorting out. That's right, during the 2007 Champions League Final, ‘towards the end of the first half, there was a Tannoy announcement, which was really loud on the pitch: “Jermaine Pennant, can you please go to the ticket office.”’ Unreasonable to ask really. Rude, even. The man’s playing a match. Incidentally, Pennant spends a lot of his book *Mental* reminding us that he was man of the match in that final. He must mention it more than ten times. We vaguely remember him having a good game but surely he was only Liverpool’s man of the match. Does that count? Milan won and must have had many contenders and indeed, if you google it, Pippo Inzaghi was the actual factual man of the match and quite right too. He did score twice as Milan got their revenge for all that ‘Miracle in Istanbul’ stuff.

Liverpool are undeniably a team well used to cup finals and here are a few more tales from the trophy room:

- The Gerrard final – we all remember Stevie G’s heroics. Some of us even remember that his late equaliser came about because West Ham put the ball out for a Liverpool injury. Instead of throwing the ball back to the opposition keeper, they threw it into the corner to defender Lionel Scaloni and immediately closed him down, rushing him into a mistake. Now that’s not illegal but it’s at the very least a bit rum. Gerrard’s version has it that ‘we took the throw-in and, compelled to be as sporting, threw it back to Scaloni. He must have felt bewildered by all the honourable play because he hoofed it straight to me.’ Nobody, and we mean nobody, Mr Stevie so-called G, has ever been so bewildered by fair play that they’ve made a mistake.
- And yes, since you ask, that is the bitterness of a West Ham fan just peeping through the cracks.
- We’re all aware of Bruce Grobbelaar’s jelly legs routine during the penalty shoot-out v Roma in the 1984 European Cup Final but we never knew it was intended to be ‘like the old “Black Bottom” dance routine’. Whatever that was.
- In the same shoot-out Steve Nicol was unfortunate enough to miss, but luckily, as he made the lonely walk

> back to the halfway line, some of that famous Liverpool team spirit took care of him, with Mark Lawrenson telling him, 'Unlucky Nico ... you dickhead.'

What is nice to read about is the chatter that goes on during a big match between those involved. At the nice end of the scale we have Dennis Tueart revealing that late on in Sunderland's famous win over Leeds, Norman Hunter approached him: 'His shoulders and his head were slumped, and through the din he said, "It looks like it's going to be your day, Dennis."' We've said it before and we'll say it again – Norman Hunter seemed more like a lovely bloke the more you read about him. In another nice bit of business, Jim Leighton tells us that when he kept goal for Manchester United in the 1990 FA Cup Final, the goalkeeper he kept out of the side, Les Sealey, 'somehow worked his way into the group of photographers behind my Wembley goal and hurled encouragement at me from there. I could hardly believe my ears when I heard that familiar Cockney voice bellowing "Come on, big man, keep going."' Brings a tear to the eye doesn't it?[93] Not as many tears as Jim's last cup final appearance for Hibs against Rangers, however, when he left the field after two minutes after having his jaw broken in two places after an accidental clash with Rod Wallace. Ouch. We're surprised Les didn't jump out of the crowd and carry him off in his arms, and then take his place in goal.

Less charitable chat came from Didier Drogba and Frank Lampard during their Champions League victory over Bayern Munich. When Bayern were awarded a penalty they noticed that former teammate Arjen Robben was stepping up to take it. Drogba recalls: 'So we went up to him, and started putting psychological pressure on him. "Arjen, you're a Chelsea player, you can't do this! Don't do it! Anyway, we'll know where you're going to shoot." And so on. We got inside his head, definitely, because his kick was weak – definitely weaker than it would normally have been – and Petr saved it.' Effective chat then, but nevertheless, bad darts.

CELEBRATE GOOD TIMES

The game's over and we have a winning team. But let's not forget the losers. Didier Drogba says that after Chelsea lost the 2008 Champions

93 Leighton also tells us that after Sealey replaced him in the side that won the replay, Les tried to give Jim his winners' medal. What a guy.

League Final, 'JT was sobbing for a long time on the pitch after the game and Avram Grant had tried, without success, to console him.' So spare a thought for John Terry. Spared a thought? Ok done. That's plenty.

In happier times for Chelsea they beat Leeds to win a bad-tempered FA Cup Final replay in 1970, leaving their opponents to struggle with defeat that time. And if we're honest, the Leeds lads come off a little like bad losers. Johnny Giles remembers: 'We didn't collect our medals. Partly, we weren't sure if the prize-giving procedure was the same at Old Trafford as at Wembley – there was no precedent for this – mainly we just couldn't be bothered.' It feels like the end of that sentence has a lot more truth to it than the start of it. We always think that when a team makes a gesture like this there must be at least someone amongst them who really wants their runners-up medal. It's nice to have a medal. Chelsea's Alan Hudson elaborates on what Jack Charlton got up to moments after telling all involved to stick their medal up their collective arses: 'I heard that he kicked the dressing-room door off its hinges. He caught a cab outside, leaving in tears, unable to bear the sound of Chelsea voices singing their victory songs in the bath in the adjacent dressing-room.' Ooh, get him. If he didn't like the noise from across the corridor then he probably shouldn't have kicked the door off should he? That can't have helped.

In further 'Leeds are bad losers' news Johnny Giles remembers when Sunderland captain Bobby Kerr ('wasn't a bad lad') tried to be nice by bringing the cup into the Leeds dressing room after the underdogs had beaten them in that FA Cup Final so memorable for Bob Stokoe's trilby and tracksuit combination. Johnny recalls 'a totally surreal experience as he handed the FA Cup around to us, so we could take a drink from it. One by one we all had a sip of the Sunderland champagne. Nobody told Bobby to fuck off. Which on a day of miracles was probably the most astonishing of them all.' It's lucky Jack Charlton was injured for the final or there might have been a Bobby Kerr-shaped hole in the dressing-room door.

Let's waste no further time on the losers. On to the winners. It's their special day and what could be better than finally getting your hands on the actual trophy. Here's little ray of sunshine Paul Scholes: 'Even though we strive all season to win trophies, I always feel a bit embarrassed to actually lift them up and brandish them in front of the fans.' Oh Paul, you've brought us down a bit here. Maybe Scholes had to be like this to balance out the shameless bandwagon jumping of David May on 'that night in Barcelona'.

Going up for the trophy is a special moment for most people. For Steve Bruce it was a boyhood dream (told you), and nothing could surely take the shine off collecting the Rumbelows Cup. 'In dreams it was someone like the Princess of Wales who stands, smiling radiantly, with the cup bedecked in red and white ribbons. When I got there, who did I find? The winner of a Rumbelows sales-incentive scheme.' Oh Diana. Why hast thou forsaken Brucey? If you look at the video of the presentation you can see Steve barely suppressing his disappointment.

Trophy collected, it's back down on to the pitch for the free-for-all celebrations. All manner of headgear is permissible, socks down and shirts untucked is a given, and chucking booze around is positively encouraged. Serial trophy winner Gary Neville even has a tip for such carefree moments: 'Luckily I was experienced enough to know that you put a towel over your suit if you don't want to sit on the bus home smelling of stale booze.' Practical, sensible advice for your moment of triumph there. Phenomenal foresight. Did he do it pre-match, we wonder, or just respond quickly when things started getting out of hand?

At this point we can give you a couple more insights from Liverpool's finest hours, should you want them. Firstly, Bruce Grobbelaar reveals that his famous walking on his hands routine at Wembley that time was brought about by a bet. Bruce was dating 'a pretty young girl named Janet whose parents had a pub near Goodison Park called the Strawberry Tavern', and the Everton loving patrons goaded him into taking the bet apparently. Secondly, and more disturbingly, Steve Nicol blows the lid off of those moments when the team huddles together and bounces while photographers get their pictures. Nicol says: 'while the snappers were clicking away and the television cameras were filming our every move and beaming the pictures all around the world, me and my teammates were singing this dirty little ditty …

Hairy growlers, paps and vees, (deep voice) paps and vees
Hairy growlers, paps and vees, (deep voice) paps and vees
There's a hairy growler over there
And it hasn't got no hair, (deep voice) got no hair!'

We will never look at that footage in the same way again. We're torn between being utterly horrified and trying to work out what the tune was.

THE DO

If you've managed to keep your suit from being covered in champagne, there's always a do to attend. And those dos will often have celebrities in attendance, sometimes even earning their keep.
Here's a rundown of some of them. Roll up, roll up, which one of them would you most like to have been at?

1953 Blackpool – Stanley Matthews: 'entertainment provided by George Formby, Richard 'Stinker' Murdoch, Norman Evans and Frank Randle, big stars of the day'.

1961 Spurs – Danny Blanchflower: 'Harry Secombe entertained us and Shirley Bassey turned up to present us with some gramophone records. I asked her to sing for us but she showed me that she had had her tonsils removed and begged to be excused. So I finished the day looking down Shirley Bassey's throat.'

1964 Preston – Howard Kendall: 'Traditionally, losers' banquets are about as lively as are wakes but, I must admit, I had a wonderful time and even managed to enjoy the cabaret which was provided by Des O'Connor, the Vernon Girls and The Batchelors.'

1973 Sunderland – Dennis Tueart: 'Mickey [sic] Most laid on all the entertainment, and Alan Price and Suzi Quatro did the honours.'

1978 Ipswich – Kevin Beattie: 'I bumped into Brian Cant, who introduced *Play School* on TV and he invited me to have a drink with him after the banquet.'

Personally, we'd plump for a night on the pop with Brian Cant. Deep down, you know you would too.

Sometimes, of course, the players are called upon to entertain everyone themselves, so we have Malcolm Allison remembering that 'Francis Lee danced on top of the piano – in his underpants', and Terry Butcher telling us that 'Ally McCoist was up on a table to treat us to one of his famous five minute raps'. Skipping straight past Franny Lee jigging in his pants like a giant baby, we have questions about Ally's 'famous five minute raps'. Just how famous are they? Does five minutes seem a bit long to you too? Are these original works or Ally's favourites? Why is everybody on the table?

Double winner Jan Molby couldn't even be bothered to stick around at Liverpool's do in 1986. Instead he slipped away up to his room to get undressed and watch *Match of the Day*, until his friends knocked him up and dragged him out to Stringfellows: 'You don't queue when you've got the FA Cup with you, so we moved right up to the front, showed the doorman the trophy and went in. All the boys were there, Kenny, Alan Hansen – and I remember having my picture taken with Alex Higgins and the FA Cup before going up into the restaurant with my friends to drink champagne all night.' This might sound like a good night out for some of you, but it's definitely a youngster's game. We can't think of anything worse than getting comfortable in your pants in front of the highlights only to have to go back out again. But we suppose the show must go on. It's the done thing. Even when Arsenal had one of their teammates in hospital, after Tony Adams dropped Steve Morrow on his head and broke his collarbone during the 1993 League Cup celebrations, the lads pressed on. Ray Parlour tells us: 'We all felt sorry for Steve but we didn't let it spoil our night out. We went to a restaurant in north London, we drunk into the early hours and had a great party.' See. What else are you meant to do?

THE PARADE

Next up, it's the glorious open-top bus parade through the hometown, which ought to be a lot of fun, even if we do sometimes worry what the toilet arrangements are on those things.

Steve Nicol reminds us that double runners-up Everton were forced to follow behind Liverpool on their own bus in 1986 because a joyous 'everyone's a winner' twin Mersey celebration seemed like a good idea to somebody at some point. That must have been awful for the Everton lads, although we're sure they found a way, either canned or bottled, to make it bearable.

Phil Thompson seems to have been on so many open-top bus parades that he even had a regular spot, saying, 'Terry Mac and myself used to always position ourselves upstairs at the back with a crate of beer for us and bottles of wine for the girls.' Could the girls have beer if they wanted it? No, no they couldn't. Don't be absurd. Brian McClair is another who suffered from parade fatigue because of all the success. At one point he describes being 'absolutely freezing, bored stiff' and says 'we told the driver to get a move on'. Treasured memories.

Of course, if you're not quite so used to winning trophies you don't get bogged down in the mundanity of glory like Liverpool and Man United. Kevin Beattie was part of that Ipswich team that won the FA

Cup in 1978 and he admits that he got a bit giddy with the celebrations and became embroiled in the case of the missing trumpets, after messing around with the parade band's equipment. The day after the police arrived to ask questions and point fingers. Kevin's memory of events is understandably hazy, saying, 'I have always wondered what actually happened to them. Just thinking about it now, had our explanation not been accepted, we could have been locked up after one of the greatest days of our lives.' Every fairy tale cup story should have some trumpet theft at the end of it.

* * *

Our look at cup glory has been refreshing as a reminder that football is sometimes about etching your name in history, rather than just the money, as some would have you believe. That's a good job in Steve Hodge's case as he recalls receiving the princely bonus of 'a box of Dairy Milk with a ten pound note sellotaped to the top!' for winning the Simod Cup with Forest. Which seems a bit tight. Not even Fruit & Nut.

Underwhelming bonuses aside, we're going to leave the final word to that dreamer of dreams, Rodney Marsh. There's real poetry and heartfelt emotion in Marsh's words here:

> There can't be anything in football to match the big red glow you feel when the whistle goes and you know that for just a few minutes you are right at the top of the mountain. You know it may never happen again so you try to soak it all up, the congratulations, the steps leading upwards, the presentation, the noise, the lap of honour, but somehow it all becomes a blur after a while. You are left with a little trophy and a tremendous sense of achievement; and then a feeling of regret that the moment has come and gone begins to roll over you. No wonder I cried.

And that was only the League Cup. Nobody gives a shit about that.

Good day to you.

FINAL WORD

As we said at the start, we hope that our look into the lives and books of our football heroes has given us all a greater insight into how they work. However, we'd be lying if we said we understood everything that was going on. There's a particular passage from Dutch maestro Johan Cruyff, for example, which has always eluded our grasp, like defenders left in his wake. We present it here in the hope that one of you out there can understand what he's talking about and take something from it.

> Numerology interests me. So, for example, I married Danny on the second day of the twelfth month, December. Two plus twelve produces the number on my back: number fourteen. The year was 1968, and six plus eight is also fourteen. No wonder we're still together after forty-eight years. Our marriage was good twice over. The same is true of my son, Jordi. He was born in '74 and I was born in '47. So both years add up to eleven. And his birthday is on 9 February and mine's 25 April. That's nine plus two and two plus five plus four. Both eleven.

This reads like a *3-2-1* clue. And we can't help but feel like we've ended up with Dusty Bin. It can't just be us that are left baffled and feeling like that Swedish defender he turned inside out at the World Cup, can it? Thank goodness for that.

ACKNOWLEDGEMENTS

John would like to thank ...

Dan for writing with me again and making me laugh, as well as the footballers for providing the inspiration.

John Greathead – forever on the lookout for second-hand books for me that I might not have read.

Mum, for her encouragement and for looking past the swearing.

Jo, for her love and endless support. This is for her, Archie, Evie and Martha. Because let's be honest, everything is.

Dan would like to thank ...

John for writing stuff that constantly made me laugh and for his insatiable appetite for footballer autobiographies, without which, I'll be honest, we'd never have read the 250 we can now boast about.

Carmen for, once again, her understanding and patience when so many evenings and weekends were taken over by this book. Totally worth it, right C? She loves really obscure football references from the 1960s, so it's all good. And Leo, who very much enjoyed wandering round Waterstones to find *Booked!* before loudly talking about how famous I must be. Hopefully he'll do that again.

Both authors would like to thank ...

Jane Camillin at Pitch for letting us do it again.

Anybody who bought the first book, and indeed this one. Thanks for your support.

Jake, Joel, Robbie and Grits for helping to take the spirit of *Booked!* into people's ears by turning it into a pretty decent podcast (exclusively on Spotify!).

Matt Holland, Alex Horne and Richard Osman for their kind words.

Finally, we'd like to recommend a few of the books we read that are particularly good and deserving of your full attention: Paul Lake – *I'm Not Really Here*; Paul Canoville – *Black and Blue*; Norman Whiteside – *Determined*; Vince Hilaire – *Vince*; and Peter Reid – *Cheer Up Peter Reid*.

Happy reading.

BIBLIOGRAPHY

Adams, Tony with Ian Ridley, *Sober: Football. My Story. My Life* (Simon & Schuster UK, 2017).

Akinfenwa, Adebayo, *The Beast: My Story* (Headline, 2017).

Aldridge, John with John Hynes, *Alright Aldo: Sound as a Pound. On the Road with Everybody's Favourite Irish Scouser* (Trinity Mirror Sport Media, 2010).

Allardyce, Sam, *Big Sam: My Autobiography* (Headline, 2015).

Allison, Malcolm with James Lawton, *Colours of My Life* (Everest Books Ltd, 1975).

Anderson, Viv, *First Among Unequals: The Autobiography* (Fullback Media, 2010).

Ardiles, Ossie, *Ossie's Dream: My Autobiography* (Transworld Digital, 2010).

Armstrong, David and Pat Symes, *The Bald Facts: The David Armstrong Biography* (Pitch Publishing, 2013).

Atkinson, Ron, *Big Ron: A Different Ball Game* (Andre Deutsch Ltd, 1999).

Atkinson, Ron, *The Manager* (deCoubertin Books, 2016).

Ball, Alan, *Playing Extra Time* (Pan; New edition, 2005).

Banks, Gordon, *Banksy: The Autobiography* (Penguin, 2019).

Barnes, John, *The Autobiography* (Headline Book Publishing, 1999).

Barton, Joey, *No Nonsense* (Simon & Schuster UK, 2017).

Bassett, Dave, *Settling the Score* (John Blake, 2002).

Bassett, Dave and Downes, Wally, *The Crazy Gang* (Bantam, 2016).

Batty, David, *The Autobiography* (Headline, 2002).

Beattie, Kevin, *The Beat* (Skript Design & Publishing, 1998).
Bellamy, Craig with Oliver Holt, *Goodfella* (Trinity Sport Media, 2013).
Bergkamp, Dennis, *Stillness & Speed: My Story* (Simon & Schuster UK, 2014).
Best, Clyde, *The Acid Test* (deCoubertin Books, 2016).
Blanchflower, Danny, *The Double and Before...* (Nicholas Kaye Ltd, 1961).
Bonds, Billy, *Bonzo* (Arthur Barker, 1988).
Bowles, Stan, *The Autobiography* (Orion, 2005).
Brady, Karren, *Strong Woman: The Truth About Getting to the Top* (HarperCollins, 2013).
Brazil, Alan with Mike Parry, *There's an Awful Lot of Bubbly in Brazil: The Life and Times of a Bon Viveur* (Highdown, 2007).
Brooking, Trevor, *My Life in Football* (Simon & Schuster Ltd, 2014).
Bruce, Steve, *Heading for Victory: An Autobiography* (Bloomsbury, 1994).
Bullard, Jimmy, *Bend it Like Bullard* (Headline, 2014).
Burridge, John, *Budgie: The Autobiography of Goalkeeping Legend John Burridge* (John Blake, 2011).
Butcher, Terry, *Both Sides of the Border: An Autobiography* (George Weidenfeld & Nicolson Ltd, 1989).
Cahill, Tim, *Legacy* (HarperSport, 2015).
Cannell, Paul, *Fuckin' Hell It's Paul Cannell* (Createspace Independent Publishing Platform, 2012).
Canoville, Paul, *Black and Blue* (Headline, 2008).
Cantona, Eric, *Cantona on Cantona* (Andre Deutsch, 1996).
Carragher, Jamie, *Carra: My Autobiography* (Corgi, 2009).
Carrick, Michael, *Between the Lines: My Autobiography* (Blink Publishing, 2018).
Case, Jimmy, *Hard Case: The Autobiography of Jimmy Case* (John Blake Publishing Ltd, 2014).
Channon, Mick, *Man on the Run: An Autobiography* (Littlehampton Book Services Ltd, 1986).
Charlton, Bobby, *1966: My World Cup Story* (Yellow Jersey, 2017).

Charlton, Jack, *The Autobiography* (Partridge Press, 1966).

Charnley, Chic with Alex Gordon, *Seeing Red: The Chic Charnley Story* (Black and White Publishing 2009).

Clark, Lee with Will Scott, *Black or White No Grey Areas* (Mojo Risin' Publishing, 2016).

Clough, Brian, *Cloughie – Walking on Water – My Life* (Headline, 2002).

Cole, Andy with Peter Fenton, *The Autobiography* (Manchester United Books, 1999).

Cole, Ashley, *My Defence: Winning, Losing, Scandals and the drama of Germany 2006* (Headline Publishing Group, 2006).

Collymore, Stan, *Tackling My Demons* (Willow, 2013).

Conroy, Terry, *You Don't Remember Me, Do You? The Autobiography of Terry Conroy* (Pitch Publishing, 2015).

Cottee, Tony, *West Ham: The Inside Story* (Philip Evans Media Ltd, 2012).

Crouch, Peter, *How to be a Footballer* (Ebury, 2019).

Cruyff, Johan, *My Turn: The Autobiography* (Macmillan, 2017).

Curbishley, Alan, *Valley of Dreams* (HarperCollins, 2018).

Curran, Terry with John Brindley, *Regrets of a Football Maverick: The Terry Curran Autobiography* (Vertical Editions, 2013).

Dalglish, Kenny with Henry Winter, *My Autobiography* (Hodder & Stoughton, 1996).

Di Canio, Paolo with Gabriele Marcotti, *The Autobiography* (Willow, 2001).

Dixon, Kerry with Harry Harris, *Up Front: My Autobiography* (John Blake Publishing, 2016).

Docherty, Tommy, *Call the Doc* (Littlehampton Book Services Ltd, 1981).

Dougan, Derek, *The Sash He Never Wore ... 25 Years On* (Lagan Books and All Seasons Publishing, 1997).

Dougan, Derek, *How to Run Football* (All Seasons, 1981).

Dougan, Derek, *Doog* (All Seasons, 1980).

Dougan, Derek and Percy M. Young, *On The Spot: Football as a Profession* (Stanley Paul, 1974).

Drinkell, Kevin, *Drinks All Round: The Autobiography* (Black and White Publishing, 2010).

Drogba, Didier, *Commitment: My Autobiography* (Hodder & Stoughton, 2016).

Dunphy, Eamon, *Only a Game?* (Penguin, 1987).

Duxbury, Mick with Wayne Barton, *It's Mick not Mike: The Autobiography of Mick Duxbury* (Pitch Publishing, 2015).

Dyer, Kieron with Oliver Holt, *Old Too Soon, Smart Too Late: My Story* (Headline, 2018).

Dyson, Terry with Mike Donovan, *Spurs Unsung Hero of the Glory Years: My Autobiography* (Pitch Publishing, 2015).

Edghill, Richard with Dante Friend, *Once a Blue Always a Blue: The Autobiography of Richard Edghill* (Pitch Publishing, 2014).

Elleray, David, *Referee! A Year in the Life of David Elleray* (Bloomsbury Publishing, 1998).

Ellis, Doug, *Deadly!* (Sports Projects Ltd, 1998)

Eriksson, Sven-Göran, *Sven: My Story* (Headline, 2014).

Ferdinand, Les, *Sir Les: The Autobiography of Les Ferdinand* (Headline Book Publishing, 1997).

Ferdinand, Rio, *#2Sides: My Autobiography* (Blink Publishing, 2014).

Ferguson, Alex, *My Autobiography* (Hodder & Stoughton, 2013).

Fowler, Robbie, *Fowler: My Autobiography* (Pan, 2009).

Francis, Trevor with David Miller, *The World to Play For: A Great Footballer's Own Story* (Granada Publishing Limited, 1983).

Fry, Barry, *Big Fry: Barry Fry: The Autobiography* (Willow, 2011).

Gemmill, Archie, *Both Sides of the Border: My Autobiography* (Hodder & Stoughton, 2005).

Gerrard, Steven, *My Story* (Penguin, 2015).

Giles, John, *A Football Man: The Autobiography* (Hodder & Stoughton, 2010).

Gillespie, Keith with Daniel McDonnell, *How Not to Be a Football Millionaire – Keith Gillespie My Autobiography* (Trinity Mirror Sport Media, 2013).

Goater, Shaun with David Clayton, *Feed the Goat* (The History Press, 2006).

Gold, David, *Pure Gold: My Autobiography* (Highdown, 2006).

Goram, Andy with Iain King, *The Goalie: My Story* (Mainstream Publishing, 2010).

Goss, Jeremy with Edward Couzens-Lake, *Gossy: The Autobiography* (Amberley Publishing, 2014).

Gould, Bobby and David Instone, *24 Carat Gould* (Thomas Publications, 2010).

Gray, Andy, *Gray Matters – Andy Gray: The Autobiography* (Pan Books, 2005).

Greaves, Jimmy, *This One's On Me* (Hodder & Stoughton, 1980).

Greaves, Jimmy, *Greavsie: The Autobiography* (Time Warner, 2003).

Grobbelaar, Bruce, *More Than Somewhat* (HarperCollins, 1986).

Groves, Perry, *We All Live in a Perry Groves World* (John Blake Publishing, 2007).

Gullit, Ruud, *How to Watch Football* (Penguin, 2017).

Halsey, Mark with Ian Ridley, *Added Time: Surviving Cancer, Death Threats and the Premier League* (Floodlit Dreams Ltd, 2013).

Hansen, Alan, *A Matter of Opinion* (TransWorld Digital, 2011).

Hasselbaink, Jimmy Floyd, *Jimmy: The Autobiography of Jimmy Floyd Hasselbaink* (HarperSport, 2011).

Heskey, Emile with Dean Eldridge, *Even Heskey Scored: My Story* (Pitch Publishing, 2019).

Hilaire, Vince, *Vince: The Autobiography of Vince Hilaire* (Biteback Publishing, 2018).

Hill, Gordon with Wayne Barton, *Merlin: The Autobiography of Gordon Hill* (Vertical Editions, 2014).

Hoddle, Glenn with Harry Harris, *Spurred to Success: The Autobiography of Glenn Hoddle* (Queen Anne Press, 1987).

Hoddle, Glenn with David Davies, *Glenn Hoddle: My World Cup Story* (Andre Deutsch, 1998).

Hodge, Steve, *The Man with Maradona's Shirt* (Orion, 2011).

Holland, Matt, *From Wembley to Moscow: A Diary of a Tractor Boy* (Greenwater Publishing, 2001).

Holloway, Ian with David Clayton, *Ollie: The Autobiography of Ian Holloway* (Green Umbrella Publishing, 2009).
Howey, Lee, *Massively Violent and Decidedly Average* (Biteback Publishing, 2018).
Huckerby, Darren, *Hucks: Through Adversity to Great Heights, My Autobiography* (Wensum Publishing, 2011).
Hudson, Alan, *The Working Man's Ballet* (London Books, 2017).
Hughes, Emlyn, *Crazy Horse* (Arthur Baker, 1980).
Hunter, Norman, *Biting Talk: My Autobiography* (Hodder & Stoughton, 2004).
Hurst, Geoff with Michael Hart, *1966 And All That: My Autobiography* (Headline, 2001).
Ibrahimović, Zlatan, *I Am Zlatan Ibrahimović* (Penguin, 2013).
Izzet, Muzzy with Lee Marlow, *Muzzy: My Story* (Trinity Mirror Sport Media, 2015).
John, Elton, *Me* (MacMillan, 2019).
Jones, Vinnie, *It's Been Emotional: My Story* (Simon & Schuster, 2013).
Jordan, Joe, *Behind the Dream: The Story of a Scottish Footballer* (Hodder & Stoughton, 2004).
Jordan, Simon, *Be Careful What You Wish For* (Yellow Jersey, 2013).
Keane, Roy with Roddy Doyle, *The Second Half* (W&N, 2015).
Keegan, Kevin, *My Autobiography* (Warner Books, 1998).
Keegan, Kevin, *Kevin Keegan* (Readers Union, 1978).
Kendall, Howard with Ian Ross, *Only the Best is Good Enough: The Howard Kendall Story* (Mainstream Publishing, 1991).
Kimmage, Paul, *Full Time: The Secret Life of Tony Cascarino* (Simon & Schuster Ltd, 2000).
King, Ledley, *King: My Autobiography* (Quercus, 2014).
Lake, Paul: *I'm Not Really Here: A Life of Two Halves* (Arrow, 2012).
Lampard, Frank, *Totally Frank: My Autobiography* (HarperSport, 2006).
Law, Denis, with Bernard Bale, *The Lawman* (Andre Deutsch Ltd, 2001).

Laws, Brian with Alan Biggs, *Laws of the Jungle: Surviving Football's Monkey Business* (Vertical Editions, 2012).

Lee, Rob, *Come in Number 37* (CollinsWillow, 2000).

Lehmann, Jens, *The Madness is on the Pitch* (De Coubertin, 2017).

Leighton, Jim with Ken Robertson, *In the Firing Line: The Jim Leighton Story* (Mainstream Publishing, 2000).

Le Saux, Graeme, *Left Field A Footballer Apart* (HarperSport, 2010).

Le Tissier, Matt, *Taking Le Tiss: My Autobiography* (HarperSport, 2009).

Lyall, John, *Just Like My Dreams: My Life with West Ham* (Penguin, 1990).

Macari, Lou, *Football, My Life* (Bantam Press, 2008).

MacDonald, Malcolm, *An Autobiography* (Arthur Baker Ltd, 1983).

MacDougall, Ted with Neil Vacher, *MacDou-GOAL! The Ted MacDougall Story* (Pitch Publishing, 2016).

Mackay, Dave with Martin Knight, *The Real Mackay: The Dave Mackay Story* (Mainstream Publishing, 2004).

Maradona, Diego Armando, *El Diego: The Autobiography of the World's Greatest Footballer* (Yellow Jersey, 2005).

Marsh, Rodney, *Shooting to the Top* (Sportsmans Book Club, 1969).

Marsh, Rodney with Brian Woolnough, *I Was Born a Loose Cannon* (Optimum Publishing Solutions, 2010).

Matthews, Stanley, *The Way it Was: My Autobiography* (Headline, 2001).

McAteer, Jason, *Blood, Sweat & McAteer: A Footballer's Story* (Hachette Books Ireland, 2016).

McAvennie, Frank, *Scoring: An Expert's Guide* (Cannongate Books, 2003).

McClair, Brian, *Odd Man Out: A Player's Diary* (Andre Deutsch, 1997).

McCulloch, Lee, *Simp-Lee the Best: My Autobiography* (Black & White Publishing, 2013).

McDonough, Roy with Bernie Friend, *Sex, Booze and Early Baths: The Life of Britain's Wildest Ever Footballer* (Vision Sports Publishing, 2015).

McGovern, John, *From Bo'ness to the Bernabeu: My Story* (Vision Sports Publishing, 2015).

McIndoe, Michael, *Wildling: My Autobiography* (Michael McIndoe, 2017).

McKenzie, Duncan with David Saffer, *The Last Fancy Dan: The Duncan McKenzie Story* (Vertical Editions, 2009).

McMenemy, Lawrie, *A Lifetime's Obsession: My Autobiography* (Trinity Mirror Sports Media, 2017).

McMenemy, Lawrie, *The Diary of a Season* (Arthur Barker, 1979).

Merson, Paul with Ian Ridley, *Hero and Villain: A Year in the Life of Paul Merson* (Willow, 1999).

Merson, Paul, *How Not to be a Professional Footballer* (HarperSport, 2012).

Miller, Charlie with Scott McDermott, *The Proper Charlie: The Autobiography* (Black & White Publishing, 2014).

Milne, Ralph with Gary Robertson, What's It All About, Ralphie? My Story (Black & White Publishing, 2010).

Molby, Jan with Grahame Boyd, *Jan the Man: From Anfield to Vetch Field* (Orion, 1999).

Morrison, Andy, *The Good, The Mad and The Ugly: The Andy Morrison Story* (Fort Publishing, 2011).

Mullery, Alan, *The Autobiography* (Headline, 2007).

Neal, Phil, *Attack from the Back* (Littlehampton Book Services, 1981).

Negri, Marco with Jeff Holmes, *Moody Blue: The Story of Mysterious Marco* (Pitch Publishing, 2018).

Nelson, Garry, *Left Foot Forward: A Year in the Life of a Journeyman Footballer* (Headline, 1996).

Neville, Gary, Red: My Autobiography (Transworld Digital, 2011).

Nicholas, Charlie with Ken Gallacher, *Charlie: An Autobiography* (Stanley Paul & Co., 1986).

Nicol, Stevie, *My Autobiography: Five League Title and a Packet of Crisps* (Trinity Mirror Sport Media, 2016).

O'Leary, David, *Leeds United on Trial* (Little, Brown, 2002).

Owen, Michael, *Reboot: My Life, My Time* (Reach Sport, 2019).

Palmer, Carlton with Steve Jacobi, *It is What it is: The Carlton Palmer Story* (Vertical Editions, 2017).

Parker, Paul with Pat Symes, *Tackles Like a Ferret* (Know the Score Books, 2006).

Parlour, Ray, *The Romford Pelé: It's Only Ray Parlour's Autobiography* (Cornerstone Digital, 2016).

Pearce, Stuart, *Psycho: The Autobiography* (Headline, 2014).

Pelé, *Pelé: The Autobiography* (Simon & Schuster 2007).

Pennant, Jermaine with John Cross, *Mental: Bad Behaviour, Ugly Truths and The Beautiful Game* (John Blake, 2018).

Pirlo, Andrea with Alessandro Alciato, *I Think Therefore I Play* (Backpage Press 2014).

Platt, David, *Achieving the Goal: An Autobiography* (Richard Cohen Books Ltd, 1995).

Poll, Graham, *Seeing Red* (HarperSport, 2018).

Powell, Hope, *Hope: My Life in Football* (Bloomsbury, 2016).

Quinn, Mick with Oliver Harvey, *Who Ate All the Pies? The Life and Times of Mick Quinn* (Virgin Digital, 2011).

Redfearn, Neil, *There's Only One Neil Redfearn: The Ups and Downs of My Footballing Life* (Headline, 2006).

Redknapp, Harry, *A Man Walks on to a Pitch: Stories from a Life in Football* (Ebury Press, 2014).

Redknapp, Harry with Martin Samuel, *Always Managing: My Autobiography* (Ebury Press, 2013).

Redknapp, Harry, *My Autobiography* (CollinsWillow, 1998).

Redknapp, Harry, *The World According to Harry* (Ebury Press, 2019).

Regis, Cyrille with Chris Green, *Cyrille Regis: My Story* (Andre Deutsch, 2010).

Reid, Peter, *Everton Winter, Mexican Summer* (The Book Service Ltd, 1987).

Reid, Peter, *Cheer Up Peter Reid* (Trinity Mirror Sport Media, 2018).

Reynolds, George, 2nd Revised edition (Blake Publishing, (2005).

Ridsdale, Peter, *United We Fall: Boardroom Truths About the Beautiful Game* (Pan Books, 2008).

Roberts, Graham with Colin Duncan, *Hard as Nails: The Graham Roberts Story* (Black and White Publishing, 2008).

Robertson, Alistair with Bill Howell, *Thou Shalt Not Pass: The Alistair Robertson Story* (Pitch Publishing, 2017).

Robertson, John with John Lawson, *Super Tramp: My Autobiography* (Mainstream Publishing, 2011).

Robson, Bobby with Bob Harris, *Against the Odds: An Autobiography* (Hutchinson, 1990).

Robson, Bryan, *Robbo: My Autobiography* (Hodder & Stoughton, 2012).

Rosenior, Leroy with Leo Moynihan, *"It's Only Banter": The Autobiography of Leroy Rosenior* (Pitch Publishing, 2017).

Rosler, Uwe, *My Autobiography – Knocking Down Walls* (Trinity Mirror Sport Media, 2013).

Ruddock, Neil, *Hell Razor: The Autobiography of Neil Ruddock* (Willow, 1999).

Ryan, John, *Dare to Dream* (Scratching Shed Publishing, 2010).

Sansom, Kenny, *To Cap It All: My Story* (John Blake, 2010).

Savage, Robbie with Janine Self, *Savage!: The Robbie Savage Autobiography* (Mainstream Publishing, 2010).

Savage, Robbie, *I'll Tell You What… My Take on the Modern Game of Football* (Constable, 2015).

Schmeichel, Peter with Egon Balsby, *Schmeichel The Autobiography* (Virgin Publishing, 2000).

Scholes, Paul, *My Story* (Simon & Schuster, 2011).

Seaman, David, *Safe Hands: My Autobiography* (Orion Media, 2000).

Sharpe, Lee with David Conn, *My Idea of Fun: The Autobiography* (Orion Books Ltd, 2006).

Shearer, Alan, *Alan Shearer's Diary of a Season* (Virgin Books, 1995).

Sheedy, Kevin, *So Good I Did it Twice: My Life from Left Field* (Trinity Mirror Sports Media, 2014).

Shilton, Peter, *The Autobiography* (Orion, 2004).

Sitton, John, *A Little Knowledge is a Dangerous Thing: A Life in Football* (John Sitton, 2016).

Smith, Kelly, *Footballer: My Story* (Corgi, 2013).

Snodin, Ian with Alan Jewell, *Snod This for a Laugh* (Trinity Mirror Digital Media, 2013).

Solo, Hope, *Solo: A Memoir of Hope* (HarperPaperBacks, 2013).
Souness, Graeme with Ken Gallacher, *Graeme Souness: A Manager's Diary* (Mainstream Publishing, 1989).
Souness, Graeme, *Football: My Life, My Passion* (Headline, 2017).
Southall, Neville, *The Binman Chronicles* (deCoubertin Books, 2012).
Southgate, Gareth and Andy Woodman, *Woody & Nord: A Football Friendship* (Penguin, 2003).
Stam, Jaap, *Head to Head* (Collins Willow, 2003).
Sterland, Mel with Nick Johnson, *Boozing, Betting & Brawling: The Autobiography of Mel Sterland* (Green Umbrella Publishing, 2008).
Stewart, Ray, *Spot on with 'Tonka'* (West Ham Football Club, 1991).
Stewart, Rod, *Rod: The Autobiography* (Arrow, 2013).
Stiles, Nobby, *After the Ball: My Autobiography* (Hodder & Stoughton, 2003).
Storey, Peter, *True Storey: My Life and Crimes as a Football Hatchet Man* (Mainstream Digital, 2011).
Sturrock, Paul with Charlie Dudby and Peter Rondo, *Forward Thinking: The Paul Sturrock Story* (Mainstream, 1989).
Sturrock, Paul with Bill Richards, *Luggy: The Autobiography of Paul Sturrock* (Pitch Publishing, 2015).
Suarez, Luis, *Crossing the Line: My Story* (Headline, 2014).
Sugar, Alan, *What You See is What You Get: My Autobiography* (Pan, 2011).
Sutton, Chris with Mark Guidi, Paradise and Beyond: My Autobiography (Black & White Publishing, 2011).
Tanner, Nick with Steve Cotton, *From A Field to Anfield* (Pitch Publishing, 2017).
Ternent, Stan with Tony Livesey, *Stan the Man – A Hard Life in Football* (Blake Publishing, 2003).
Thomas, Clive, *By the Book* (HarperCollins, 1984).
Thomas, Mickey, *Kickups, Hiccups, Lockups: The Autobiography* (Century, 2008).
Thompson, Phil, *Stand Up Pinocchio: Thommo from the Kop to the Top – My Life Inside Anfield* (Trinity Mirror Sport Media, 2013).

Thornley, Ben with Dan Poole, *Tackled* (Pitch Publishing, 2018).
Tomlinson, Barrie, *Real Roy of the Rovers Stuff* (Pitch Publishing, 2016).
Toshack, John, *Tosh: An Autobiography* (Arthur Baker, 1982).
Trundle, Lee with Chris Wathan, *More Than Just Tricks* (Mainstream Publishing, 2010).
Tueart, Dennis, *My Football Journey* (Vision Sports Publishing, 2011).
Van Den Hauwe, Pat, *The Autobiography of the Everton Legend* (John Blake Publishing Ltd, 2015).
Vardy, Jamie, *From Nowhere: My Story* (Ebury Press, 2017).
Venables, Terry, *Born to Manage: The Autobiography* (Simon & Schuster UK, 2015).
Vieira, Patrick, *Vieira: My Autobiography* (Orion, 2006).
Walcott, Theo, *Theo: Growing Up Fast* (Corgi, 2012).
Walsh, Paul, Walshy, *My Autobiography: Wouldn't it Be Good* (Trinity Mirror Sport Media, 2015).
Walters, Mark with Jeff Holmes, *Wingin' It: The Mark Walters Story* (Pitch Publishing, 2018).
Ward, Mark, *From Right-Wing to B-Wing… Premier League to Prison* (Football World, 2009).
Wark, John, *Wark On: The Autobiography of John Wark* (Know the Score Books, 2009).
Warnock, Neil, *Made in Sheffield: My Story* (Hodder & Stoughton, 2008).
Warnock, Neil, *The Gaffer: The Trials and Tribulations of a Football Manager* (Headline, 2013).
Webb, Howard, *The Man in the Middle: The Autobiography of the World Cup Final Referee* (Simon & Schuster UK, 2017).
Whelan, Ronnie, *My Autobiography. Walk On: My Life in Red* (Simon & Schuster UK, 2011).
Whiteside, Norman, *Determined: The Autobiography* (Headline, 2007).
Windass, Dean, *Deano. From Gipsyville to the Premiership* (Great Northern Books, 2011).
Winter, Jeff, *Who's the B*****d in the Black? Confessions of a Premiership Referee* (Ebury Press, 2006).

Woodcock, Tony with Peter Ball, *Inside Soccer* (The Book Service Ltd, 1985).

Worthington, Frank with Steve Wells, Nick Cooper and Ian Worthington, *One Hump or Two? The Frank Worthington Story* (ACL & Polar Publishing, 1994).

Wright, Ian, *A Life in Football: My Autobiography* (Constable, 2016).

Yorath, Terry, *Hard Man Hard Knocks* (Celluloid, 2004).

Yorke, Dwight, Born to Score: The Autobiography (Macmillan, 2009).

John Smith and Dan Trelfer are the co-authors of *Booked! The Gospel According to Our Football Heroes.* Along with Robbie Knox and Martin Gritton they host the Spotify original podcast Football Legends – inspired by these books. You might like that too.